Forgotten Lincoln.

Monks' Abbey.

Forgotten Lincoln.

A History of the City from the Earliest Times.

BY

HERBERT GREEN

Reprinted from the " Lincoln Gazette & Times."

EP PUBLISHING LIMITED
1974

Copyright © 1974 EP Publishing Limited
East Ardsley, Wakefield
Yorkshire, England

Additional material, updating lists of officials, by
G. F. Morton

This is a facsimile of the 2nd edition
originally published Lincoln 1898

The publishers wish to thank Lincoln City Library
for their help and co-operation

The publishers point out that, as this is a photo-
graphic reproduction of the 1898 edition, the
quality of this reprint faithfully represents the
standard of printing of the original, and not that
to which present-day readers may be accustomed.

ISBN 0 85409 966 2

Please address all enquiries to EP Publishing Limited
(address as above)

Printed in Great Britain by
REDWOOD BURN LIMITED
Trowbridge & Esher

PREFACE.

THE Series of Articles under this title proved a most popular feature in the "*Lincoln Gazette & Times*" from week to week. They were compiled by Mr. HERBERT GREEN, a member of our Staff, from various authorities previously published and from sources of which there are no previously printed records.

No attempt has been made to deal with the subjects from the strictly antiquarian or the historical aspect, but the writer has endeavoured—with what success our readers will judge—to describe in interesting narrative form the main features of interest and the associations and traditions of so much as remains in the Lincoln of to-day to connect it with the Lincoln of the past.

The first edition in volume form was published at the close of 1897, and was entirely sold out in less than a month. We printed a number which we believed would be sufficient to meet all demands, and destroyed the stereotype plates from which the impression was taken. The edition, however, proved wholly inadequate for the wants of the trade which far exceeded our most sanguine expectation, and encouraged by this evidence of public appreciation, we determined to print a second edition.

By means of our Linotype Composing Machines we have been enabled to re-set the whole of the volume in an improved form with such emendations and additions as will make the book more acceptable as a historical retrospect of our ancient city. The chief addition to the letterpress is a list (not previously published) of the City Sheriffs from the earliest date to the present time ; whilst the value of the book has also been further enlarged by a series of illustrations reproduced from rare prints of "Forgotten Lincoln." We have, therefore, no hesitation in saying that the volume constitutes the most complete and reliable history of Lincoln that has ever been published.

THE EDITOR.

Lincoln, May, 1898.

INDEX.

FORGOTTEN LINCOLN.

A history of the City from the earliest times.

I.—THE ROMAN CITY.

Citizens of modern Lincoln, who dwell where once was the cradle of East Anglian history, the very stones around and beneath whose homes are full of the doings of past ages, are, by the necessities of fin de siecle business competition, or by the thousand and one distractions of daily life, to be forgiven for falling into any forgetfulness of the noble and important part Lincoln has played in the history of the nation since the first Roman invasion 55 years B.C. Familiarity breeds—forgetfulness in this case at all events, and this, to some extent, is perhaps due to the absence of any thoroughly comprehensive and readably written history of the city. Self-evident places and facts do not need to be reviewed, but Lincoln has a history second to that of no city in the kingdom, and dating back as far as the annals of the country itself, a history that a great proportion of her sons and daughters have only a slight knowledge of, and that, we believe, mainly requires to be presented in an interesting and attractive form for due regard to be given to it.

One does not need to be told, for instance, of Lincoln's continuous growth. The very fact of the spread of its building area from year to year gives a ready conviction of that. And as regards the population much the same thing applies. In modern or comparatively modern times the establishment of manufactories and railway depots has largely aided the increase. It is noteworthy in this connection that the population in the year 1800 was 7,398, which had risen in 1840 to 13,919, in 1873 to 30,000, and is now considerably beyond 40,000. But Lincoln under the wise and glorious governance of Victoria and the city as we know it to-day is almost wholly of a growth from the Saxon and Danish landing on these shores. Earlier than this, however, we have relics of a Roman city, the chief of which is that remarkable archway spanning the division between Newport and Bailgate, which we call Newport Arch. It is well-known that this, absolutely the oldest arch in England, was built in the year of grace 42.

Earlier still was the British town of Lind-coit, as most writers name it, which stood to the northward of our present city and also of the Roman town. Of this Lind-coit there are now really no remains. Some declare that the inequalities of the ground north of Newport Arch mark the site of the early British town; but there are others who affirm that this particular ground was the pasture-land of the succeeding Romans. Assuming that it was the actual site of Lind-coit, we can hardly wonder at the non-existence of any undoubted remains, for the ancient Briton's dwelling was, as a rule, composed of interwoven boughs plentifully beplastered with clay and loam, the whole thatched or roofed over with rushes, long grass, or straw. The date of the founding of this, the first town of which we have any record on or near the site of the present city, cannot even be estimated. Stow, in his annals, computes the arrival of these founders of our island-race as 1108 years before the dawn of the Christian Era, and there is a space of over 1050 years without any definite history save that of Geoffrey of Monmouth, who, in his turn, procured his information from the Welsh Bards. So that Lind-coit may have been established at almost any time before the first Roman invasion. It was enclosed by earthworks, these being a bank and a ditch, with palisading, or, more probably, a stockade. There is a record, or what purports to be a record, of the British king Vortimer having died there; and Sir Charles Anderson gives it as his opinion that the British tribes in Lincolnshire were less civilised than those in the south and south-west of the country, which is hardly complimentary to the fen county. The Lincolnshire tribes had the not ungraceful name of the Coritani.

These statements practically exhaust what is known of Lind-coit, and, indeed, reflect much of the early history of the whole country. In the year 55 B.C., however, Julius Cæsar's legions sighted the shores of Albion, and, following their invasion, came a second landing under Augustus. It was not until after this second invasion that the Romans did very much to establish themselves, and the Roman colony at Lincoln is generally dated about A.D. 100. "Lindum Colonia," as it was called, was one of nine Coloniæ, which consisted of veteran Legionaries, who held their lands on condition of rendering military service whenever required. The eight other Coloniæ were London (Londinium or Augusta), Colchester (Camelodonum), Bath (Agri Solis or Thermæ), Gloucester (Glevum), Caerlon (Isca Silurum), Chester (Deva), Richborough (Rutupiæ), and Cambridge (Camboricum). The Roman cities were named and classified in accordance with their privileges. Every one of these ancient place-names has a meaning, which, if not always recoverable, still existed in the cities' first days.

But this name of Lindum is not, be it known, of strictly Roman origin. It is old British, though bearing a Roman stamp. The site of our present city, below-hill, was then one wide pool. "Lyn" was the British name for a "clear, still pool." "Dun" signifies "a hill fortress," and the late Precentor Venables defined the meaning of the name Lindum as "the pool under the stronghold on the hill." London's name was derived from the same root. At all events, it cannot be gainsaid that the Romans made a veritable stronghold of this same Lindum. Their city, which measured some 500 yards from east to west, and 400 yards from north to south, was planned as a fortified camp reproduced in stone. In its centre was a milestone, put up 267 A.D., and now in the Cathedral Cloisters, and of which something will be said in another article. The city's northern entrance was the present Newport Arch, and there was a southern gate (called Bail Gate) about the site of the Leopard Inn. Its our roads or viæ are now replaced or represented by the upper part of Steep Hill and Bailgate from north to south, and Eastgate and Westgate from, of course, east to west. Eastgate, however, is much deflected from its original course, as it ran in a line with Westgate, that is, striking into Bailgate opposite where St. Paul's Church now stands. The enclosed area to the north some authorities believe, as has been stated, to have been the pasture-ground attached to the Roman town. A reason for this belief is that the British camps never, these disputants say, followed the natural configuration of the ground, and were never rectangular. It is quite certain that it was usual for Roman settlements to have a fortified pasture-ground annexed, into which the sheep and cattle were driven on the occasion of an attack by the hostile and driven-out British tribes.

As time went on, the space within the Roman walls became too small for its inhabitants, and the city was extended southward, down the hill. The new east and west walls were built on a line with a gateway on the site of our venerated Stonebow, extending from the north side of Brayford (where a small tower was built later) to Broadgate. This side of the city was further defended by the swampy Witham, the early name of which stream, says Mergand, was Gantavon or Grantavon. The western wall ran northward from the Brayford to near the present above-hill reservoir. The eastern wall ran almost parallel with it, up the hill, across the site of the Cathedral and west of the Chapter House, across Eastgate to a point due east of the fragments of the north wall still to be seen in fields east and west of Newport Arch. Another wall crossed just above the ruins of the Bishop's Palace to the west wall, and the gate connecting the lower town with the upper or military portion was situate not far from the summit of Steep Hill. The western gate of the upper town was in 1836 unearthed, nearly perfect, in excavating on the west side of the Castle Dykings, having been covered up when the Norman wall was built. It is probable that a number of villas and country houses were built outside the walls of the extended city. Of the many and valuable discoveries of remains of this epoch adequate mention will be made later.

All these discoveries tend to prove that Lindum Colonia lies some nine or twelve feet beneath the present city. The old main road lies eight or nine feet below the level of the existing High-street and its continuants, both below and above hill, and excavations for drainage purposes some years ago even showed the tracks of wheels on portions of the ancient thoroughfare. The Roman roads were called "Strata," whence we obtain our word street, and there can be no better testimony to their splendid construction, or of the permanency of the buildings which bordered them than the existence locally of so many relics—a number of them in almost faultless condition—nearly 2,000 years after their construction.

Outside the city the Via Herminia, or, as it was called later, Ermine-street, still preserves its severely straight course to the Humber, whence, in former days, a ferry connected it with another road that led direct to York. In some Lincolnshire villages it is yet called the Old Street.

There was an organised British church in Lincoln before the Romans left Britain, and certainly gravestones with Christian inscriptions. At the Council of Arles, in France, A.D. 314, three British Bishops were present—Restitutus of London, Eborius of York, and Adelfius of Lincoln. There is little doubt that it was on the site of the present church of St. Paul's that the first Christian church in Lincoln was raised.

But the full extent of the Roman city will probably never be revealed to us; Lindum Colonia is buried beneath our feet, and despite the relics which are brought to light from time to time, the majority of the massive beauties and imposing designs of the city are verily dead. When the Romans left Britain in the year of grace 426, they left behind them a city already remarkable in history, and destined to take a still greater part in the annals of future ages.

II.—AFTER THE ROMANS.

The Roman settlement in England was not of great length; before the end of the fourth century their great empire at home was falling to pieces. The Roman troops which had invaded and settled in other lands were hastily summoned to defend their home-country. The Saxon Chronicler says that in 418 A.D., "the Romans collected all the treasures that were in Britain, and some they hid in the earth, and some they carried with them to Gaul." Britain being practically deserted, it was not long, as might be expected, before other invaders arrived. A conglomeration of tribes, whom we nowadays term the Anglo-Saxons, swarmed into the country, and, with true heathen passion, did their best to sweep away all traces of previous occupation, not sparing the most elaborately-carved stone or princely building. Lincoln suffered with the rest, and the whole town east of Eastgate was utterly wrecked. So great, in point of fact, was the destruction wrought, that it was found more practical to re-build on other ground than attempt to restore the remains of the destroyed area. The town being re-constructed, it became of increasing importance, the whole surrounding district being named Lindisig, or Lindsey as we call it now—the "eye" being the island of Lindum. In those times, however, Lindum was still occasionally the scene of war, but the history of the period in general and—though we give no special reason for it—that of Lincolnshire in particular is by no means clear or complete.

Following the Saxons came the Danes, a race who, some will say, have made their mark on Lincoln stronger than any preceding or succeeding invaders. Their first landing on these shores seems to have been unostentatious and unchallenged—it may have been because they came in small numbers. They were in England long before the accession of Ethelred (866), and soon after that an armament under Hubba and Hingvar landed in East Anglia. Their most noteworthy invasion of Lincolnshire took place in 865-7, when Hubba and Hingvar, after taking York, crossed the Humber, destroyed the Abbey of Bardney, and, some affirm, the church of Stow also. Osgot, the Sheriff of Lincoln, thereupon collected 500 men, and, with Earl Algar and others, advanced to meet them. The Danes were defeated for the time being, three of their chiefs, or kings, being slain. The surviving village of Treking or Threckingham, commemorates the battle.

But in 873 a large body of the Danes, after spending some time at Torksey (then rejoicing in the refreshing name of Tiolfingcaster), subjugated a very great portion of northern and eastern England. Later, Lincolnshire became a part of the Danelaga, the district under Danish laws. No county map, declares one authentic writer, bears clearer traces of Norse occupation than that of Lincolnshire. There are, however, very few undoubted remains of the period yet found within Lincoln city. One of these few is a stone to the memory of Havelock the Dane, who astonished everyone by the distance which he "put the stone" at an athletic contest in the city. Some think that the stone is in honour of this feat.

One special mark of Lincoln being a Danish city is the frequent recurrence in its present-day street nomenclature of the word "gate," anciently "gat." The word signified a thoroughfare rather than the entrance thereto, and many old Lincoln streets were called "gates" in this way. Our well-traversed High-street was designated Micklegate, and the names of Eastgate, Westgate, Northgate, Saltergate (the street of the drysalters), Flaxengate (devoted to the flax-spinners), and others still cling to those streets. Hungate was then Hundegate, or Houndgate, where the hunting dogs' kennels were situated, and Danesgate was the scene of the early settlement when one street sufficed for the local Norse population, before they overflowed, as is evident, into the surrounding thoroughfares.

There were gates, of course, in the defensive sense of the term, with gatehouses for the accommodation of soldiery. There were Bail Gate, the arch to which reference has been made as crossing the Steep Hill near the Leopard Inn, Clasket Gate, or Claxlede—where there was also a prison—near the Bull's Head Inn; Thorn Gate, near the present Magpies' Bridge; the Stanbow, or, as we term it, the Stonebow; and others. In a map of Lincoln, dated 1610, are marked Potter Gat, Ball Gat. and Clasket Gat.

Passing just outside the city walls, traces of Norse occupation still recur. Swallowbeck is possibly the modern corruption of Svali-bekkr (cool stream), and Riseholme is traceable to the old Norse hris (shrub or brushwood), a name frequently found in Scandinavian districts. Some of the land round the city was at this period beginning to be reclaimed. A lengthy raised causeway ran from Cross o' Cliff Hill across the marshy ground to where the High Bridge now stands, fording the Witham there, and up to the Stanbow Gate. The tide flowed unchecked from Boston to Lincoln, and raised the waters of Swanpool; and it is interesting to recall that a boat, fastened to a stake, beneath our present High-street (where the pool then extended) was discovered in excavating some years ago.

Lincoln owes much to the Danes. When William the Conqueror appeared the city was a Danish municipality, governed by twelve law-men, three of whom were in holy orders. The excellence of their rule may perhaps be best judged from the fact that William did not materially interfere with it. Tochi, son of Outi (a Dane), is reported to have possessed at this time thirty mansions, besides his own hall, the patronage of two churches, and the moiety of another. A lower town had sprung up on the river banks, called

Wikenford—a name corrupted into the modern "Wigford," of th⟩ same district. The population of the whole city in this memorable year of 1066 was of some importance, and was possibly not very friendly to the Conqueror, who built the Norman castle, as Sir Charles Anderson frankly expresses it "to keep them in order." In 1069 no less than 166 houses were ruthlessly destroyed to make room for this fortress on the hill, where, however, earthworks had previously existed. The castle has a history of its own, which, though deeply interesting, cannot be touched upon in this article.

In 1079, that gem of Lincoln city, and pride of every one of her sons and daughters, the Cathedral Church of Saint Mary, was commenced, so that, for some little time, cathedral and castle were rising side by side, and stone by stone, to form pages of history for many future generations. As with the castle so with the cathedral—we must not pause here to dilate upon its history. During their infancy, a river trade was established to Boston, which became, in one sense, a port for Lincoln. The river banks were strengthened, and vessels sailed from the city to the sea.

There is a tradition that the present towers of St. Mary-le-Wigford and St. Peter-at-Gowts Churches were being constructed at the time Aemigius was commencing that cathedral, which he and so many of his successors were to leave unfinished. Colsuen, or Colswegen, a wealthy inhabitant, most likely a Dane, is credited with building the towers in question.

Henry II. was crowned at Lincoln, but is stated to have worn his crown only at Wikenford, outside the walls of the city proper. The reason is not stated, but it is worthy of mention that there is an old legend which threatens that

"The first crowned head that enters Lincoln's walls,
His reign proves stormy, and his kingdom falls."

Could the monarch, living in a superstitious age, have been influenced by an old-wife's tale?

Next came the great battle of Lincoln, fought in 1217, between Henry III.'s adherents and the rebels, the latter aided by the French Dauphin, in which the insurgent leader, Count de Perche, was killed. Another tradition states the young monarch was hidden in a cowshed at Bardney, but this record of kingly precaution is not fully authenticated. In 1224 timber was given from Sherwood Forest to the Bishop of Lincoln for the hall of his new palace, the ruins of which yet give some idea of the building's former magnificence.

We hurry on to 1648, the year of the famous civil troubles which ended so disastrously to the unfortunate Charles the First. The Parliamentarians encamped on Canwick Hill on Monday morning, May 6th, 1644. The troops were in charge of the Earl of Manchester; Cromwell had been sent to intercept Lord Goring, who, it was reported, was coming to the relief of the City with 6,000 men. As history shows, the Castle was stormed and taken, and the Cathedral itself desecrated and ransacked. When Evelyn visited

Lincoln in 1654 he records to have been "an old confused town, very long, uneven, steep, and ragged, formerly full of good houses."

But, despite all this, Lincoln not only survived but grew and flourished. Many excellent buildings were added, some of which still exist, and some, of which it is proposed to treat hereafter, are gone. To take another rapid leap, it was not until after the year 1792 that the Witham at the High Bridge became navigable. Many will deem it incredible, but it is a well-attested fact that, towards the end of the last century, a ropewalk crossed the High-street near the Cornhill, and that the work was not interrupted by vehicular traffic more than five or six times a day!

We have endeavoured, in this breathless rush through Lincoln's history, to give a mere outline of the records of one of the most interesting cities in the realm. That it is incomplete is obvious, but it at least serves the purpose of pointing out the origin of a few of our "landmarks of history," and now we may briefly hint at the series of articles to which this historical summary has been by necessity prefatory.

There are yet remaining many ancient buildings full of absorbing interest. But there are—or rather were—other erections, of which little or no trace remains, that will teach many that Lincoln has a record that they probably never surmised or only half suspected. There was, for instance, the House of the Carmelites, or White Friars, now replaced by the Midland Railway Station; the Chapel of St. Thomas of Canterbury, which stood on the High Bridge; the Church of St. John, on the site of or near the present Cornhill; and the Bargates, of which but the name is left.

III.—THE CHURCH OF ST. BENEDICT.

Picturesque, as seen from the High-street, the least artistic taste must admit; quaint, a glance at the dwarfed tower and the general aspect of the building alike prove; ancient, its history and its archæological traces equally and indisputably assert; and an indefinable old-world flavour goes with these to make St. Benedict's Church unique in Lincoln. Existent right in our midst, where it has suffered storm and strife for ages past, shall we not be right in saying that in the minds of tht many the church is, to all intents and purposes forgotten? Eyes there are, keen for business and the things of life in general, which pass and repass the Church of St. Benedict day after day, and year after year, and practically never, never see it! And the old church itself seems to feel the spirit of the times, and to desire to raise an impenetrable ivy veil before its walls, to hide itself and its appealing uselessness from the gaze of the multitude. Yet, we venture to think, if its history were more widely known, in like measure would grow a veneration for that green spot in the rush and grind of the main street of our busy city. The edifice we may look upon to-day, however, is but a fragment of the original building. It extended much further to the westward, and there is reason to believe—though, so far as we are aware, there is not now existent any original plan—that it was of important proportions. Similarly, the tower stood further westward, the present tower being built from remains of the old one and of the nave, etc., of the original church. Very rudely carried out was the re-building of the tower, which gives but little idea of the architecture of the former one. It is strange that one old writer, usually accepted without question as an authority on matters of the kind, should have fallen into the error of describing the present tower as the original one, and commending to his readers' notice the quaint formation of a narrow window, built some centuries after the period to which he attributes it!

But the present tower was a re-building from old material, as just stated, sometime in the 17th century, and some little distance from the original position assigned to the first tower. Of the whole building, it is doubtful to what period its erection may rightly be credited. It was largely altered, and at great expense, in the 14th century, and it would probably be safe to state that it was built at least 150 years previous to that. These alterations included the insertion of some very richly traced flamboyant windows. One of the original windows yet remains in the south wall. Probably some of the finest windows were placed along the nave.

The nave, however, together with the former west front, is gone. The existing church gives us but the chancel of the old one, with a side chapel to the memory of Agnes de Tateshale (modern Tatter-shall, of which more anon. There is, or was, a brass plate to the memory of one A. W. Becke and family, with the effigies of himself, his wife, and children, and the date 1620. As this brass is under-stood to have been formerly affixed to one of the piers (where there is a place fitting it) which now adjoins the tower—but almost lost in the deep shadows—it appears fairly evident that the curtailing of the church took place after that date. Sympson says of the building, "The Church of Saint Benedict, of antient time, belonged to Roger Bigot, Earl of Norfolk, who gave it Deo et S. Mariæ de Lincolniæ et Roberto Episcopo et Successoribus suis, which grant was confirmed by King Hen. I., as we learn from the Monasti-con. It is parcel of the prebend of North Kelsey, the prebendary patron."

At one time, the late Precentor Venables assures us, it was the church of the richest and most important merchants in Lincoln. This may account to some extent for the numerous chantries en-dowed in it. A citizen named Robert Dalderby endowed a chantry at the altar of St. Mary in this church, for two chaplains, in 1352. Roger de Tateshale, also a citizen of Lincoln, endowed one at the altar of St. Katherine, for one chaplain, 28 years later. His wife, Agnes, bequeathed her body to be buried in the church near that of her husband, in 1394. Robertus Appulby, citizen and mercnant, gave his body to be buried with Johanna, his wife, in the chapel of St. Thomas the Martyr, in this church, 1407. Robert Rotherby, merchant, bequeathed his body in 1417.

In the year 1318 there is an entry in Bishop Dalderby's Register, an indulgence of thirty days to all who pray for the souls of Robert de Gaddesby and Agnes, his wife, buried in the Church of St. Benedict, while among later interments was that of Dr. Caesar Primrose, 1719, and George Kent, twice Mayor of the city, who died in 1731, and was buried with Anne, his wife, whose age is given as 58, and who died some seven years earlier. From this it will be plainly learnt that the church, in its palmy days, was one of considerable rank in the city, and the passing allusions to the various chapels attached to the edifice show that the complete building was one of somewhat extensive area. The most obvious evidence of the original further extension of the church lies in the fact that the present tower stands upon a pointed arch, which un-unqestionably formerly spanned a division between two portions of the church.

The arcading within the remaining part of the building is very beautiful, and has elegant capitals of foliage. The richness of the architecture inside the church, and the almost perfect condition in which some of it still remains, is indeed the most remarkable feature of the present interior, and deserves the attention of archi-tects and students of the art in Lincoln schools. Particularly worthy of mention is a magnificent canopied sepulchral recess in the south wall. It was debated for a long time amongst the present-day authorities what the original import of this recess was, but, by direction of the present Rector of St. Peter-at-Arches, the Rev. Canon T. S. Nelson, much encumbering rubbish and decayed and fallen material were cleared away some years ago, and the recess fully revealed. It had contained a recumbent effigy, and though this has not been confidently identified, we believe that most authorities are agreed that the probabilities very largely favour its having been commemorative of Robert Dalderby. The church suffered much in the great rebellion, when such fearful havoc was wrought in churches all over the country; indeed, it was hardly to be expected that so important a church, as this then was, would be spared. Probably this may have been the cause, or one of the causes, which led to the pulling down of the nave and tower, and the use of the materials for restoring the sadly-stricken chancel and re-erecting the tower.

One of the best remembered institutions of the olden times, perhaps, is the Curfew. Its use is widely known. Its duty was to warn the law-abiding citizens of the hour for extinguishing their lamps and other lights. Very finely is the Curfew written of—almost immortalised, it might be said—in that remarkable poem, "Curfew shall not ring to-night," dealing with the Royalist and Roundhead period, and telling of the peril and heroic adventure of a maiden to save her captive lover. Most cities had their curfew, and that of Lincoln hung in St. Benedict's tower. It was the gift of the Barber Surgeons in 1585, and was famous for the beauty of its ornamentation. It was rung at six o'clock each morning as a signal for the labourers and workmen of olden Lincoln to go to their work, and at seven o'clock in the evening to bid them cease the day's toil. The parish clerk, by name John Middlebrook, was the ringer, and at his death the office was continued to Mary, his widow.

Now, the parish clerk's house was but a mean affair, a lean-to, built against the church tower. Mary performed her work methodically and satisfactorily for many years, but as she grew old she found the ringing of the Curfew a task of increasing difficulty. Thereupon she hit upon what must be conceded an ingenious plan. She caused a hole to be made in the wall dividing the bell-chamber from her own room, had the bell-rope conveyed to her bed's head, and thus was able to perform her duty while enjoying the rest to which her years and a life of honest toil entitled her. The same bell, it is interesting to state, now hangs in the tower of St. Mark's Church, a little further doyn the High-street.

Within recent years the extent of the churchyard has been greatly curtailed, the roadway past the office of the "Lincoln Gazette and Times" and "Lincolnshire Echo" offices widened, and the square generally improved. The patronage of Saint Benedict formerly belonged, as we have stated, to the Prebendary of North Kelsey in Lincoln Cathedral. But by an order in Council, dated April 7th, 1854, the perpetual curacy was united with the rectory

of St. Peter-at-Arches. A year later the Rev. Canon T. S. Nelson
was appointed to the perpetual curacy of the parish, and as rector
St. Peter-at-Arches, which position—over 40 years later—he still
holds.

An inspection of the building at the present day, decayed to
some extent though it is, is not without interest and instruction.
The quaint, high, stiff pews, the uncompromising, prominent pulpit, and the recess before mentioned, are all worth noting. The
tower is now the home of a flock of pigeons. An ascent of two
ladders—there is not, and never has been, a stairway to the present
tower—brought the writer, on the occasion of a recent visit, to a
beam immediately beneath the roof, at which altitude (which is
not reached without some peril, and should not be attempted by
the nervous) were several dainty nests of pigeons' eggs, and a
number of newly-hatched birds.   The parent birds, however,
viewed the intrusion on their presence with obvious dislike.

A number of stones on the floor and on the walls bear scarcely
decipherable inscriptions, and some of the flooring is rotten.
Whether the church will ever again be used for religious service
it is hard to say. The expenditure of a few pounds, we are informed, would put the edifice in good condition, and the additional
provision of a curate's modest stipend restore it to the worship of
God, a monument for veneration and good work.

IV.—THE HIGH BRIDGE.

Our High Bridge is of four-fold iterest. Firstly, it has its own particular history; secondly, it spans the river Witham at a part which has not been navigable for much more than a hundred years, and concerning which much of interest might be written; thirdly, it once bore a chapel of more than ordinary importance; and, lastly, it was formerly a mark dividing two portions of the city for the apportionment of common-rights. History, some say, is dry stuff, but the most sceptical will admit, if they care to peruse a brief sketch of its annals, that the High Bridge at Lincoln has a chapter at once interesting and unique.

We have said that the Bridge has its own peculiar history. It may not, perhaps, be generally known that it is the only mediæval bridge in England that preserves the houses built upon it, and that upon one side only. The date of the erection of the structure is doubtful. A chantry was founded in the chapel on the Bridge in the reign of Edward the First, says one authority, and if it is safe to assume, as is generally agreed, that this is the same chapel (St. Thomas of Canterbury) as was pulled down in the middle of the last century, then the Bridge must be some five and a half centuries old. We could quote no better authority than Mr. E. J. Willson for a description of the structure as it formerly appeared. From his account the High-street of his day must have been a narrow thoroughfare, differing vastly from the present one, while the approach from the Cornhill has been greatly improved. Speaking of the High Bridge, Mr. Willson declares it to have been "a very ancient structure, arched with ponderous ribs of a semi-circular curve, and formerly covered by two ranges of houses, forming a dark and narrow street, with a chapel of curious structure, coeval with the Bridge itself." We must not omit to mention a somewhat singular error which prevailed amongst the citizens, in a former time, to the effect that the Bridge once possessed eight arches. In a Charter of Charles the First, dated 1628, a passage runs thus: "Whereas, our Citye of Lincoln in the County of our City of Lincoln of long time hath been a City very ancient and populous defended with walls and towers and one of the chiefest seats of our whole kingdome of England for the staple and publique markett of Woolsellers and Marchant Straingers meeting together: Whereas, through the middle of the City the River of Witham which from thence doth run into the Ocian is graced being built over with Eight several stone Arches," etc. Some printed copies of the Charter quote the passage as, "the bridge thereof is graced with eight several stone arches"—a widely different wording. The first quotation, however, may be taken as correct. The passage in

question is blamed by some as being wrong, but it was the inter-
pretation of it that founded the error. What the Charter meant
by "eight several stone arches" was, more reasonably, the eight
several (i.e., separate) bridges over the various branches of the
Witham. The High Bridge itself was one, Thornbridge (near the
present Swing or Magpies' Bridge) another, the two Bar Gate
Bridges in the lower portion of the city, and the four old Gowts'
Bridges making up the remainder. This is probably the meaning
of the Charter, as several authorities have it, but Stark printed a
history in 1810, and the author suggests that small supplementary
land arches, required to meet the declivity of the roadway, may be
meant. Leland, usually the most correct of historians, says, "High
Bridge hath but one great arch," and later on speaking of the Witham's two arms entering the city, he says, "over each of them is an
arched bridge of stone to pass the principal street. . . High
Bridge to pass over the great arm."

It is quite certain that the width of the river at this point was
no greater in Charles's time than it is now. If it had been wider,
it must have extended to the south, or lower level, as the land rises
to the northward. But on the south were ancient buildings (not-
baly, Scotch Hall, of which some remains were to be seen a few
years ago). within a very few feet of the river's edge, which must
have been there in Charles the First's time, and two or three centuries before it, and it is equally certain that the river never extended further to the north.

We have made passing allusion to Scotch Hall. In Sympson's
time (1740) it was called Scotch Court, and was a mansion of considerable size. Two widely different reasons are given for its title.
One is to the effect that it "was so called because William, King of
Scots, was here entertained when he came to swear fealty to K.
John, A.D. 1200." The other, to which greater credibility attaches, is furnished by Sympson, writing about the date above
given—1740. He affirms that "it got this name within memory,
by a Scotchman living in it, and entertaining many of his travel
ling countrymen as lodgers. I believe the place to be of great
antiquity, from the manner of the building and the curious painted
glass and coat armour which was in the windows about fifteen years
ago, but now gone and demolished." A coat of arms was on a
doorstead within the court, and he pronounces it to be that of the
Gegge family, and long quartered by the Granthams, who married
the heiress, temp., Henry VIII. The same coat of arms was once
to be found in a window of the neighbouring Church of St. Benedict.

Which of the two stories above given is correct it is hard to say.
bue certainly in the year 1200, "William the Lion," King of Scotland, did, it is recorded, make homage to King John on Bower Hill
at Lincoln, for the lands of Lothian and the earldom of Huntingdon.

The history of the navigation of the Witham from here is very
interesting, in many ways. It seems remarkable that, though the
city was of growing importance the river was not made navigable

until 1793, and still more remarkable that even then a strong and lengthy opposition was offered by the Corporation to the scheme Previous to this the river had been shallow, and even fordable at dry seasons of the year. To quote Sympson again, he says: "Horses and carriages pass through the water underneath, in summer time and dry seasons, when the water is low." Of course, the lock near the Stamp End Works of Messrs. Clayton and Shuttleworth was not then in existence. Very little to the west of the Bridge, between it and Brayford, was a ford, which stopped the navigation. However, it was at last thought that the river should be deepened and rendered capable of navigation.

A report, dated 1792, was furnished by Mr. Jessop, and the Horncastle Navigation Act was obtained in the same year, one of its provisions being that the Witham should be connected with the Fossdyke by deepening the shallow parts through the city. The report laid down that Brayford Head should be lowered two feet, and Thornbridge should be removed; a "swivel" bridge (on the site of the present one) being built at the lower end of Broadgate. An outlet was recommended for the Sincil Dyke, so as to enter the Witham to the east of the city, below Stamp End. There is reason to believe that the old junction of the two waterways was somewhere a little above Stamp End. Prior to the commencement of the work a dance took place beneath the High Bridge, planks being specially laid down. But, as we have intimated, the improvement was not commenced without strong opposition. The grounds of this opposition are given as the fear lest the town should lose the porterage business at the ford between the Bridge and Brayford, where, of course, cargoes had to be unloaded and re-shipped.

Tradition, in this case well-founded, asserts that the Corporation was only brought to reason by the threat of Sir Joseph Banks, of Revesby, who had land lying lower down the Witham, that he would cut a canal to carry the trade completely outside the city, and thus rob Lincoln of the traffic altogether, if the opposition were persisted in. Bravo, Sir Joseph! But for his public spirit the advance of Lincoln, tardy though it was in some things, must have been considerably impeded.

We now come to the mention of the chapel which stood on the Bridge. Various authorities state it to have been dedicated to St. Thomas of Canterbury (Thomas a Beckett, or St. Thomas the Martyr) or St. George. The balance is overwhelmingly in favour of the former. It seems curious to modern minds that a chapel could have stood upon so confined a space, but the late Precentor Venables says it was the custom in the middle ages to have wayside chapels on bridges. There seems to have been a foundation here as early as the reign of King John, as appears from a charter in the Dodsworth M S., granting the advowson of the Chapel on Lincoln Bridge to Peter of Paris, who was to place there a chaplain to say masses for the soul of the king, his father, and all his ancestors and successors, etc., dated at Porchester, April 28th, in the first year of his reign. But the chapel here mentioned was most probably a different one from that which was dismantled at the Reformation, as the eastern wing of the bridge on which the latter stood is evidently built since the time of John, being distinguished from the rest (which is of the manner of his reign) by diagonal ribs. There was in it a Chantry, founded by Thomas de Wykford, and another was in course of foundation when the Reformation occurred. This was to have been given by Archdeacon, afterwards Dean Heneage, a member of the family of which Lord Heneage of Hainton is the present most prominent member. In 1541 the common Town Council ordered the edifice to be converted into dwellings, and, two years later, the bell was taken down and sold. On November 3rd, 1569, the building was made over to the Butchers and Tanners as their Hall. Some entries in the Cordwainers Guild Roll show that certain Guilds had been in the habit of mustering at this chapel on their anniversaries, and from there went in procession to the Cathedral.

Mr. J. G. Wilkinson, of Melville-street, has a number of curious little bars, which were discovered on making some alterations several years ago on Mr. Henry Kirke White's High Bridge premises. What they were formerly used for is not quite clear, but the Rev. Canon Maddison, the Cathedral librarian, hazards the opinion that they were possibly a kind of tally used before the days of the ledger, or an adjunct to some forgotten game. They are of four or five different sizes, and Mr. Wilkinson would gladly show them to anyone interested.

The whole of the buildings on the east side of the bridge were removed in the last century for the widening of the street, and the obelisk erected. In his "Walks through the Streets of Lincoln," commenting on this obelisk, the late Precentor Venables makes a curious slip. On page 30 he says "The Obelisk was erected in 1763," while on page 56, again commencing a sentence, he says "The Obelisk was erected in 1762." It was completed, however, in December, 1763, Mr. Gale, of Hull, being the architect, and was built to contain a cistern for a conduit of spring water. Of this conduit we shall have something to say in connection with the ancient Friaries.

The obelisk is regarded by some with the veneration accorded to a local Cleopatra's Needle, and, certainly, in its early days, was a finely-sculptured and noteworthy erection, and yet forms a striking column in the line of High-street.

Lastly, we touch upon the common-rights division. At the bridge foot were two pillars of the Doric order, built in 1725, with a chain between. The chain marked municipal divisions as "above the chain" and "below the chain." It is most likely that other pillars had stood there previously. As we stated in our first article, Wickenford or Wigford was in late Roman times practically a separate town from the older one, and in the respect

of common-rights the distinction appears to have still held good.
Till within the last seventy years it was usually appealed to in
city business to settle pasturage rights.

V.—WHEN TRAVELLING WAS YOUNG.

Let the man whose business or pleasure takes him from town to town say what he will, he lives in excellent times, so far as travelling facilities are concerned, at any rate. If he desires to make a journey of, say, a hundred miles, he can cover the distance in almost as few hours as it formerly occupied days, so that in point of time alone, not to speak of the vastly improved comfort of the journey, he has a great advantage over the travelling of fifty, eighty, or a hundred years ago.

It is quite a matter of taste, this modern yearning or pretended yearning for the "good old days," but if one of these sentimental malcontents were to be transmitted, by some Mahatma-like process, to a coach ploughing its way through, or remaining partly buried. perhaps, half a bitter winter night in a snowdrift, having been already some two days on his journey, his ardour might be somewhat chilled, and a preference admitted for the distance-annihilating express of our time. Of course, it is very picturesque to conjure up a scene like this: A long stretch of broad white road meandering by fields of waving corn, bridging a rippling stream, rising to a hill whence a glorious panorama of field and forest presents itself, dipping to a quaint, many-gabled village, where, beneath the swinging sign of the one inn, waits the ostler, a relay of horses ready to take the place of the spanking team drawing the stage-coach, which has not yet come into sight, but from whose roof the winding notes of the guard's horn can be heard faintly echoing from a distant rise. This is coaching as it is pictured, and, to some extent, must be admitted to have been the real thing, but the worst part is hidden.

After all, it is not so many years since the stage-coach clattered through the streets of Lincoln, or woke the echoes from the old Stonebow and the inns on either side. Present-day residents of the city, with its railways and manufactories, perhaps need to stretch the imagination somewhat to believe that coaching scenes such as we see on old prints or read of in the pages of Dickens, in Cockton's "Valentine Vox," and the works of other writers took place regularly in our own streets, even for some time after the railway engine first puffed and steamed into the town from Nottingham. Not only that, but the coach was able, for a short time, to hold its own with the railway in various parts of the country, and even beat it in point of speed sometimes! Of this, however, we shall say more anon.

When the coach, and the coach only, was the popular travelling conveyance, passengers needed to be philosophic and by no means in a hurry. The late Sir Charles Anderson, writing in a preface to one of his works in 1880, says: "In days gone by men were content to jog along in jackboots on palfreys of sober and constitutional pace, or to crawl through miry lanes in leathern conveniences called coaches or flies, truly like flies in a gluepot."

Perhaps the best manner in which the harassment and actual danger of this travelling can be conveyed to the popular mind is to state the fact that people frequently made their wills before taking the coach from London to York, which, according to an old advertisement, probably still hanging in the Black Swan coffee-room of that city, "performed the journey to London if God permitted) in four days."

Coming to our own city, the principal inn from which the coaches started appears to have been the old Saracen's Head, a timber building of apparently the Tudor period, while the Spread Eagle was a noted carrier's inn a hundred years ago. Formerly there was a toll-house at the southern entrance of the city (about the site of the Bargates), which was subsequently removed some 200 yards further down, to where the Newark and Sleaford roads meet to enter Lincoln.

A coaching journey from Lincoln to London, some fifty years ago, is graphically described in Sir Charles Anderson's old "Pocket Guide." He says: "Leaving Lincoln by the mail at 2 p.m., supping at Peterborough at 9 p.m., the traveller, after composing himself for an uneasy slumber about Yaxley Barracks (from whence the waters of Whittlesea Mere might be seen shimmering in the moonlight), grumbling through a weary night at the obstinate legs of his opposite neighbour, and sorely pinched in the small of the back, was only delivered, cold and cross, at the Spread Eagle, Gracechurch-street, about 5 the next morning."

Earlier than this, in 1786, on the opening of a new road, a coach had begun to run from Lincoln to London, by way of Newark, Grantham, Stamford, etc., on Mondays, Wednesdays, and Fridays, starting from the King's Head at eight o'clock in the morning, and, after a stoppage of four hours at a point about half-way along the route to give the passengers a chance for sleep, reached London, or was timed to do so, in the afternoon of the following day. Inside passengers had to pay a fare of £1 11s 6d for a seat on this journey, or, if they cared to brave the elements from a seat on the roof, could be conveyed at a charge, really moderate under the circumstances, of 15s 9d per head.

In the year 1816 it is recorded that a coach ran from Barton-on-Humber, and through Lincoln to London, performing the journey between the two last-named places, under favourable conditions, in 22 hours. There was a favourite country inn at Spital in those days.

Footpads and their kindred abounded, as is well-known, and it was no uncommon thing for a coach to be "held up" and the passengers rifled of their cash, jewellery, and such other portable property as the "knights of the highway" took a fancy to. Dick

Turpin's famous ride from London to York is stated by some to be absolutely mythical, but there are many who have persistently asserted that the notorious highwayman carried on his "business," very often, to the southward of Lincoln, and was not infrequently to be seen galloping across Bracebridge Heath.

With George Stephenson's memorable application of steam power the knell of the stage coach may be said to have been sounded. The railway lines gradually spread over the country, and in August, 1846, is recorded the opening of the first railway into Lincoln. Naturally it was a gala day in the city, the bells of the Cathedral and churches ringing peals at intervals, while considerable decorative work had been done. The band of the 4th Irish Dragoons played the "Railway Waltz" as the two trains left Lincoln (Midland) Station, and cannon were fired, and lusty cheers came from the throats of the thousands of enthusiastic spectators. All the way to Nottingham groups of people gave an occasional cheer as the trains passed, and the destination was reached in about two hours. After a dinner celebrating the occasion, a start was made back to Lincoln in a heavy downpour of rain. A banquet took place in the evening in the National Schools (now the Corporation Offices), Silver-street, Lincoln. A slight accident is reported during the day, one Paul Harden having his leg shattered by the bursting of a cannon in the station-yard. He was removed to the Hospital—the old one opposite to Christ's Hospital-terrace, and now put to ecclesiastical uses—and the leg amputated.

From this time most of the Lincoln coaches began to run to suit the times of the trains, and the rail gradually superseded the road as well in local as in general favour. Even before its supremacy was established, however, statisticians were busy showing the probability of the train service wiping out the coach. One writer pointed out that the number of horses needed to work one coach between London and Manchester was 200, and further computed that this number of animals consumed on an annual average the produce of very nearly 700 acres of land! It is interesting to note, however, that the coaches, during the struggle between road and rail for public patronage, had one great champion in the Press, this being nothing less than the "Times" newspaper, which, in July, 1837, pointed out that certain parcels were longer on the journey by rail than by coach.

We have alluded to the fact that certain coaches for a time beat the railway in point of speed. The same issue of the "Times" says: "We have already strongly recommended that coaches should be kept on the road, from the conviction that a great part of the public will prefer the punctuality of the coach to that of the railway. One coach, the Manchester Telegraph, continues to perform the journey in nearly the same time as the coaches and railway are accomplishing it," this latter referring to the plan of some coaches being carried part of the journey by rail.

The proprietor of the "Shrewsbury Wonder" seems to have been

one of the most obstinate fighters against the steam innovation.
There is a well-vouched-for record to the effect that his coach left
London one Monday morning at the same moment that a train
left Euston-square, and the coach reached Birmingham exactly
twenty minutes before its rival! The Birmingham coaches, indeed, seem to have carried on the war some time after Lincoln had
capitulated. That our city has benefited by the railroad, by means
of which its engines and machines are carried and made famous
throughout the civilised world, is an accepted truth, and could one
of the old coachmen re-visit the city he would probably be im-
measurably astonished at its growth and vigour.

VI.—THE BLACK FRIARS.

It would be a difficult task to gauge exactly what Lincoln owes, directly or indirectly, to Friardom. When these good men, in their peregrinations, came to our city they found it very sadly deficient in many things, and unselfishly set themselves to work to improve the faults and supply the wants so far as in them lay. The water supply seems to have received great attention at their hands, and a number of places in the present-day city yet remain as memorials of the good old Friars. At the same time they prodigiously exercised themselves in learning the manners and customs of the country, and became amongst the most learned men of the city. But never for a moment did they forget their first great object and work, that of preaching the gospel from day to day, and from door to door.

It was in the thirteenth century that the Friars arrived in England, and they do not seem to have been very long in reaching our city. Though different bodies, their lives appear to have been led in one simple, staid fashion. "Man wants but little here below" was never stronger exemplified than in the mode of life of the good Friars. They proposed to live, it was stated on their landing in this country, supported only by their own labour, such as were able to work, or upon the alms which they received at the hands of those to whom they preached daily in the city of their choice.

The first body to arrive was that called the Dominicans, otherwise the preaching Friars. A number of other sects, if the term is permissible, for all were Friars, followed at intervals, amongst the principal being the Franciscans, or Friars Minors; the Carmelites, or White Friars; the Augustines, or Gray Friars; and the Black Friars.

Much more interesting matter could be written of each of these bodies, but in the limits of the present article we have but space to speak of one, leaving others for consideration at an early opportunity. The reason for our choosing the Black Friars for first discussion is because, of all the buildings the Friars have left us, Monks' Abbey presents the most remarkable appearance. And not only remarkable, but strongly and plaintively suggestive of past dignity and power. Isolated from the busy streets, yet within sound of the clangour, and within sight of the rising smoke of the works which have made Lincoln what she is to-day, it almost seems as though the old ruin had voluntarily withdrawn itself from the modern crowd, and chosen to make its long fight against Time's ravages in calm and in solitude. And so, save when he casts a passing glance at it from the window of the excursion bearing him to his beloved Cleethorpes for a few hours' well-earned relaxation, many a working man never sees it. Young people, tempted by the strikingly beautiful lane running alongside it, and arched over with leafy branches, stroll by here, all too familiarly note the crumbling walls and pass on. With few exceptions, only the antiquarian cares to visit it with a reverent regard, which is its due. Truly is Monks' Abbey worthy of inclusion in a collection of information on "Forgotten" Lincoln!

Of course, for the matter of that, there is but little to see, and for the average man it is a long way to go and see it. It cannot at all be said to convey an adequate idea of its original dimensions. As in the case of Saint Benedict's Church, which we discussed recently, the edifice extended considerably further than its present walls suggest. Moreover—and this is important—what remains of Monks' Abbey is not a part of the original foundation at all, but a section of an addition of later date. What is left, however, has a certain picturesqueness of its own, and we have even heard of an enthusiastic antiquary, who declared that, so far as it went, it reminded him a good deal of the much-sung Abbey of Melrose!

"If thou would'st view fair Melrose aright,
    Go visit it by the pale moonlight,"

sang Scott, and we venture to say that, given a rising moon just peeping over the trees to the eastward of our own Abbey ruins, small though they be, and seen through the skeleton window of the building, an artist would concede them to have an undeniable beauty of their own.

To turn to the history of the building. It was founded, it appears, in the reign of the first Edward, and was a cell subject to the Abbey of Saint Mary at York. It combined a chapel with a dwelling, the latter being to the westward and of fair size. The eastern part of the building seems to most authorities to have been the chapel or oratory, though they throw some doubt on their statement by admitting that, so far as they have been able to learn from the ruin, none of the attributes of the ancient church are in evidence. The northern wall of the chapel yet remains to its full original extent, and is terminated by the pier or respond of an arch, which was apparently some twelve feet in width. At a little distance from here a wall has been carried across, and this was no doubt the western limit of the chapel. If all these statements and deductions are correct, as there is good reason to believe, we get the length of the chapel as about 60 feet.

But there was another building attached thereto, which we are not able to trace so far in detail. On the southern side of the south wall, at a distance of one foot from the pier, there may be traced the eastern wall of a vanished southern transept, but that building has long been entirely destroyed, even to the extent of the foundation being taken out. Fairly well preserved is the eastern wall, though the apex of the gable is broken off, and, it is to be feared, lost. A number of authorities have noticed the

absence of any corbel or other support, and from this it seems
reasonable to believe that there was a ceiling of wood, on the
same lines as those existent in sacred edifices of a date coeval with
this one. This exhausts practically what is known of the main
building, three sides of which are left us to-day.

At a little distance to the westward—forty-seven feet, to be
exact—from the pier previously mentioned, there stands a piece of
wall which conveys no hint of its former use or of what building
it formed a part. It was a portion, we are told, of the domestic
part of the Abbey buildings, hardly to be classed, however, as a
part of the religious edifice itself. Some idea of the general uses
of this part may be obtained from the perusal of the lives of the
Black Friars in further detail, though, probably owing to its unostentatious character, there is but little record of the local doings
of the devoted band. At the eastern end of the building, or buildings, to be correct, was a water mill, doubtless used by the Friars
to perform the work which they desired to spare the miller of the
adjacent city.   That the miller would have gladly assisted the
Friars we may rest assured, for charity   seems   to   have   been
showered richly on the Friars whenever and wherever they solicited
the divine quality.

The deep humility and apparent suffering of the good men—we
are speaking now of the whole body general of Friars (for it is
from   the   French   freres,   brothers)   in   Lincoln—seems to have
awakened the greatest sympathy in the popular mind, and the
Friars found their lines, according to many accounts, cast in exceedingly pleasant places. Alas for human nature! Friars, be
they never so devout, and resolutely shut up in heart against the
lures and wiles of the world, are of the self-same flesh and blood
as ourselves, and the saint and the sinner are moulded from one
common clay! Far be it from us to be other than regretful at
the Friars' fall, but the failings of a good man were ever more
glaring, because of their white background, than those of his weak-
hearted or weak-headed brother.

Monks' Abbey might be an object lesson for us all; if ever "sermons in stones" appealed to the imaginative mind, here is food
for thought. Once the cell of a great religious building (or the
Chapel) of Saint Mary, modern manners and minds have retained
remembrance of its dwellers only, and "Monks' Abbey," as its
name is now corrupted into, is as widely known in the city as
the designation of a brand of locally-manufactured aerated water
as the ruins of the home of the once powerful body of Black Friars.
Life, however, now abounds near the old walls; a recreation ground
for children is hard by, and the laughter of innocent youth at play
echoes across the land where once only sounded the tolling bell at
frequent and regular intervals, calling the band of saintly brethren
to prayer, penitence, and praise.

VII.—THE JEWS' QUARTER.

Of the many ancient buildings standing in our city at the present day, there is none, with the exception of the Cathedral and the Castle, that has the widespread fame of the Jews' House. If ever a dramatist or a novelist were in need of a theme, we would commend him to the history of this house and its surroundings, for really the stirring scenes which have occurred there could be shaped into a remarkable story or notable play. The poets have already done it justice, even so far back as Geoffrey Chaucer.

Those who have read Zangwill's "Children of the Ghetto" will recollect that that was the name given to the Jews' quarter in Rome, where they were practically confined. Although we can find nothing to show that the treatment of the Jewry in Rome and Lincoln was the same, the fact is substantiated that from some little distance above our present "Jews' House" to the lower end of the Strait was a region wherein the Jewish population had matters pretty much to themselves in 1250, and for some time previously. The lower boundary was marked by a gateway or barrier, closed and secured at night, and beyond which no Jew was permitted, at all events after sunset. The name of this gateway was Dernestall Lock, which, by the error of an old-time Local Board, became corrupted into St. Dunstan's Lock, under which name not a few historians and guide-booke describe it at the present day. A similar mistake—also accredited to a Local Board—crept into the name of the "Greezen," which became Greestone Stairs, by which name it has been known ever since.

How it came about that the name of Dernestall Lock was changed is inconceivable, since it is quite certain that there was not, and never had been, a St. Dunstan's in the city. Even Dernestall Lock is given by some authorities as a corruption of "the Dernestall," the place where little St. Hugh was born. St. Martin's Church is alluded to in some old documents as "St. Martin upud le Dernestal," and there is a certain amount of evidence which goes to show that some place called "the Dernestall" stood thereabouts. Old St. Martin's Church, by the way, was most probably the first Christian Church in the city below hill, as St. Paul's (written of in our first article) was of the upper city.

Before we turn to a discussion of the famous Jews' House, however, we must take the reader further up the hill, where, at the left-hand corner of Christ's Hospital-terrace, stands the house once occupied by "Aaron the Rich," also a Jew. Aaron, with his brother Benedict and one Fitz Isaac and his sons, was one of the chief money-lenders, temp. Henry II. So rich were the Jews then that they had practically a monopoly of the ready cash of the realm, and not a few notabilities were clients of Aaron and his family, even the Abbey of St. Albans being heavily in his debt. In fact, it is recorded that once, when the convent was "in arrears," Aaron appeared at the Abbey gates, and informed the monks that the place, even to the shrines of their saints, was his, and if he wished he could seize them at once. When this important individual paid his last debt—the debt of nature—his property was forfeited to the Crown. But the Crown was destined never to enjoy it, for Henry, having made over a portion of his wealth to his heirs, reserved an ample share for his own person, and, crossing to Normandy in 1187 (two years previous to his death), some of his ships were wrecked, and, consequently, money-lending Aaron's riches lie in the bed of the English Channel.

Between this house and the Jews' House known to fame, is the historic Mayor's Chair. At this spot, in 1732, the then Mayor, Mr. William White, had a bench erected for pedestrians to rest on. The present terrace and rail, which turns all vehicular traffic from Steep Hill into Danesgate or Well Lane, has a curious history, for it is reported (though we do not vouch for its accuracy) that the diversion of the traffic was effected in order to prevent any foolhardy individual from emulating the feat of the late Colonel Sibthorp, who drove a four-in-hand down Steep Hill for a wager! So, at least, the story goes. The Mayor's Chair was at one time the northern boundary of municipal jurisdiction.

And now we come to the Jews' House itself. It will be noticed, even by the casual observer, that the building is of remarkable solidity, and is of stone. The Jews built their houses of stone because they had a wholesome, and a by no means unfounded, dread of housebreakers, who found it no difficult task to break through ordinary house-walls, consisting, as they did, of timber-framing, the spaces being filled with "wattle and daub;" many old villages, indeed, yet cling to that form of structure as the bset. The house under review belonged, as first noticed in records, to a Jewess, Beleset de Wallingford, and this lady, in 1271, betrothed her daughter Judith to one Aaron, giving the young pair 20 marks and a very precious manuscript of the Hebrew Bible, written on calfskin. Four years later the marriage took place, but Beleset was hanged in 1290 on a charge of clipping the King's coin. That year was a disastrous one for the Jews, as they were expelled from England, and not allowed to return until the Lord protector held the reins of the country, 350 years afterwards. Both this house and that of Aaron, it may be mentioned, are of the Transition-Norman period, with round arches and carved capitals, while in each the chimney of the only fireplace is supported on an arch of the chief doorway.

A most horrible practice, and one that brought down the severest condemnation on the heads of its perpetrators, was the Jews' alleged ceremonial of torturing and slaughtering Christian children for the purposes of their so-called sacred rites; at least, that charge was brought against them, and being proved to a sufficient extent for the Christians of the day, largely assisted in bringing about the then hated Jews' banishment. Widespread indignation was especially aroused by the murder of one child at Lincoln, whom the Jews are stated (and wth, it would appear, full proof) to have crucified in commemorative mockery of Christ's death. This took place in the year 1255, and a screen-wall in Lincoln Cathedral now marks the site of a shrine erected to "little Saint Hugh's" memory. Of the original shrine there are no remains whatever, and even its site was forgotten when Bishop Fuller set up a memorial tablet in a place where, it is nearly certain it could never have stood.

The tiny skeleton was seen about a century ago, when the stone coffin enclosing it was opened. Geoffrey Chaucer spoke of

Young Hew of Lincolne slaine also
With cursed Jewes, as it is notable
For it n's but a litel while ago."

The story, in verse, of our little local saint is given by the late Precentor Venables, who says that as a child he used to hear the following Buckinghamshire version of it:—

It rains, it hails in merry Lincoln,
    It rains both great and small,
For all the boys and girls to-day,
    Do play at pat-the-ball.

They patted the ball so high, so high,
    They patted the ball so low,
They patted it into the Jews' garden,
    Where all the Jews do go.

Then out spake the Jew's daughter,
    As she leant over the wall,
"Come hither, come hither, my pretty playfellow,
    And I'll give you your ball."

She tempted him in with apple so red.
    But that would not tempt him in;
She tempted him in with sugar so sweet,
    And wiled the young thing in.

She led him in through one dark door,
    And so she has through nine,
She's laid him on a dressing board,
    And sticked him like a swine.

Then out it came, the thick, thick blood,
    And out it came the thin,
And out it came the bonny heart's blood,
    There was no more within.

She's rolled him in a cake of lead,
    Bade him lie still and sleep,
And thrown him in St. Mary's well,
    'Twas fifty fathoms deep.

When bells were rung and mass was sung,
    And all the boys came home,
Then every mother had her own son,
    But Lady Maisy had none.

Any Jew, it is to be noted, seen in England after All Saint's Day
1290, was sentenced to be hanged, and his property confiscated.
So fierce had grown the uprising the country over against the Jews,
the flame of hatred having grown from the spark kindled by such
deeds as the murder of unfortunate little Hugh.

VIII.—THE GREY FRIARS.

There were formerly three Priories and five Friaries in Lincoln. Of the Black Friars we have already written at some length, in connection with the Monks' Abbey. We now propose to devote our attention to the Augustines, or Grey Friars, whose local history is full of interest.

At first blush there seems but little union—to the non-historian. that is—between Lincoln Grammar School and St. Mary's Conduit, in front of the Church of St. Mary-le-Wigford. Yet we are indebted to the Grey Friars for both.

The Augustines first appeared in this country in the beginning of the 13th century, and much that we have written concerning the Black Friars applies equally to their brothers of the grey cloak. Their house in Lincoln was built, says an authority, "in the south-eastern angle of the Roman town, being bounded on the south and east sides by the Roman wall, and on the north and west by Silver-street and Free School-lane." The site is, in point of fact, where the present Lincoln Middle School, of which it forms a part, stands.

The meekness and piety of the Friars won for them the popular approval, and they speedily found themselves possessed of considerable means. Prevented by their vow from the possession of land, they expended their surplus money on the subsantial character and architectural beauty of their houses, and, indeed, contributed some really valuable work of this kind to the city.

The principal building associated with their name is the house mentioned, but there was another of their houses in the Bail, while they are also responsible for St. Mary's Conduit.

We have stated that the Friars appeared early in the 13th century. They settled in Lincoln in the year 1220. The first-named house continued in their possession nearly 300 years—in fact, until the Dissolution, when Mr. Justice Monson (one of the Judges of the Court of Common Pleas) purchased it from the Commissioners appointed by Henry the Eighth, who suppressed the Friars in 1536. There seems to have been considerable hostility at this time between the Friars and the Monkish orders and secular clergy; and Henry also put down some 376 small monasteries, with revenues under £200 per annum, confiscating most of the belongings.

In the early part of Elizabeth's reign there is mention of two schools in the city of Lincoln. One of these was in the Bail, under the governance of the Dean and Chapter, and the other in the lower part of the city, supported by the Corporation. Both appear to have been very dilapidated. Mr. Justice Monson, as we have said, had purchased this latter, and it is on record that he, "in

consideration of the affection he bore towards the city of Lincoln,
and also for the desire he had for the maintenance of a free grammar school, or school house in the city," covenanted the "site,
convent, and precinct," he had purchased, and described in the
documents bearing upon the transfer, as the "Graye Freres," for
that commendable purpose.

Accordingly, by feoffment, bearing the date of December 18th,
in the seventeenth year of good Queen Bess's glorious reign, the
"Graye Freres" was conveyed and assured to feoffees, to the use
of the Corporation and their successors in fee. Soon after this
desirable end had been accomplished a Grammar School was established, supported by the Corporation of the city. Nine years later
the Dean and Chapter entered into a Deed with the Corporation
to unite the school in the Bail with that in the city, with the
object of maintaining a Grammar School there at a later period.
This was brought about, and in recent years developments of the
scheme have taken place, resulting in the existing Grammar and
Middle Schools. Of the value of these institutions little need be
said ; many a Lincoln boy has had founded there an education that
stood him in good stead in after life, and given him grip to climb
above his less fortunate fellows on the precarious rungs of the
ladder of life.

The Friary, as it now stands, is not strictly the original edifice.
Here, as elsewhere in the city, the ground is much higher than in
the days when the place was built. The very fact that our present High-street is several feet above the old Roman highway
alone proves this, as a general rule, while excavations in various
parts of Lincoln have strengthened our knowledge of the subject.
Consequently, in the case of this particular building, the lower
storey is but partially seen from the outside. A long vaulted
apartment, up to a few years back used as a Mechanics' Institution, yet remains of the old Friary, over which is the School itself,
the latter having been a chapel, or a refectory.

The original roof is also existent, and a very interesting construction it is, consisting of a series of semi-circular timber arches
at alternate rafters, and ceiled on the underside with boards placed
in a zig-zag manner. This ceiling, which is of oak, was originally
beautifully illuminated ; we are unable to state what subjects were
depicted. But doubtless they were the same as have been seen on
the ceilings of similar edifices built by the Friars.

But not only do we indirectly owe the gift of this school building
to the Grey Friars, but we also, indirectly, owe to them a distinct
improvement in the water supply of the city. It appears that the
Grey Friars first brought the water into Lincoln from the neighbouring hill, somewhere close by the monastery of the Black
Friars, and probably from the same spring as supplied the Monks'
Abbey stream, since it was certainly on lands owned by the latter
brotherhood. It is quite certain, too, that water-pipes did not
reach beyond St. Mary's Conduit at the time of the Reformation.

But when the Commissioners disposed of the Grey Friary to Mr. Justice Monson, at the time the monasteries were suppressed, we find in their correspondence that the Mayor and Commonalty of Lincoln besought them to grant to the town the conduit in question. This zeal, or, as we should probably call it now-a-days, this Pure Water Crusade, is one of the happiest traits the Grey Friars have left to us. They, at all events, before they found themselves in affluence, devoted their attention to the condition of the poverty-ridden. They built their home in one of the slums of the city, giving themselves up to works of charity. This continual contact with the lowest orders convinced the Friars that pure water was "an essential element in their work of evangelisation," and so they set themselves to obtain it. A tremendous task it must have been, too, in those days, when hydraulics were immature, labour slow and only partly competent, tools rudely-fashioned and not always applicable, and materials not at all bearing comparison with modern sanitary appurtenances. But the great work was accomplished, and as Precentor Venables puts it, in a nutshell, "the water we now enjoy, though not so good as in the time of the Friars, is a perpetual memorial of these self-sacrificing men." Here, very probably, is the root of the vast popularity of the Grey Friars—that popularity which subsequently brought about their downfall.

St. Mary's Conduit is built of materials from the dissolved convent of the White Friars (of whom we shall have something to say hereafter), and Leland, in his "Itinerary," states that it had been erected shortly before his visit in 1540. While some authorities make it out to have been built of fragments from the convent or one of its chapels, Mr. E. J. Willson gives it as his opinion that it is possibly of the remains of the Chantry itself, transferred at the dissolution from the convent, and converted to its present use. "The appearance," he says, "of this little structure is that of a chapel; and the ornamental tracery, niches, and other carved works on its sides look like the fragments of some richly-decorated chantry, perhaps of one built by Randulph de Kyme."

In an old wall, which formed an adjunct to the Conduit on the south side, were two recumbent figures. one at the foot of the other, but the wall has been taken down. The male figure is doubtless that of the Randulph de Kyme mentioned above, the effigy having been brought from the White Friary. Leland also says "there lay in a chapelle at White Freres a rich marchaunt callid Ranulphus de Kyme, whose image was thens taken down and set at the south ende of the new Castelle of the Conducte of Water in Wikerford." The female is stated, not on reliable authority, to have been that of his wife.

At the back of the Conduit are some coats of arms, which originally adorned the gable of a roof, as is proved by the oblique form of the panels in which the shields are inserted. The style of the whole of the details is very late, and the building to which they belonged could have been built only a few years previous to the destruction of the convent itself.

The date 1672 on the north end of the Conduit is misleading to the casual observer, as it refers, not to the erection of the building, but to some repairs at that time, when the two balls terminating the gables were set up, and on the suitability of which considerable division of opinion existed amongst the authorities of the day.

A number of sculptured fragments, corresponding in appearance with those built into the Conduit, were dug up on the site of the White Friars' Conduit in 1832, but of the actual Friary of that order, we believe not a trace now remains.

IX.—THE ELECTION AS IT USED TO BE.

In previous articles we have discussed, for the most part, events which have transpired outside the area of living memory, and the history of buildings and institutions established in past centuries. But a chapter devoted to scenes and times which, while having occurred within the lives of many of our present citizens, and yet which are "forgotten" except when some circumstance of present-day life lights the closed chamber of the memory, cannot be out of place. Some of the events to be mentioned have taken place within the last five-and-twenty years; indeed, the last date we propose to draw upon is the year 1874.

The excitement, the party feeling, and the keen fights for votes of modern Parliamentary elections are well known to us all, but if we may trust the records of the "good old doys," the modern excitement may hide its diminished head in shame, for words of to-day were blows then, and the cheering and the chairing of our time had their prototypes in fanatical party demonstrations thirty, forty, and fifty years ago.

The Corrupt Practices Act may be held largely responsible for the check placed upon these proceedings. Bribery, as we know it now, had another name in the times of which we write, and the man with the longest purse had the best chance of gaining the seat he coveted. The woes of a modern Parliamentary candidate are unquestionably extensive and deep, but his pockets are not drawn upon to the extent of the demands—for they practically amounted to that—made upon his forefathers on the thorny road to St. Stephen's. Lincoln, we suppose, was no worse in this or other respects than that of towns elsewhere in the country, and probably a little better than some, and it may be taken for granted that there was many a man on the Burgess Roll who scorned the openly proffered or indirectly hinted bribe, and voted as his heart and head prompted. Still, there was a large class, and possibly the balance of the gift of the seat lay in their hands to a large extent, whose votes were only too easily to be secured by the highest bidder. We cannot stay here, of course, to discuss the arguments for and against bribery of this kind, further than to say that it cannot be denied that the vote-sellers benefited very considerably by the sale of their convictions to the opposing candidate, and that a number of homes were bettered by this questionable means.

But there were other ways in which candidates put money into the hands of electors. The canvassing, for instance, was done on a much more elaborate scale than now, and a candidate was frequently accompanied on his visits to likely or "wobbling" sup-

porters by a hired band of musicians, who played a selection out
side the house while the candidate was negotiating with the voter
on the other side of the door.   Whether the idea was to "charm"
the   good   man   and true, after the manner of an Indian snake-
charmer, with his sinuous companions, or whether the show of
pomp and circumstance was intended to impress him, is not recorded.

Voters had often a considerable distance to come, and it is stated
that on one occasion Sir William Ingleby hired every donkey and
cart in the city, and a great number of boats, to bring electors from
the Fen district, all the way from Lincoln to Boston, in which
latter town were several of his supporters, and who thus travelled
to Lincoln, and recorded their votes for the enterprising and ultimately successful candidate.

Another way in which the independent elector put money in his
purse occurred during the famous agitation against the Slave
Trade.   Lincoln may be taken as a very faithful reflex of the
country, which rang with the indignation of Englishmen and Eng-
lishwomen against the continuance of slavery within British Colo-
nial dominions.   The abolition of slavery in our Colonies in 1834,
and the name of William Wilberforce will never be forgotten.   A
candidate for Lincoln Parliamentary honours hit on a happy idea
during this agitation.   He engaged a number of boys and men to
"make-up" as and impersonate the unfortunate slaves, and these
were marched up and down High-street, with overseer and whip
complete, several times, the desirability of voting for the candidate
in question, of course, being duly impressed upon the commiserat-
ing electorate.   An old resident, now, of course, well on for nono-
genarian honours, still tells with great gusto of the impression
created upon the crowd by this re-production of the slave picture
at so opportune a period.   Granville Sharp, Clarkson, Buxton, and
Macaulay were, in their day, also workers for freedom, and Harriett
Beecher Stowe's graphic story aimed not the least blow that eventually snapped the chain.   Well may we re-echo the words of
Cowper :

> Slaves cannot breathe in England : if their lungs
> Receive our air, that moment they are free,
> They. touch our country, and their fetters fall.

It has not always happened that the right man has been returned
at the top of the poll at Lincoln—the right man, that is, in the
opinion of the noisier portion of the inhabitants.   By inhabitants
we do not necessarily infer voters, for the blatant man who airs
his opinion so freely is usually missing from the electoral list.   But
there has ever been a class who, if "their" candidate has been defeated (and it is deplorable to have to relate that he very often
was, if we may judge by consequences), forthwith revenged themselves by rioting in the streets of the city.   As may be expected,
window-breaking was the chief form of this amusement, though a

stack of hay or wood, or even a house, sometimes received a fiery baptism, and woe to the man of the hated colour who ventured to show his head. It is in no party spirit, but solely by the records, that we place the majority of the rioting at the doors of the Liberals. The solid fact exists, however, that Liberal members were more than once returned (in the days we write of Lincoln had two seats in the House of Commons), and everything was afterwards as quiet in the city as if no untoward event had stirred it to its deepest depths, while, when a member or members of the Tory party have been returned, a long line of broken windows and a night illuminated by flaring torches and fiery tar-barrels, and rent with shouts of partisanship and general defiance of law and order, has followed. Processions of men with party flags were common, and it was a frequent occurrence for the Tory procession to be met (on the Lindum-road for choice), and stripped of its bunting. "We met 'em on the New-road," said an old gentleman interviewed for the purposes of this article, his eyes sparkling at the reminiscence, "and they often had as many flags as men; we went at it hammer an' tongs, and in five minutes there wasn't a Tory flag left." The proud air with which the victory was announced defies description, except from the pen of a Dickens.

In connection with broken windows, probably no building in the city could approach the record of the Saracen's Head Hotel, but the White Hart, Spread Eagle, and Queen Hotels have suffered too, as well as a great number of private houses, party leaders coming out prominently here—and retiring just as conspicuously at the time.

Hoping to profit by experience, a barricade of considerable strength was once erected before the White Hart, but proved useless, it being destroyed by the mob, who retaliated by not only breaking the windows as before, but brought out a considerable number of bottles of liquor from the Hotel, and drank what they listed, and smashed the remainder. When Mr. Seely was returned on Saturday, Nov. 9th, 1861, the Saracen's Head lamp and eighteen panes of glass, the Spread Eagle and Queen lamps and other glass was shattered. The police interfered, and, being pelted with flambeaux and stones, deemed discretion the better part of valour, and beat a retreat. The police got the worst of the encounter on a number of occasions, and the military had to be called in. In February, 1874, when Messrs. Seely (grandfather of the present member) and Chaplin were elected, and Mr. Hinde-Palmer's memorable defeat took place, Mr. Alderman Maltby, then Mayor, found it necessary to read over the Riot Act from the steps of the Great Northern Hotel, previous to a body of soldiers clearing the streets. On another occasion the military were sent for, and were expected to arrive from the south end of High-street. The rioters, determined that their orgies should not be interrupted, erected a stout barricade across the street, near St. Mark's Church. It is recorded that when the Commanding Officer rode up at the head of his men (it was a section of a cavalry regiment) he laughed, set spurs to his horse, galloped forward, and cleared the barricade with a stentorian "Houp la!" and the troops dispersed the astounded mob in double-quick time. Nor were these scenes without a humorous side. A particularly obnoxious rioter, a High-street tradesman, had defied the red coats near Butchery-street. He hurled a missile at one of them, and ran into his shop, hastily securing the door. While concealing himself beneath his counter, however, a pair of thunderous hoofs crashed upon the door, which gave way, and horse and rider advanced into the shop, the chuckling soldier menacing the paralysed fellow with drawn sword. Another citizen, who had hurled an object at the soldiers, was pursued by one of them down Guildhall-street, and brought to bay in Water-lane. He backed up against a wall and begged for mercy, but the soldier put on a fierce look, and thrust at the man with his sword, the weapon striking him and grating the wall beyond him. The terror-stricken man fell, mortally wounded, as he supposed, and his assailant ran back to his comrades. It was only on the arrival of his wife that his victim found that the sword had only passed between his arm and his side, and that he had not so much as a scratch to bear witness to his encounter. Other incidents, humorous and tragic, might be written at some length, did space permit. But we have attained our limit for the present article, and there is a host of other matters in the history of "Forgotten Lincoln" to record.

X.—THE WHITE FRIARS, AND THE STORY OF QUEEN ELEANOR'S CROSS.

Having written at some length, and we believe, also somewhat exhaustively, of the local fortunes of the Black Friars, of whom a souvenir remains to us in the remnant of Monks' Abbey, and of the Grey Friars, we propose to discuss the doings of the White Friars, and the other brotherhoods which made a sojourn within our city.

Unfortunately, the doings of any or all these bodies are but meagrely recorded, and he must research long and deeply who would possess himself of any fair knowledge of their work. The fact that these men went about their duties, as they conceived them, in a simple and unostentatious manner, and preferred seclusion and privacy, in no ordinary sense, to mingling with the busy world for the purpose of mere chatter or publication of their own work, has robbed the historian of much that is interesting. They were not the men, perhaps, who helped to make history, and the historian might have lost sight of them and their deeds for that reason. We are dealing, of course, with the brethren in a local sense. Of the landing and general history of the Friars we have made mention in an earlier article.

If, as Shakespere avers, the deeds that men do live after them, they are deeds other than those of the Friars. They devoted themselves to the people of their time and place, and their good works lie buried in the graves of those who benefited by them. Their buildings are also gone to a great extent, the Grey Friary, wherein the Middle School is now carried on, being by far the best relic of their time. Therein we may recollect the Augustines or Grey Friars; while, wreck though it is, the little ruined chapel of St. Mary, bordering on Monks'-lane, and now termed "Monks' Abbey," is evidence of the local habitation of the Black Friars.

But if we look for the house of the Carmelites, or White Friars, we find ourselves at fault. Anything more widely differing from itself than the site of the White Friary, in the day of that Brotherhood and now, can hardly be conceived. We may well imagine the quaint, quiet edifice, simple and plain as the Friars themselves, which constituted the White Friary in the 13th century. To-day its site is occupied by a busy railway station, and the clangour of the platform bell, the shrieking whistle of the engines, and shouts of porters are heard where the tolling of the Friars' bell scarce disturbed the silence six hundred years ago! The locality, indeed, was formerly rich in places of worship, church, chapel, and friary almost elbowing each other. To-day one of the churches is pulled down, and re-placed by another, and one (St. Edward's) has dis-appeared entirely, not a single stone remaining to mark its site.

The House of the Carmelites must have been one of some size and importance, since it is recorded that it was once used for a sitting of Parliament in the reign of Edward II., a distinction which, we believe, has been accorded to no other religious edifice in Lincoln, excepting the Chapter House attached to the Cathedral. When the Friary, or part of it, was pulled down, the Conduit before the Church of St. Mary-le-Wigford was erected from the remains, as recorded in our account of the work of the Grey Friars. A prominent member or patron of the Friars appears to have been Ranulphus de Kyme, who probably built a chantry at the Carmelite House, and whose effigy was laid in a chapel there, and subsequently removed to the Conduit at St. Mary's. Whether the Conduit is a reproduction of a Carmelite Chapel as it stood, or whether a collection of general fragments were built haphazard, we cannot say, but there is sufficient verification of the fact that the stonework, much of it really beautiful, is from the White Friary, and is, so far as we are aware, the only remnant to be found. The two balls, it should be noted, which surmount either gable, were of a later date. We may again point out that the date on the building is misleading, and refers, not to the erection, but to the time of certain repairs which had been rendered necessary.

But we have one other relic of the White Friars, between the Conduit and the site of the Carmelite House. It is a private dwelling, and is situated in the rear of No. 333, High-street. The front elevation faces south, and is a most excellent piece of workmanship, apart from its historical interest and importance. As an example of timber building, it is well worthy of study; a finer specimen one could not wish to meet with. However, alteration and repair, many times repeated, have changed it considerably—so much so, in point of fact, that neither original window nor door remains in the lower part. There is a danger, by reason of its being out of the way, that the house may be overlooked by the casual visitor, which is a pity, for if he delight in ancient architecture, it is certainly a building he should see. It is reached by a passage running beside the shop of F. Lansdown, plumber and gasfitter, half-a-minute's walk from the Great Northern Station.

That this house belonged to the White Friars is only a tradition, but the tradition is in this case well-founded, and we believe it may be taken for granted that the house is what it pretends to be. But, even apart from that, it should be seen.

From the White Friars we pass to a discussion of the Gilbertines (the only Order, by the way, of English origin), whose building, rather than themselves, has much to interest. The Order had been established by one Gilbert of Sempringham, the son of a personage of some importance, residing near Bourne. The peculiar distinction of the Order was that it combined religious persons of both sexes under a common rule. The house at Lincoln consisted of a convent of monks, and one of nuns, which, while under one roof, were really two separate houses.

The Priory, which stood on the west side of the High-street, in St. Catharines, and is sometimes referred to as the Hospital of St. Catharine's (not to be confounded with the Leper Hospital, which stood about 100 yards away), was founded by Robert de Chesney, fourth Bishop of Lincoln, in 1148. Being situated outside the city walls—for the Bargates, in the south wall, did not extend further than the line of South Park and Altham-terrace—the Priory had thrown upon it many hospitable duties—duties which, inns and other houses of entertainment being scarce, devolved upon the monasteries in those days.

The principal guests recorded as spending a night within its walls were the bearers of the body of Queen Eleanor. The sad story of Edward the First's Queen is a matter of the history of our land rather than of the city itself. While with her liege lord at Clipstone Castle, in Sherwood Forest, where he was holding a Parliament, Eleanor was taken ill, and, presumably for quiet or a change of air, was removed to the house of Weston, one of the knights of her train, at Harby. Medical aid was summoned from Lincoln, but she sank slowly, and, after two months' illness, wasted away with inward fever, and died on November 29th, 1290.

Thus we get the beautiful story, unique in history, of how a broken-hearted king decreed that she should be embalmed and taken to London, her nightly resting-place being marked by a memorial cross. The first stage of the funereal journey was at St. Catharine's Priory, where the body was embalmed. A portion of her remains were placed in the Cathedral, and a splendid altar-tomb, with an effigy in gilt copper, erected under the east window, but this was destroyed in the Civil War in 1644, when the Cathedral was taken by the Puritans of the Earl of Manchester. The tomb was recently restored by the munificence of Mr. Joseph Ruston.

In accordance with Edward's wish, a cross, stated to have been a most beautiful piece of tabernacle work, adorned the statues of the deceased Queen, and similar to the Crosses at Northampton, Geddington, and Waltham, was designed by Richard of Stowe—the artist to whom we owe our glorious Angel Choir in the Cathedral. The Cross was erected on Swine's Green, opposite the Priory, and was repaired at the Corporate expense in 1624, but, like so many of our best local monuments, suffered demolition at the hands of the Puritans twenty years later. We are informed that one fragment, and one only, remains, and this, the lower portion of one of the statues of the Queen, was to be seen in the garden of Mr. E. M. Burton, in Eastgate, but was presented by him to the Castle Museum, and now stands just within the Castle-gate. On December 4th, 1290, the funereal train, accompanied by the bereaved Edward in person, set out from St. Catharine's Priory for Westminster Abbey, and the course of the long journey was marked by the series of Crosses which stretched from Swine Green at Lincoln to the little village of Charing, which latter is the Charing Cross in the heart of busy London to-day.

When St. Catharine's Priory was pulled down, a stately mansion was erected on the site by Sir Thomas Grantham's family, and here King James the First took up his quarters on the occasion of his visit to Lincoln on March 17th, 1617. The house of Sir Thomas, indeed, seems to have been famous in all the country round for its hospitality and generous board.

There is a remarkable statute of our Cathedral to the effect that the Bishops of Lincoln are bound to sleep at Catharine's the night previous to their enthronement, and from thence to walk barefoot to the Cathedral. The late Precentor Venables, who affirms that this statute is still unrepealed, observes that he is inclined to think that it was always more honoured in the breach than in the observance.

There is a record that the only De Sacco Friary (Friars de Penitentia), was at Lincoln, but of their house there is not a trace remaining.

XI.—THE STONEBOW AND GUILDHALL.

"Now," says the average reader, "how can a building be classed as 'forgotten' which we see a dozen times a day? The Stonebow is not forgotten, and never will be whilst Lincoln has an inhabitant left!"

Quite so; but we dare affirm that nine-tenths of the people who pass beneath its arches are unacquainted with its history, except in a very general way. It is very old, of course, and has been a gate at one time, but at present it is rather in the way than otherwise. Then the man who has read his guide book steps in, and supplements this with a description of the images and carvings on its surface; but we believe we are right in saying that so extended a notice as we purpose giving has not hitherto appeared in any one compilation.

We may divide our subject into three sections, viz., the Stonebow, the Guildhall, and the Ancient City Prison.

Proceeding up the High-street from the lower part of the city, the Stonebow is seen at its best. Mr. E. J. Wilson in his "Picturesque Antiquities" speaks of the Stonebow as "a large gatehouse crossing the street with a very stately front towards the south. The date of its erection has been differently stated, some accounts making it 1592, whilst others refer it to the reign of Richard II., two centuries earlier." However, there is much doubt on the point, and it is quite possible that neither of the dates is correct. The statues of the Virgin and of the Angel Gabriel, which are placed conspicuously on the south front, would decidedly not have been affixed there in the time Elizabeth. "when the barbarous zeal of the Reformers warred against the finest monuments of art as so many profane idols, nor does the style appear so early as Richard the Second's reign."

The fact is, that the ornamentation of the Stonebow has been so added to from time to time that the original work has been to some extent obliterated in order to make room for embellishments of later date, but several authorities agree that it is probable that the gate was built late in the 15th or early in the 16th century, perhaps not before Henry VIII.'s time, the balance of opinion, perhaps, inclining to the latter. But it must not be taken that the situation of this gate was a new thing. As we stated in the historical summary with which this series of articles opened, the first gateway was placed in the southern wall of the Roman city of Lindum Colonia. Like the vast majority of Roman buildings, this existed for several centuries, and a renewal of the structure is recorded in the 14th century.

But, though it has thus been a gateway since the first century, it is interesting to note that its entrance has never been barred by doors. It appears to have been guarded by an iron chain, stretched from pillar to pillar across the roadway, and secured by a lock. This was a common mode of forming a barrier against the progress of horsemen and vehicles, and was probably similar to the chains which guarded several of the principal streets of London up to as late as the reign of the Second Charles. It also formed a breast-work, as a provision where a guard of pikemen might oppose the advance of an enemy.

Fancy our old Stonebow under such conditions—how picturesque it would appear! The gateway itself, strong, imposing, its central arch forming a fitting framework to the group of pikemen with their formidable weapons held ready to check the advance of the enemy crossing the Witham, the great chain constituting a powerful ally to the array of men gathered there to defend the city!

But even in our own time the Stonebow has been in danger. Numerous proposals have been made to demolish it, on the ground that traffic was seriously impeded by it, and that it blocked up a lengthy view of the main street of the city. The improvement of Mint-lane (now Mint-street) some few years ago has drawn off the Newland traffic, which now passes northward of the Stonebow, by Smith, Ellison, and Co.'s Bank, and by a gradient emerges into Newland at the upper end of Water-lane. Still, there is certainly something in the argument that traffic is inconvenienced by the relatively small passage of its archway, which can only accommodate one vehicle at a time. Yet this cannot be accepted as anything approaching a sufficient reason for the demolition of the old relic. We recollect one proposal was to the effect that a fitting position for the old gateway would be at the lower main entrance of the Arboretum, and for a time this found a certain amount of favour, but eventually died out.

We may take it for granted now that where there is one person who desires the Stonebow removed or destroyed, there are three who would prefer it to remain where and as it is. It would be a hard matter to prophesy which will eventually gain the day. The growth of the capital city of England has necessitated the pulling down of many historical buildings and the obliteration of several landmarks, and the march of progress seems to be greedily, if gradually, doing the same in many of our large towns. Whether this will be the eventual fate of our central gateway, time will tell. But we may be certain that it would not be lost without a great struggle on the part of those who admire and revere it, both for its beauty and for its historical associations.

To come to a closer description of the Bow, the old gateway may be said to consist of a large pointed central arch, guarded on either side by a round tower, each bordered, in turn, by a lesser gate or postern, of flat or elliptical character. Over the central arch is a coat of arms, now greatly defaced, with the motto "Ave gratia plena Dominus tecum"—"Hail full of grace (highly favoured) the Lord is

with thee." On the central arch, to the south, according to the
Rev. — Simpson, son of the antiquarian, are the Royal arms, and
to the north, on the eastern side, a Red Rose (Lancaster) crowned;
with a Fleur-de-Lys (Lincoln), also crowned, on the western side.

The Annunciation, represented on the southern front, was a
favourite subject for sculpture, and though the two figures on the
round towers are now "the worse for wear," they are still fine specimens of early work in this direction. The Virgin, standing on a
dragon, is on the one side, and the Archangel Gabriel on the other.

The old clock, given by Mr. J. Fardell, who represented the city
in Parliament 1830-1, had got very unreliable, when some few years
back Mr. F. H. Kerans, then Member for Lincoln, re-placed it with
the present timekeeper. Many humorous stories, for which, however, space refuses insertion, are told of the waywardness of the
old clock. To sum up, the Stonebow is one of the oldest—some say
the oldest—gateways in the Kingdom, and one of which we may be
justly proud.

Over the arches is the Guildhall, now used for meetings of the
Lincoln City Council, and for other meetings at the discretion of
the Mayor. It is a capital specimen of a timber-roofed chamber,
in which are some particularly notable Royal portraits. It is
worthy of note, in passing, that there were at one time four wards
in the city, a number to which there appears a growing desire to
return.

For a considerable time the Guildhall was used for the City
Sessions and Assizes, in fact, until a more suitable building for this
business was erected. The inner hall was formerly appropriated to
the Aldermen, and of late the chamber in which were kept the
Corporation records. It is unfortunate that these documents go no
further back than the time of the Reformation; the cause of this
deficiency seems to be unexplained. In this inner hall, too, suc-
cessive Mayors have robed themselves on assuming the duties apper-
taining to the civic chair, and a long and worthy list these gentlemen make.

The whole building, then, is a notable one, and Mr. Pearson,
called in some years back by the Corporation to secure the continued
stability of the erection, has earned the thanks of the citizens for
the successful measures he took to deal with what, ere now, must
have threatened our most southern existing gateway's safety.

The eastern wing of the building, now in use as the offices of the
Town Clerk, and others, deserves mention, inasmuch as it was
formerly the city prison, even so late as 1809, presumably to be near
the justice-room, which we now call the Guildhall. The prison was
a most loathsome place; in fact, nowhere in the city do we find
record of anything so repulsive, or so horrible, or so condemnable.
Strange that it should be found under the only roof devoted to local
temporal justice! It was a most insanitary place, with unglazed
windows. Howard, the renowned philanthropist, who visited it in
1784, and again four years later describes it in unqualified terms as

the worst in the kingdom, while Nield, in a letter to Lettom in 1802, calls it "a disgrace to the city and shocking to humanity."

The prisoners are declared to have been half-starved, half-suffocated, and in a state of continual intoxication. The allowance was 2½d a day, and the prisoners were able to beg alms through the windows, the latter being invariably spent in drink. Water was an unknown luxury, and straw was not a portion of their allowance, while they were also without a square inch of exercise ground. It was a good thing for all concerned when, after receiving the condemnation of every humane person, this hole was abandoned in favour of the new gaol and court-house, Monks'-road (now the Sessions House, where the city magistrates sit daily, and where other Courts are held) in 1809.

Taken as a whole, therefore, the Stonebow buildings have been the locale of very opposite acts, from the highest civic proceedings in the city to the lowest degradation ever perpetrated in Lincoln in the name of the law.

XII.—THE CATHEDRAL CHURCH OF ST. MARY.

Can any compilation, however small or however great, dealing with the city of Lincoln be brought together without having mention of the Cathedral as a central feature? No building in the city comes less under the head of "Forgotten Lincoln," yet it would be discourteous, not to say quite impossible, to endeavour to ignore the noble edifice which, seen near or afar, dominates the surrounding landscape.

We have complained before now that the history of Lincoln is scattered and fragmentary. This hardly holds good in the present instance, for we have fairly ample records of the the establishment, erection, and subsequent history of our Cathedral to afford matter for a dozen such articles as the solitary one we are able to devote to it. But there is a host of other matter and an array of other buildings awaiting our attention, and a brief notice of the Cathedral must be taken, not so much for the space it occupies, as evidence of our desire to give as much of the city as possible.

In the large quantity of matter, and comments and criticisms on that matter, which is written, so to speak, round the Cathedral, we must "choose the best, and leave the rest." But the stirring scenes both during and after its erection, which have occurred there are unequalled in the records of any other building in Lincoln, as, indeed, fits the Queen of them all !

One looks at the stupendous edifice, at the lengthy and intricately-worked West Front, at the imposing and dignified Galilee Porch, at the shorn but yet beautiful South Porch, and then up at the noble towers, only to marvel, in spite of oneself, at the patience and ability and talent and genius, which conceived and carried out its erection, under the comparatively crude architectural resources of eight and nine centuries ago. A view of the interior, still bearing mute token of the robbery and destruction wrought upon it by the Puritans, a glance from the western end along the glorious nave, through the open doors at its further limit, and across the Choir beyond this, and one is simply lost in wonder how the people of the past ever got stone upon stone and pile upon pile.

An ascent of the Rood Tower, with its weary round of stairs, and final emerging upon the lead-covered roof, leaves the problem still unsolved, in fact, further complicates it. What a feast for the eye and the brain ! The best description of the view from the summit of this tower is, in our opinion, that of the late antiquarian enthusiast, Sir Charles Anderson, Bart. ; and it is so good that we quote it from his "Pocket Guide to Lincoln" in full. He writes: "Let anyone ascend the broad tower of the Minster on a sunny day before harvest, when light clouds are sailing calmly in the blue sky, and passing shadows and catching gleams play over the surface of the landscape, he will have a grand panorama. To the north, fields yellow, green, brown, and crimson, teeming with agricultural wealth, interspersed with plantations, among which may be seen the modern Palace of Riseholme, with many a substantial farm gleaming like white spectres towards the distant Wolds. To the east, the woods of Sudbrooke, and, beyond, a long stretch of level fen, equally varied in tints, with the Castle of Tattershall, and the lofty tower of Boston, commonly called 'the Stump,' in the horizon. On the south, the green slope of Canwick (the abode of the Sibthorps), the tower of Washingborough, and, below, the River Witham, the Cow Paddle, the dusky factories of the great chiefs of agricultural machinery, the ivied ruins of the Palace, the Vicars' Court, and the long, straggling city, with the towers of St. Peter-at-Arches, St. Peter-at-Gowt's, and St. Mary-le-Wigford, with the new spire of St. Mark, now dwarfed by the lofty chimneys around them. Beyond, to the south-west, the drained and cultivated flat where the Corporation swans once sailed in their pride on the broad expanse of Swanpool. Still farther, in the lengthening distance, that Vale so dear to foxhunters, with many a graceful spire, terminating in the ducal towers of Belvoir. To the west and north-west, the old hall at Doddington, rising over the woods of Skellingthorpe, the groves of Burton (the residence of the Monsons), the lumpish tower of Saxon Stow, the marl hills of Nottinghamshire, and on a very clear day the faint outline of the Derbyshire Moors."

Though eight hundred years old, Lincoln Cathedral is one of the youngest in England. At the same time, it is representative of two Sees that belong to the very earliest period of the English Church, viz., that of Lindsey, founded in 678, after the conversion of its inhabitants by Paulinus of York, and that of the Middle Angles, the seat of which latter was placed at Leicester in 680. The fire-reddened walls of Stow Church to this day bear testimony to the flames kindled there by the Pagan Danes, when they drove the Bishops of Mercia further inland, and effaced the Bishopric of Lindsey altogether.

These Christians next planted their church at Dorchester, which became the Cathedral Church of the whole stretch of country, from the Humber to the Thames, and including no fewer than 10 counties —Lincoln, Rutland, Cambridge, Huntingdon, Bedford, Buckingham, Oxford, Hertford, Leicester, & Northampton. But William the Conqueror granted the transfer of the See to Lincoln, on the application of Remy (Remigius), to whom, for his services on the Conqueror's invasion, the latter had promised the first vacant Bishopric. Remigius, however, had ben accustomed to the comparative splendour of a Norman Monastery, and looked with probably something akin to contempt on the modest episcopal See at Dorchester, which, by the death of Wulfry, was first vacant, and preferred a more central site than that on the very border of his extensive diocese.

He chose Lincoln.   Gradually, but surely, there arose on the northern hill of the city a building, which, altered and added to from time to time, is the building which crowns the city to-day.

But what a labour the building, aye, and the defending of it, was! How heart-breaking it must have been when, after years of toil, a portion was completed only to be almost utterly demolished by some uprising of the period.   What vigilance we read of as being displayed in the watching of the great and grand pile in troublous times.   Yet, despite the number and severity of the blows launched against it, the Cathedral grew and extended.   Many of these struggles, though an attack upon the lordly Cathedral was included, partly because it offered too many temptations for wreckage to an angry mob to be disregarded, and partly because some of them were of a "religious" nature, are really more concerned with the history of the city itself than of the Cathedral Church, and as such we hope to deal with them, in noting various buildings, institutions, and times.

But the Cathedral suffered from other than human enemies. Bishop Alexander had completed some important work, when, in 1185, on April 15th, a shock of earthquake rent the great church from top to bottom.   We may note here that, by reason of Henry the Second's notorious neglect, Lincoln, in common with other dioceses, had no Bishop, the King preferring that the revenues might help to fill his own ever-ready coffers.   However, the next year, Hugh of Avalon was appointed, and though he found his Cathedral half in ruins, at once set about its restoration.   While one stone of our Cathedral remains above another, Bishop Hugh's name will be venerated.   Truly, he was a practical enthusiast, for not only did he direct the work to which he personally largely contributed, but could from time to time be seen shouldering the hod, and carrying the cut stones and the mortar for the use of the builders.

His death unfortunately prevented the full completion of his scheme, though part of it was carried out subsequently.

Time marched on, and the next important incident we read of as affecting the Church was the fall of the Central Tower, during Grostete's Bishopric.   We all know the story, surely—how Grostete was at variance with the other authorities of the building, and how he, preaching there one day, declared if he were silent on the subject of their misdeeds the very stones would fall, upon which the Central Tower did crash down!

Is there, we wonder, any sculpture more beautiful in any Cathedral than the Angel Choir?   It is worthy of more than interested contemplation; it is worthy of study.   And then the quiet calm of of the Cloisters, which come next, what retirement, what peace they speak of!   Last of all, there are the Western Towers, which, with various little Chantry Chapels, completed the Cathedral as we have it now.   The history of its erection is one of struggle and indomitable perseverance all through, and should make us the more proud as we reflect that it is not only the keystone of one of the oldest dioceses in England, but also a memento of the zeal and energy and deep-rooted faith of our forefathers.

This is no place for a detailed description of the present interior. The reading of a guide-book, pure and simple, at any other place than that described is apt to be uninteresting and irritating. Besides which, there are sufficient books to be had which deal at length with the Cathedral and its monuments.

XIII.—THE MINT.

To many it will seem remarkable that Lincoln once possessed a Mint—a place where current coin was struck, and whence it was issued for circulation; while to the historian, it may be that this article will appear almost unnecessary, as his class is mostly familiar with the fact and its circumstances. But as the avowed object of these articles is not so much to serve historians with new matter as to interest others whose knowledge of Lincoln's past is slight, we perceive a real need for the inclusion of as complete a budget of information on the subject as we have been able to obtain.

The Mint of Lincoln is verily a thing of the past now. We may walk along the street which is named after it without observing the slightest indication that here stood in bygone days one of the most important institutions in the whole city. One corner is still very appropriately occupied by a bank, that of Messrs. Smith, Ellison, and Co., and a most imposing frontage it presents—a remarkable contrast from the street front represented in a scarce old print we have been privileged to see, and which depicts the street as it was more than 50 years ago. The Mint Lane of that day has been widened, and the thoroughfare has pierced through into Newland, taking upon itself at the same time the more dignified appellative of Mint-street. The walls of the "Mint Hall" were taken down some time ago for the widening of the street.

The earliest date of the existence of a Mint in Lincoln appears to be a matter for much controversy. That noted antiquary, Mr. Maurice Johnson, the founder of a Literary and Scientific Society at Spalding in 1710, gave a local origin to several coins issued under the authority of the Roman Emperors. On these, or some of these, coins appear the letters L.C., and these he interpreted as the initials of Lindum Colonia.

But at the annual meeting of the Archæological Institute of Great Britain and Ireland, held at Lincoln in July, 1848, Mr. Edward Hawkins, keeper of the antiquities at the British Museum, took exception to this. He admits, of course, that the Roman name of the city was Lindum Colonia, but he considers that the initial L may have stood for Londinium (London) or even Lugdunum (Lyons), while the C might imply Civitas, which was applicable to any of the towns. It may also have meant Cura, a term used upon many coins as signifying that the coin was struck at the place indicated by the preceding letters.

However this may be—and Mr. Johnson's opinion seems entirely influenced by the two letters L.C.—there can be little doubt that a Roman Mint really did exist in Lincoln. Mr. Hawkins hardly goes so far as to deny that. Indeed, he considers it by no means improbable that Lincoln may have been one of the places where coins were struck when Britain was under the Roman sceptre.

Like the majority of historians, however, his conjectures are conjectures merely. There appears to be absolutely no evidence, so far as an assiduous search has been able to find, to conclusively prove that a Mint was established in Lincoln in Roman times, and we can hear of no coins indisputably of the origin of the Mint—if there was one—of this period. Mr. Johnson's assertion we cannot take into account, since opinions are so strongly divided upon it. For ourselves, we are inclined to attach the more weight to the contentions of Mr. Hawkins and others, for the mere basing of an argument on the two letters above quoted is not nearly sufficient proof, to say the least. As a matter of fact, it is by no means certain that the coins in dispute were struck in Britain at all—Mr. Hawkins himself quotes Lyons as an instance, and the side-issue might certainly be followed further, did space permit.

The question may be asked, and has been asked by a number of people, do the letters on the coins really refer to the places where they were minted?

A close comparison of the opinions of some of the leading authorities appears to prove conclusively that they do. Enthusiasts in numismatics will be quite well aware that the privilege of coining was enjoyed by an appreciably large number of cities in various parts of the empire and its colonies.

The "Mint wall" pulled down some years ago, but which may probably be remembered by older citizens, was certainly of Roman construction. A notable authority, whose opinion on this matter is for many reasons valued very highly, gives it as his belief that while the wall was of indisputably Roman origin, and very probably a part of the premises where a Mint stood also, it was not part of a Mint-house in Roman times. He proceeds to explain the apparent paradox by the statement that it was very likely the site of a Mint of a later age, when all authorities are agreed that a Mint really did exist in the city.

Coins professing to be Roman were certainly manufactured in the city, "but whether," says this same authority, "forgeries by individuals, with a view to deception for their own particular profit, or by persons, perhaps officials, whose practices were connived at, though not regularly authorised, is a question upon which antiquaries are not at present agreed, and probably never will be." Moulds consisting of flat pieces of clay, having on either side an intaglio impression of a Roman coin, have been found at Lincoln, but—and this is rather remarkable—not, we believe, within the boundaries of Roman Lincoln.

Several numismatic writer (Ruding, for instance), establish Lincoln's claim to a Mintage not earlier than the reign of Edgar, but Mr. Hawkins again steps forward, this time with the bold assertion that there was a Mintage at Lincoln in the time of Alfred, fifty years earlier, and, what is more, makes good his case. He attributes the mistake on the part of other antiquaries to the fact that the monograms of Lincoln and London were somewhat alike, and several people must have passed over the Lincoln monograms as those of London. It is certainly curious that Ruding himself should give an engraving of a coin of Alfred, with the Lincoln monogram, and at the same time assert positively that Lincoln had no coin of its own minting in that reign.

Another coin to which attention is drawn is one bearing the inscription LINCOIA CIVIT., and the name of St. Martin. This was struck early in the tenth century. It resembles a number of the coins struck between 927 and 951 of Eric of Northumberland, and as Saint Martin was generally esteemed Patron Saint of our city at this period, the coin is attributed to a Lincoln Mint. Coins bearing the name of Saint Peter were certainly known to have been struck at York, where Paulinus, Archbishop there, had dedicated a church to that Saint. Paulinus is accredited with having built a Christian Church at Lincoln, and this was afterwards known as that of Saint Martin.

It is lamentable, however, that no coins bearing the names of either Edward the Elder, Æthelstan, Eadmund, Eadred, or Eadwig are now extant. From this point the public records show that the Mint of Lincoln was rapidly advancing in importance and increasing in wealth. In the reign of Edward the Confessor the city paid £30 to the King and Earl, and when Domesday Book was compiled it paid £100, and the Mint £75. This sum, so far as the records may be relied upon, was larger than that paid by any other Mint, and egotistical citizens may feel inclined, with more or less truth, to attribute it to the important place held by the Mint at that period.

We are unable to learn that any coins of the reigns of John or the first Richard are now in existence, but records yet preserved prove that the Mint was still flourishing. Richard granted certain privileges to the citizens of Lincoln at the commencement of his reign, from which the King's officers and moneyers were excluded. John, in the ninth year of his reign, commanded the moneyers and officers of certain cities, of which Lincoln was one, to seal up their dies with their own seals and appear at Westminster, within fifteen days of the morrow of St. Denys, to receive there the King's commands.

A puzzle to numismatics for some time was a number of coins bearing the word NICOLE, as the word of a town. Not having referred much to written documents, they were unable to locate it, but it is now positively known that Nicole and Lincoln are and were one. The reason of the extraordinary change of name is supposed by many to have come from the propensity of our Continental neighbours to alter and transpose every name they had occasion to use.

A consultation of the rolls of Prliament from Edward I. to Henry VIII., shows whenever an entry referring to Lincoln is made in the

French language the name of this city is written Nicole. In the proceedings and ordinances of the Privy Council the same thing occurs, but in these latter documents the name Lincoln is occasionally used in French as early as the reign of the fourth Henry. The word NICOLE, however, only appeared upon what were known as the "short-cross pennies," which some writers suppose to have been struck by Henry II. in 1180. This monarch certainly did introduce in 1180 a French artist, one Philip Aymary, of Tours, to superintend a new and improved coinage, and this, it is admitted, strengthens the assumption.

Later than the reign of the first Edward we have no reliable record of a Mint at Lincoln, and we must now be content with the coinage issued from the Mint standing almost under the shadow of that mighty queen of fortresses, the Tower of London.

XIV.—EXISTING RELICS OF ROMAN DAYS.
PART I.

There have been unearthed in modern Lincoln a number of relics, large and small, of the period of the Roman colony, but there must be many articles or portions of buildings yet hidden beneath our feet. Every time an excavation for gas, water, building, or other purposes is made within the limits of the site of Lindum Colonia the eyes of the antiquarian are keenly alert, and his vigilance rarely goes unrewarded. Yet we have not found one-half, probably, of what exists underground, and as the removal of the houses in Bailgate en bloc is somewhat unlikely, whatever may lie beneath them, we are afraid, will not be revealed to us, unless it is by the agency of an earthquake or other unlooked-for visitation.

But our immediate purpose is to deal with what has been found from time to time of Roman Lincoln, not to conjecture on what may or may not be hidden from us.

Let us take first the walls of Lindum Colonia. Newport, the northern gate, yet stands to mark the old exit. We can find traces of the southern gate near the Leopard Inn, but the others are gone. It will be remembered that the western gate was lost for many years, and only discovered after long and wide search. Now, this need never have been, had the searchers closely studied their map. Ermine-street ran straight as a die to the Newport Gate. The old Foss Road ran, before its course was diverted for stone quarrying and other purposes, exactly straight for the Eastern Gate, and the Burton Road ran unswervingly straight to the lost Western Gate. before it was turned aside. The modern map of Lincoln strikingly reveals the Burton and Foss Roads running from east and west, and making straight for these gates. How it was, as an old antiquary said the other day to the writer, that the Western Gate was missed so long, when the solution lay practically under the noses of the searchers, is a mystery.

But where are the walls now? Of the north, portions remain near the Arch; of the east, there is a remnant in the garden of Mr. Alfred Shuttleworth; there is, or was, a bit of the south near the Sub-Deanery; and a part of the west beside Motherby Hill. Indeed, some state that the Park and Motherby Hill are built upon the south wall itself, though we have not seen any convincing testimony on this point, if any such exists.

Part of the extended east wall (when the Roman city was doubled in size, and brought down almost to the Witham), was discovered in digging for the insertions of the foundations of the new Constitutional Club at the corner of Silver-street and Broadgate. It was from eleven to twelve feet in thickness, and had to be blasted away,

that portion, at least, which was absolutely necessary. It is due to
Mr. W. Watkins, the architect of the building, to say that he took
care that only that part absolutely in the way for the new flooring
was removed, the remainder being left. Doubtless, more of the
wall remains—at least, towards the north, and it may also be mentioned that the uncovered portion was quite straight, and evidently
making for a point about Thorngate.

Most people interested in the ancient town will have seen the
remnants of a Roman portico existing under the house of Mr. George
Allis, Bailgate. This is, perhaps, one of the most important relics
of the period we have. It was not discovered all at once—by all,
we mean the nineteen bases in a direct line, of which three are
beneath Mr. Allis' house—but at various periods, and caused much
excitement when the first were unearthed in 1878. Three of the
bases, as we have said, may be seen in a specially-adapted cellar of
Mr. Allis' house, two are beneath the property of Mr. Wilson Blaze,
and the remainder are under the street (Bailgate). Having once
been discovered, however, it was not intended that the spot beneath
which they stand should be lost again, and accordingly each is
marked by white Hopton setts, presenting a distinct appearance
from the other paving. What manner of house the building before
which these pillars stood could have been, is not quite clear, but
some of the best authorities, including a beloved Bishop, now dead,
have expressed the opinion that so large a building—for the front
measures 283 feet in length, and the building evidently extended
236 feet back—was probably a storehouse for food, at a time when
the Governor of the colony—as was customary—received provender
for the people, and was responsible for it. Others, amongst them
the late Precentor of Lincoln, inclined to the opinion that the
building was the Basilica, or Hall of Justice. The bases to be
seen are massively built (indeed, the wonder would be to find anything of this period that was not built for strength, yet, nevertheless, with a beauty of its own), and of imposing appearance.

It will be fresh in the memory of citizens that further excavations
—this time for the express purpose of finding the missing pillars—
were made early in last year, with the result that the columns, it is
believed, of the completed front are now located. There are now
one triple column, and clear evidence of another, four double
columns, and thirteen single columns, the full length of the frontage
being 283 feet. The triple columns can only be accounted for, perhaps, on the assumption, held by many antiquarians, that these extra
pillars, as in the case of the double columns, were placed there for
the purpose of giving an air of strength to the building. Other conjectures, of course, there are, but we fail to see a case made out in
any other direction. Nineteen pillars are now defined, but only one
of these exists triple. It is worthy of note with regard to this last
discovery, that the moulding is rather different to the others. It
has frequently been asserted that the Romans never adopted a pattern of moulding which would hold water. The mouldings on this

particular column are decidedly Roman, and certainly hold water.

Further along the Bail, near Mr. Elderkin's shop, there was unearthed, also in excavating, a portion of a base of great strength. It was not taken out, but was built round, and is yet beneath the ground. The best authorities incline to the opinion that it was the base of a pedestal or column supporting a statue of some notable. Possibly, it was a local Governor or other person of importance.

But we have not done with Mr. Allis and his relics and explorations. An old sewer, presumed to be Roman, was accidentally discovered near the shop of Mr. Wilson Blaze some years ago, large enough in circumference to admit the passage of a man's body. Mr. Allis walked along this for a considerable distance—nearly to Newport Arch, he judges—and found no sign of an end, while the sewer evidently ran a long way southward. It has been suggested that an entrance to this sewer be constructed from the apartment in which are the portico bases, but Mr. Allis has declined for sanitary reasons. Asked as to the feeling when penetrating the long-disused sewer, our informant replied that the place was very dark and very damp. There were breaks in the upper portions, evidently communicating with the old street.

Mr. Allis also possesses a small museum of an absorbingly interesting character. Most important in his collection is a Roman sword, found in the Fossdyke several years ago. Mr. Roach Smith, the great antiquary, judges this to be unique, and many visitors have expressed great interest in it. We believe Mr. Allis has had a tempting offer for the weapon, a portion of the scabbard of which he also preserves, but he resolutely declines to part with any of them. Then there is a notable mould, most probably of soft Lincoln top clay. This has been pressed by the right hand, and the impression taken with the left. It is particularly worthy of note that the mould bears, not only the finger-marks, but the very lines on the skin of the worker's fingers! Professor Freeman, the late historian, held the Romans were cleverer with the right hand than with the left. The figure on the mould is half a female head. There is, further, a great quantity of pottery, and some flat bricks, one of which is branded with the maker's name—it being, says an authority, the custom in Roman times to brand one in each hundred. Mr. Allis has also a cast of the moulding on the eastern Roman wall, discovered when the Dean and Chapter of the Cathedral were making a heating chamber near the Chapter House.

The owner of these relics tells with a chuckle the story of Dean Blakesley's visit, with his wife and little son, some seventeen years ago. The youngster was particularly impressed with Mr. Allis' bits of pottery ware. He made a number of comments on them, his mother vainly endeavouring to silence him, so that the company might have the benefit of the Dean's expressions on the remains. But the sight of so many pieces of ancient crockery was too much for the little fellow. "My!" he broke out at last, "what a great many housemaids they must have had, to have left all these broken pots!"

The most interesting of the Roman relics of Mr. Allis is preserved in the Cathedral Cloisters. It is the milestone which stood in the centre of Lindum Colonia, and is about eight feet in height. It bears the following inscription:—

IMP CAES
MARCO
PIAVONO
VICTORI
NOP F INV
AVG PONT
M A X
TR P PP
AL S M
P X IIII

A translation runs thus: "Under the Empire of Cæsar Marcus Piavonius Victorinus, the pious, fortunate, unconquerable Augustus, chief pontiff, invested with tribunician power, father of his country. From Lindum to Segelocum fourteen miles." Lindum, of course, was the Roman colony at Lincoln, while Segelocum was Little-borough.

This stone was found in 1879; the only similar one we know of in this country is also a milestone, discovered at Pyle, near Neath. The reason of this may be found in the fact that the reign of the licentious but powerful monarch was an extremely short one, from 265 to 267 A.D., when he was murdered at Cologne by one of his officers as a revenge for an act of profligacy.

In the rear of Mr. Allis' house there still remains a portion of the "Mint wall." This, we believe, practically exhausts the list of that gentleman's collection, but we cannot conclude this notice without, firstly, thanking him for the kind assistance he has rendered in its compilation, and secondly, by quoting from his "Visitors' Book" the names of a number of well-known people who have been to see the portico and museum.

These include the signatures of Roberts, F. M. (General Lord Roberts); G. Roach Smith; George R. Wright, F.S.A., hon. Congress Sec., B.A.A., etc.; W. De Gray Birch, F.S.A.; Mary Walpole, Hampton Court Palace; William Grantham, Judge of Assize, Midland Circuit; Joseph Ruston, High Sheriff; Roland Vaughan Williams, Judge of Assize; Lady Hawkins; F. J. Furnivell, Chairman of the Wyclif, New Shakespere, Shelley, and other Societies; William Butler, Dean of Lincoln; Dr. Merry, Rector of Lincoln College, Oxford; Lady Lawrance; General Fielding; Earl of Stamford; Bishop Wordsworth and Bishop King; Sir G. M. Humphrey; Wallcott Horsley, R.A.; Dr. Creighton, Bishop of London; Professor J. H. Middleton; Cecil Carus Wilson; and a host of clerical legal, and antiquarian notables at home and abroad. On the occasion of Mr. Gladstone's visit to the Dean of Lincoln, Mr. Allis was invited to the Deanery to explain Roman Lincoln and its remains to the venerable statesman. Mr. Gladstone appeared quite charmed with the subject.

XV.—EXISTING RELICS OF ROMAN DAYS..
PART II.

In the previous article we dealt at length with various Roman relics discovered within the confines of Lindum Colonia—principally of the original colony. But there have been found a number of remains of that period without the walls of the first Lindum, and one of the most interesting of these is the altar dedicated to the Fates found when digging the foundations for the fine tower and spire of St. Swithin's in March, 1884. It is a wonderfully perfect piece of work, this Roman altar, and as it was found lying face downward on a bed of gravel, the inscription was almost as clear as the day it left the mason's hands. It was discovered some 13 feet below the present ground level, is 3 ft. in height and 1ft. 8in. broad at the base, and 1ft. 3¼in. in width at the upper part.

The altar stone was hewn from a single block of oolite, and many make no doubt that it is from the same bed as the stone forming Newport Arch. Some authorities place its date at about the same period—A.D. 42—and some early in the Second Century. The right side bears some carving, a pitcher containing wine for the libation, and on the left there is the long-handled dish for pouring wine on the offering. The sacrificial knife, usually represented on an altar of this kind, is absent.

There had previously been found only three altars dedicated to the Fates in Britain—at least, Professor Hubner records but three—and all these were in the Carlisle district, two being in Carlisle itself, and the other in Silloth. Roman monuments, as a matter of fact, are not uncommon, in commemoration of these goddesses. One was found some years ago in Lincoln, and is now, we believe, in the British Museum.

The following is the inscription, with the late Precentor of Lincoln's translation:—

> PARCIS DEA
> BVS ET NV
> MINIBVS AVG
> C ANTISTIVS
> FRONTINVS
> CVRATOR TER
> AR D SD.

"To the Goddesses, the Fates and to the Deities of Augustus Caius Antistius Frontinus, being curator for the third time, erects this altar at his own cost."

Professor Hubner, to whom a description of the altar and a copy of the inscription were sent—and who, it is needless to add, ranks amongst the very highest authorities on the Roman period, dates the relic as belonging to the end of the Second or Third Century. He does not agree with the opinion that Frontinus was a person in holy orders, but that he was more probably a worthy Roman soldier or veteran, held in such high esteem by his comrades that they chose him three times " chapel-warden " of the little place of worship of the troop which, twelve or thirteen hundred years ago, stood on the site of the present handsome church of St. Swithin's.

There are several interesting Roman remains deposited in the Cloisters of Lincoln Cathedral, and there appears to be no mention of them in any of the pamphlets dealing with the edifice. How it comes about that these are not included in the visitor's guide-book to the Cathedral we are unable to say, but Mr. Hague, the master-mason, has an excellent knowledge of them—or most of them—and has been at considerable trouble to arrange them, to a great extent chronologically. But, all the same,, we are of opinion that there should be an authoritative pamphlet, giving a description and history of these relics. The known history of these, in some cases, is meagre, but a very readable booklet might be written upon them.

The collection includes a notable piece of Roman tesselated pavement, removed from its original place in the Cloister Garth some years ago; a number of Roman amphoræ; and some ponderous monumental slabs, of considerable beauty of design.

A sculptured stone was discovered in February, 1884, when digging the foundations for the Schools of Science and Art, and nearly opposite to the eastern gateway of the extended Roman colony—the entrance being known later as Clasket-gate. It consists of a quadrangular pilaster or " cippus " of a tapering form, and is crowned by a projecting cornice carved with inverted acanthus leaves of great beauty of execution. On either sides are carvings of similar foliage, and the face of the stone bears an elegantly draped figure, in the left hand of which is a " cornucopiæ." The right hand also probably carried something, but this, owing to the mutilated character of the stone, cannot be determined. The features are quite gone, but the head was obviously covered with some kind of hood. Various authorities have decided, some that the figure is that of a man, others that it is that of a woman. Like the altar at St. Swithin's Church, it is executed in Lincoln oolite.

A Roman villa was brought to light in digging for ironstone in Greetwell fields in 1884—or at least a part of one. The discoveries made, as described by Dr. O'Neill, of Lincoln, include a bath-room, with tesseræ running round the room, and a bath three or four feet deep; a particularly deep well in an adjoining apartment; two long walls, thirty yards apart, with several chambers between, having tesselated pavements and red tile flooring, and fragments of well-finished wall-plaster. On one piece of plaster was a well-worked figure of a swallow. Dr. O'Neill writes of the building: "The house must have been the home of a Roman gentleman of taste and opulence. The site was well chosen, with a direct southern exposure, but in consequence of the villa being built on the brow of a hill, the lower rooms were on different planes. Doubtless if careful diggings were extended on either side of the mining trench other Roman discoveries of a valuable character might be made." True enough, in 1889 excavations to the eastward of this field revealed a portion of a tesselated pavement of a plain pattern formed of red and white tesseræ, and this by the direction of the then Mayor, Mr. Edwin Pratt, was taken and preserved for that city museum which is yet an institution of the future. A word of thanks to Mr. Ramsden, the Resident Manager of the Ironstone Works, for his interest and assistance in the discoveries on the ground under his rule, is due from ever archæologist in the country, particularly for the detailed account and ground plan of the remains.

A quantity of roofing and flooring tiles were also found dispersed over the site of the villa, bearing various markings. In addition to these was a lead spoon, a bronze ear-ring, a number of small urns, stag's horns, human bones, portions of a human skull, animal bones and a large collection of oyster shells, fragments of glass and black pottery, iron nails, etc. There was an evidence of fire in nearly all the rooms, and charcoal was plentiful. A key brick was also found $1\frac{7}{8}$in. thick at one end, by $2\frac{7}{8}$in. at the other, 11in. long by $5\frac{1}{4}$in. wide.

In 1877, during the progress of drainage work, a narrow, straight trench was discovered in the east end of Newport. It was bordered by rows of "loculi," or pigeon-holes, each containing a stone coffin. These "loculi" were constructed of flags or slab stones, and some were placed upright to form partitions, while others were laid so as to form roofs and floors of the "loculi." Dr. O'Neill, who has written a paper on the discovery, from which we quote, states that he has been informed that in parts of the street several of these "loculi" are not more than six inches below the surface of the road. The find was certainly a startling one, and the Doctor offers this solution of the apparent enigma : That the present road from close to the Roman Arch to about the Training College does not follow the straight path of the old Roman road, but has deviated from it by bending several yards towards the north-west, and in the course of its deviation has encroached upon an ancient burial ground. His idea, he says was confirmed on learning that patches of the old Ermine-street, the foundation stones of which were laid in concrete, had been laid bare during gardening operations behind certain Newport houses. The doctor's theory is certainly plausible, and has found considerable acceptance. We agree that it is quite possible indeed, very probable, that Ermine-street proper has been diverted from its original course, but we should like more particulars of the " ancient burial ground," which may or may not have existed there. It must be admitted, however, that the find just spoken of goes some way to prove it.

A crematory furnace was discovered in Bailgate, just opposite the White Hart, on June 6th, 1884. The remains had lain undisturbed not more than six inches below a shop floor for considerably more than a thousand years ! Nay, there had probably been previous houses here, and yet the old furnace, its fires dead, its heat gone, had reposed silently beneath the changes of the passing centuries for—did we say a thousand?—some seventeen hundred years ! Three feet below the level of the crematorium was discovered what is described as a sarcophagus, in shape very like an ordinary coffin. " Under cover of the rough slabs was a layer, fourteen inches thick, of fine sand, under this a layer of dark-coloured vegetable ashes, and again under this a layer of lime embedded in which were ten vases of various shapes and sizes, all except one being in an upright position."

It seems probable that the crematorium was the property of the inmates of a gorgeous Roman villa the basement rooms of which were discovered during the drainage work in Exchequer-gate. A tesselated piece of the pavement is on view at Mr. Allis's, Bailgate. Near the crematorium was found a quaint looking Roman arch, six or eight feet north-east of the sarcophagus. This arch formed a right angle with the sarcophagus, and was some 6ft. in height and two feet in width, resembling to a great extent the Newport Arch, and, like it, having no keystone. Between the arch and the sarcophagus was a semi-circular path of concrete. A number of urns, containing ashes of the dead, were also found here.

Not far from the sepulture buildings was found the opening of a well in the centre of a broad, flat stone four feet square, the stone having been much worn by the feet of those who came to draw water.

A particularly interesting discovery was made some years ago beneath the Precentory. Very little of it is publicly known, the reason given being the late Precentor's wish that his dwelling should not be invaded by the curious. It is a Roman heating apparatus, and consists of a number of round columns 24 inches high, alternating with a number of square columns. The floor is tesselated, and the whole construction is very interesting. Mr. Allis, of Bailgate, has a plan of the apparatus.

It is remarkable to say the least, that Lincoln, where once was a strong Roman colony, a prominent Danish township, and where at various times events important and vital have made English history, has no museum that can receive the relics discovered from time to time. Particularly does this apply to the Roman period. We have relics in the city that the British and other museums would give much to possess, and yet we have no public storehouse wherein to place them for safety and public inspection. A number are described in this and the preceding article, and there are a number of private collections which it is, perhaps, not advisable to mention in detail. But there are Roman relics in private hands—some of them almost priceless, certainly unique—which the present owners would gladly present to a museum could one be established in Lincoln. A loan collection was exhibited in the city some time ago, and proved very successful. An agitation was worked up to secure a museum worthy of the ancient place we live in, but after seeming fairly on the road to realisation, the proposals fell through. Surely it is not too late for a museum to be established? Is it a question of finance? There are gentlemen, we dare assert, whose purse-strings would readily be loosened for such an object. Is it a matter of room? The Schools of Science and Art, the Church House, or the Castle could surely help there—the Cathedral is out of the question for the remains now there, we are afraid, are perishing by exposure. Or is it a question of lassitude? We can make no reply to that, only regret it, if such be the case.

The time has passed, never, as we hope, to return, when it was necessary for ponderous and strong gateways, with bolts, bars, or chains, to guard the entrances to our city, forming the only breaks in a series of walls of as great strength as it was then found possible to make them. Unquestionably we, the modern residents of Lincoln, owe something to the gates, and to their builders, and lovers of architecture at least will be grateful for the remnants of them that are left to us.

We propose to touch upon these barriers in the course of the present article. Some of them are yet left to us, some perfect, and some but partly remaining, while others have vanished into that "Forgotten" Lincoln, in which we are endeavouring, in these writings, to interest the citizens.

The gate to first claim our attention needs no selection. In this respect Newport Arch, from its great age, has a priority that none other in the city—or, for that matter, in the country—can dispute. Of course, it is but a relic of itself, and repairs, which became absolutely necessary, have inevitably helped to take from it its former appearance, but it is still a remarkable span, and one which visitors from distant lands as well as those nearer home, have viewed with the deepest interest.

The centre arch consists of twenty-six stones. Mr. Essex says: "The whole seems to be built without mortar, but time has penetrated so far into the joints that it is difficult to determine whether it was or not." There is no keystone, but a joint in the crown. The height is given as 22½ feet, several feet being now buried. On each side of the arch, several courses of horizontal stones or springers are laid, some of them being six or seven feet long, and intended to take off the lateral pressure from the arch. The diameter of the side arch is 7½ feet, and the height, in all, 15 feet.

With regard to the breadth of each pier, Gough, whose dimensions seem to have been generally accepted and followed says, "Breadth of the piers 39," and refers to Essex. This is probably an error of the Press or in transcribing, as Essex has it 3 ft. 9in. The whole width of the front is given as 22½ feet, and the whole height 37½ ft. Most of the mouldings are broken off, and says a historian, the whole appears to have been almost ruined long before the parts above it were erected, the ancient work being distinguishable from the modern by the remarkable length of the stones. Stukeley, writing in 1724, says the stones are 4ft. thick at bottom.

It hardly needs to be added, perhaps, that Newport Arch is the oldest arch in England, the reputed date of building being the year 42. There is ample food for reflection, did space permit, on the scenes enacted within the vicinity of the old gateway—the Romans in toga and breastplate, repulsing an attack of a tribe of painted, skin-clad Britons, driven out by the foreigners' invasion; the haughty Danish sea-kings striding proudly through the gateway of the old city; the fair-haired, indomitable Saxon; the bewigged, knee-breeched courtiers of a later date; "my ladye" being borne in her sedan-chair by obsequious chairmen, with, if it was night, a link-boy, with flaring torch, preceding; her husband, falcon on wrist, riding forth for a day's sport; and the picturesque list could be continued to practically any extent. May the old gate's shadow never grow less!

Some little distance away was the western gate of the old town, discovered in 1836, nearly perfect, in excavating on the western side of the Castle Dykings, it having been covered up when the Norman wall was built. The eastern gate was situated at or near the point where the wall crossed the present Eastgate—at least, so Sir Charles Anderson affirms.

Potter Gate, so called from the tradition that a Roman pottery existed in the locality, is one of the most picturesque old gateways left us. The northern front is a very fair specimen of the military keep, embattled, pierced with loopholes, and grooved for a portcullis. A fine gateway it must have appeared in its original state, and of great strength, as is evident to the most casual observer.

The Cathedral Close was fortified in former days, and the Exchequer Gate formed the principal entrance thereto. The outer portal of this, crossing the road at the west end of St. Mary Magdalene's Church, fell into sad disrepair, and was pulled down in 1800, the stones being used in the construction of St. Swithin's Church. At the west end of the 'Chequer Church there stood, somewhat earlier than 1855, a corresponding gateway, called Priory Gate, the gate-house being taken down in 1815-16. The name, Precentor Venables assures us, was a complete misnomer. A row of grand specimens of old dwellings stood along here, on wooden pillars, forming a picturesque, if rude, kind of piazza. These appear to have been demolished some eighty years back.

The manner in which the Close came to be thus fortified is in itself interesting. A petition was addressed by the Canons to King Edward the First in 1285, informing him of the peril in which clergy stood when going to midnight services, owing to the number of cutpurses—who would not scruple at becoming cut-throats—and other bad characters who lurked habitually in the shadows of the sacred building. Edward graciously inclined his ear to the petition, and had a wall begun round the Close, and with double gate-houses at either entrance. Edward the Second was also favourable to the plan, and had the wall embattled and towers added in the first year of his reign. Of these towers two yet exist in the garden of the Chancery.

Now come with us a little further westward, and turn down Steep Hill—an appropriate name, if ever one was. We will pause near the Leopard Inn, where the road is at its narrowest. Here was the south Roman Gate, portions of which were standing as late as 1783. Gough, visiting Lincoln in that year, wrote that it was taken down at the beginning of the last century by the proprietor of the house on the east side of the street. In a chamber occupied, in the year of Gough's writing, by a barber, might be seen the eastern postern entire, but nothing now remains of the principal gate except the foundation stones on either side of the road, and one jamb between the houses on the west side, with two or three cuneiform stones just above the springing of the arch.

It says not a little for the stability of the erection that it was not without difficulty that the venerable pile was demolished. Not much "jerry-building" there! If the descendants of the "contractors" were in business now-a-days, what an excellent testimonial this would furnish them. The workmen set to knock down the arch were armed with a huge beam shod with iron, which they used battering-ram fashion, and with this they battered into pieces one of the stones in or near the crown of the arch, expecting, of course, the whole structure to fall, "but every stone being as it were a key, the rest shrunk together and fixed as firm as ever!" Yes, it's rather a pity we don't know the descendants of the builders of an arch like that! It is interesting to note that this gate was connected with Newport Arch by a straight line of street in Roman times.

Further down the hill, says Precentor Venables, stood the southern gate of the Bail. This was a mediæval archway, and was cleared away in 1775. In olden times it was decorated with hangings on Palm Sunday, while the choir from the Cathedral sang before it the Latin hymn, "Gloria, laus, et honor."

Going down the hill we reach the site of Dernestall Lock, which was fully described in our seventh article.

We may, therefore, proceed along Grantham-street towards the Bull's Head Inn, near where stood the gate-house of Clasket, as it is generally called, but more properly Claxlede-gate. It was originally outside the city walls, and from the Roman period guarded the south-eastern entrance to Lincoln. When the land was required for building purposes, many years back, the foundations were discovered, and were so solid that they could only be removed by blasting with gunpowder. A little more "jerry (?) building!"

The gate-house in which the Knights Templar were confined previous to their trial, and afterwards used as an armoury by the city, seems to have been a building of no ordinary strength, with a low archway, and narrow slits for the discharge of firearms. The name is apparently derived from the Anglo-Saxon "hlid-geat," a back door, or postern gate, and from thte Norse "Klaka" (a personal name), also found thrice in our county in villages named Claxby. Claxlede-gate was pulled down in 1786, when the " New " Road was constructed.

Passing down Silver-street, we leave the Stonebow—already done justice to—and reach the site of Newland Gate, which was the entrance to Lincoln from Saxilby and district. From a drawing in the Bodleian Library, we are able to gather that it was a tall gatehouse with gables, of probably 14th century erection, with additions when the city was defended against Cromwell and his Puritans. It had wide pointed archways, above which were arched windows of four lights. Of this gate, which stood at the foot of Motherby-hill, we are not aware that any trace now remains.

Reference to a plan of the city in James the First's reign shows a line of wall from the Great Bar Gate in the High-street round to the Little Bar Gate, which stood further east. We can find no trace of the former. Both gateways were standing about 1730, and portions of the adjoining city walls, inscribed and showing the date of repair, were remaining at least ten years after that. Each gate-seems to have been the scene of a stirring military fight.

At the Great Bar Gate there took place the last scene of the great struggle between the French Dauphin and his opponents. The forces of the Dauphin had been surprised outside the Castle walls, and had lost their commander, Count de Perche; a panic had spread amongst them, and away they rushed down the hill towards the southern gate. This gate, however, was arranged so that when it had been thrown open, a wooden cross-bar mechanically re-closed it. The alarmed troops—or rather the first amongst them—dashed the gate open and rushed out of the city, but the remainder found it closed in their faces. Consequently the Royal forces were enabled to capture nearly the whole of them, and this, remarkable to add, without bloodshed, three men only falling in the whole engagement! The captured included fourteen barons, some of these being of the highest rank, some four hundred knights, and others. This battle, as history proves, put the final veto against the Dauphin's attempts to gain the throne of our land.

At Little Bar Gate another battle took place, some four hundred years later, and formed part of the local scenes of the struggle between Cromwell and the Crown. But these same scenes are of sufficient importance to merit, or rather demand, a special article later on. The Little Bar Gate was taken down about the middle of the last century, and the bridge itself removed in 1826 on the improvement of the drainage. A pinfold afterwards stood there. Buck took a drawing of the gateway in 1720, and this is now in the Bodleian Library, showing "a low round archway flanked by two short drum towers pierced with loopholes," and approached by a pointed arched bridge. We have the name Bar Gate applied twice or thrice in the vicinity, Little Bar Gate being within a stone's throw of its namesake, the original archway.

Swine's Gate was below the Great Bar Gate, whereon was erected the cross of Queen Eleanor.

A gate of less formidable pretensions existed until within comparatively recent years at the lower end of High-street. We allude to the old toll-gate.

While on the subject of gates, no one can fail to notice the frequent recurrence of the word "gate" in our street nomenclature. All the old streets are thus named. It is of Danish origin, and proves clearer than, and independent of, anything else how strong a hold the Danes had of local affairs.

Happily our gates are now purely ornamental, and that they are this, lovers of architecture generally will agree. Our Stonebow and Newport Arch are the envy of many who see them, and have been the pride of the citizens of Lincoln through many, many generations; may these, and other arches yet standing "to tell their silent tales," be no less the pride of those who shall follow hereafter.

XVII.—THE EARLDOM OF LINCOLN.

Who is the Earl of Lincoln? Can one person in five, we wonder, answer the question? Can one person in ten tell how the Earldom originated, how it progressed, how it fell, and rose again?

Few people but have read the story in verse of the ill-fated White Ship, or of that King whose son was lost when the vessel sank, and who "never smiled again." No one but has heard the story of Godiva's ride through the streets of Coventry to lift the poll-tax from Leofric's people. And who has not heard of the Battle of Lincoln? All these things affect the Earldom of Lincoln, and two at least profoundly.

To trace the descent of our local Earldom is no light task. It has had as chequered a career as the estates and title of any novelist's hero, and has even passed out of the direct line altogether, for a time. Even recognised historians have themselves been confused and misled by the strange turns which circumstances have given it, and we owe much to the efforts of those whose long and shrewd retrospections have cleared the clouds away, and let in the light upon the intricate but deeply interesting history of the ancient dignity.

The claims of inheritance to the Earldom of Lincoln were originally derived from Anglo-Saxon ancestors. This does not mean that the Earldom existed before the Conquest, though Camden commences his enumeration of the Earls of Lincolnshire with the Saxons Egga (Printed Eggo by Mr. Kemble in the Anglo-Saxon Charters) and Morcar. Egga, Camden declares, flourished in 716. But Egga is a purely fictitious name. Long search finds it only once, and that among the witnesses to the false foundation-Charter of Croyland Abbey, which document was a forgery of the monks of —mark this—a later date.

Morcar, described by Camden as the maternal uncle of William de Roumare, the first Norman Earl of Lincoln, is a person with better credentials. He was a son of the Earl of Mercia and brother to Harold's Queen, Edgiva; but in history he is noticed as the Earl of Northumberland—by Dugdale, amongst others—and not as Earl of Lincoln.

Now here it was that chroniclers seem to have got right off the line at once. The Croyland chroniclers give it that Morcar had an only sister named Lucia, apparently forgetting or, for some unaccountable reason, ignoring Edgiva, and Lucia is written down as the mother of William de Roumare. Upon this statement Camden and the majority of writers on the peerage have based their chronicles, and here they must unhesitatingly be contradicted.

To credit their statements one must believe an obvious impossibility, namely—that Countess Lucy (of whose existence there is no doubt) was at once the sister of Earl Morcar, the wife of Ivo Taillebois, married 43 years later to the father of William de Roumare, and yet again to the Earl of Chester, by whom she had issue two sons and two daughters.

Later historians offer as a possible explanation—and with this we must agree, seeing no other—that there were two Lucys, mother and daughter, the former the wife of Ivo Taillebois, and the latter twice married, the mother of William de Roumare and of Ranulph, Earl of Chester. The name of Lucy, by the way, occurs in a charter of her husband's, dated 1085, and as giving the Church of Spalding to the priory of St. Nicholas at Angers. The first recorded Earl of Spalding is one Turold, mentioned in Domesday Book as giving land to the Church of St. Guthlac at Croyland, and in the charter of Taillebois as kinsman of Lucia, his wife. This same Turold is affirmed in the false charter of Croyland to be a brother of the famous Lady Godiva, and considerable credence attaches to the statement, though, of course, the charter is repudiated as a whole. But it is quite certain that Godiva (styled in a Saxon charter as Godgife) and Leofric joined in that work of piety, the foundation of the Monastery of Stow.

Ivo Taillebois died in 1114, and was buried at the Priory Church of Spalding, his daughter Lucy was married to her first husband, Roger de Roumare, some years previously. Roger's only recorded child is William de Roumare, afterwards Earl of Lincoln. Lucy's second husband was Ranulph de Briquesard, eldest son of the Vicomte de Bessin, of Normandy. His cousin Richard was drowned with other nobles, and King Henry's son, in the unfortunate White Ship, and Ranulph then became Earl of Chester. Some authorities incline somewhat towards the opinion that Ranulph was Earl of Lincolnshire also, but proofs are hardly strong enough for general acceptance. Ranulph died in 1129, and the rights of his widow in Lincolnshire then became fully recognised.

Lucy inherited her father's lands in this county, and became bound under the penalty of 500 marks of silver not to take another husband within the next five years, without the license of the Crown.

William de Roumare, who brought the Earldom into great prominence had distinguished himself both at home and abroad before his accession to the title. He is first mentioned as governor of the frontier fortress of Neufmarche en Lions, in 1118, where he was for some time the sole supporter of Henry's authority in Normandy. In the next year we find he is one of those who had intended to proceed to the English Court in the White Ship, but he and others refused to voyage in her "because they perceived the ship was filled with too numerous a company of wanton and arrogant youth."

So William de Roumare, Earl of Lincoln, stayed on the foreign shore, and watched the White Ship spread her wings and glide away over the dancing waves towards England and home. On board we can imagine the rejoicings of the flower of the English

Court, the central figure of which was the heir to the throne of our land. We can imagine the development of those rejoicings; how care was flung to the winds, prudence trampled underfoot, and forethought banished from the scene. We can picture the panic which overtook the company when the ship was in danger, and they realised too late that revelry had cost them dear; we can almost hear the shrieks of the hapless beings as the White Ship sank for ever beneath the tossing billows. And we can mark with especial sympathy and sorrow the waters close over the head of the boy for whom a king father waited on the distant homeshore, longing to see that face which was the gem of all the jewels that were his, but which, monarch though he was, he was powerless to summon from the clutches of the merciless deep. For the eyes were closed in a sleep that not the voice of a king, nor the fanfare of trumpets, nor the cheers of loyal populace could ever wake him, and Henry could never see his beloved son again until that other great White Ship bore him on its mysterious wings towards the Unspeakable Land.

.	.	.	.	.	.	.

William de Roumare found that though he had not perished in the White Ship, her foundering had a serious effect on his fortunes As already stated, Ranulph, Earl of Chester, obtained that dignity by his predecessor going down in the White Ship, and on obtaining the investiture he was induced to surrender to the King a large portion of the estates of his wife. This aroused William's ire, for he thus lost the prospect of his inheritance. He demanded the restoration of the land, but the King refused. Angered by this, William communicated with those favouring the claims of the son of Duke Robert Curt-Heuze to the sovereignty of Normandy, and a bitter war was waged upon the Normans.

For two years the war waxed fiercely, and William only withdrew from the strife when the King had yielded complete satisfaction to him. The claimant to the throne of Normandy died in 1128, and William was one of the first to be reconciled to the King.

Henry died seven years later, and Stephen, his successor, appointed the Earl of Lincoln one of the Justiciars of Normandy. In 1141 we have the rebellion of William de Roumare and the Earl of Chester against Stephen, and the seizure of Lincoln Castle; but this is not the place wherein we purpose to write of Lincoln in time of war, for the subject is one fully meriting at least one article to itself. This period, however, was the most stirring of all the many interesting epochs of Lincoln's history, and the rebels were for a long time able to hold their own against the Crown.

We may just point out here, in passing mention of Lincoln Castle, that the Lucy Tower, forfeited by the Earl of Chester's mother, yet exists under that name, and that after the rebellion was quelled, and Stephen reasserted his dominion over the city, the Earl of Chester still held possession, with the King's acquiescence, of the Lucy Tower. The first witness to this charter was the Earl of Lincoln.

The date of William's death is uncertain, but it was earlier than

1168. The old castle of Bolingbroke, where Henry the Fourth was born, is attributed by some to William de Roumare. William's son died before his father, and the next heir, the first William's grandson, never seems to have been confirmed in the Earldom of Lincoln.

But we must return to the Battle of Lincoln in 1142, when the Earldom was divided, and there were two Earls at one time—Gilbert de Gant and William de Roumare, while at the same period the Earl of Chester was virtually a third, inasmuch as he was actual lord of the Castle! When the Earl of Chester took Stephen prisoner, he also captured Gilbert de Gant, who was the representative of a family which possessed much land in this county. He was compelled to marry the Earl of Chester's niece, and we have evidence that the title of Earl of Lincoln was used by him, contemporaneously with William, until his death.

The Earldom of Lincoln was now vacant, and enterprising Richard the First, ignoring the claims of William de Roumare's descendant, sold or let to farm the custody of the Castle of Lincoln and the revenues of the county to one Gerard de Camville, who was subsequently ousted from them by Chancellor Longchamp. In 1216 the nominal Earldom is assigned to the second Gilbert de Gant, nephew to the preceding one, and termed "Gilbert the Good." Ranulph, Earl of Chester and Lincoln, succeeded him, in whose time many stirring events occurred to which full justice will be done in our account of Lincoln's battles. John de Lacy became the next Earl in 1232, and his son Henry followed in 1258.

The latter, by marriage, united the Earldom to that of Salisbury, and died at his house in the suburbs of London, which has since then retained the name of Lincoln's Inn. Next, Thomas, Earl of Lancaster, Leicester, and Derby, acquired the Earldoms of Lincoln and Salisbury by his marriage with the previous Earl's only daughter. Probably the access of so much land was the cause of him literally "losing his head" at Pontefract on March 22nd, 1322. His widow became Countess of Lincoln, and, on her death, his nephew Henry was created Earl of Lincoln in 1349, and of Lancaster two years later.

His daughter Blanche married John of Ghent, Earl of Richmond, and fourth son of King Edward III. John was created Duke of Lancaster, and his privy seal shows that he used Earl of Lincoln amongst other titles. He died in 1399, and his son Henry of Bolinbroke, ascended the throne as King Henry IV. Thus a son of Lincolnshire was crowned King of England, and the Earldom of Lincoln was merged in the Crown as part of the Duchy of Lancaster.

The title was revived in 1467, when Edward IV. conferred it on his nephew, John de la Pole. The new Earl dying twenty years later without issue, Henry VIII. conferred it in the same way upon his sister's son, Henry Brandon. This Earl died in childhood.

Last of all, Elizabeth—"good Queen Bess"—conferred it on the Lord Admiral Clinton in whose family it was retained and descended, until to-day it is merged in the Dukedom of Newcastle.

We think readers will agree that we have kept the promise we made at the outset, and that the history of the Earldom furnishes not merely interesting but absorbing matter for perusal. How strange a thing is Fate, and what toys of Chance and Mischance, hurled back and forth, now high in the air, now fallen low in the mire, we poor mortals are; and how the king may have his purple robe torn from him and be forced to hide in the purlieus of the city, and the beggar be elevated unto the throne, and a crown of gold and gems be placed upon his brow !

XVIII.—THE VEINS OF THE CITY.

Lincoln is somewhat poorly served in the matter of watercourses, especially when the importance of her river traffic is considered. Several of her near neighbours are better favoured. Gainsborough and Newark, for instance, have the broader waters of the Trent; Grimsby is practically close by the sea; Boston has her docks and a direct way to the ocean; but Lincoln has a comparatively narrow stream, the course of which, seaward, is broken by locks.

Yet we see the Witham undoubtedly at its best. Many, many years ago, when the Romans were in possession, the tide surged up from Boston right into the waters of Swan Pool. Both the river and the fenlands of the county were then uncared for, and the Romans were not here long enough to improve them. Of the other watercourses, the Sincil Drain or Dyke is the chief, and this joins the Witham eventually, and they then flow in company to the sea.

The Witham has played its part, and that creditably, in the advance and rise of Lincoln, and this will be found interesting to trace.

Everybody knows the name of Wigford. It is now applied to the district formerly known as Wikenford or Wickerford. It arises from the old vik or bay. The "ford" crossed the Witham near our present High Bridge in early times—in fact, as has already been told in these articles, it was not until after 1792 that the river became really navigable.

But what was this Swanpool? We have heard of people stating that it was simply the modern Brayford, but this scarcely gives a true idea of its extent. Brayford is certainly Swanpool confined and narrowed, but the ancient pool seems to have extended over the Holmes and elsewhere. The fact that a boat, tied to a stake, has been discovered under the present High-street may point to the fact that it extended thus far eastward.

Nor is this confinement of the pool of very distant date. Swanpool was drained early in the present century, and there were two others, Nicol-pool and Cuckoo-pool, somewhere in the direction of Boultham.

A very refreshing sight it must have been to see the Judges at the Summer Assizes being treated to a day's fishing in the waters of the Swanpool! And a stately function it must have proved when the Corporation barge, with their august lordships on board, was conducted from Brayford through some channel not now existing, and so into the waters of Swanpool for the angling expedition! Let us hope they had good sport, and caught something more than a cold, and that, if fickle fate sent them home with untasted bait, the unhappy prisoners awaiting trial were not made to suffer for the sins of the finny tribe.

As we have said, Brayford is the remains of the greater pool, or, we might add, the chain of pools that probably existed in the vicinity. From Brayford it is an easy stage to turn to consideration of the Witham itself. The Witham, then, seems to have had quite a number of names at different periods. Its earliest appellation appears to have been Ganthavon or Grantavon. Later, it is alluded to as the Lindis. Leland, in his "Itinerary," writes "the river Lindis fleatith a little above Lincoln towne." The Sincil Dyke, or "King's Ditch," was anciently called the "Old Ea," and there are those who incline to the opinion that this was the original course taken by the Witham .

Formerly, too, the Lindis, the Till, and the unbanked Trent combined to make the northern division of the county an island, hence, several writers think, its name of Lindisse, now Lindsey. The first attempt to drain the fens was a car-dyke, cut from Peterborough to Washingborough, to catch the watershed and convey it seaward by the river.

But when the Danes came to Lincoln, they—people of the sea as they were—seem to have set themselves to thoroughly re-construct the Witham. Vessels and tide alike had come from Boston to Lincoln practically at their own sweet will, and the city suburbs jutted upon the very edge of the genuine fen. But in the times of the Danes and the succeeding William the banks of the river were kept up, and trade established between the low country and Boston, the latter becoming a kind of port for Lincoln.

Until the year 1265 there was no bar in the river to the tide, but in that year tolls were taken from upgoing vessels at Dock Dyke, a place easily recognisable in the modern Dogdyke. However, floods still occurred, and, as before, seriously hampered the progress of commerce. Floods, indeed, seem to have been severe in our county, and a momentary digression here to mention them may be pardoned.

As early as the year 95 there is a record of the Humber overflowing, and flooding the country for fifty miles around. Again in 245 there was an inundation of the sea into the fen country, which laid under water many thousands of acres, unrecovered to this day. In 1288 a great part of Boston was drowned, and in 1570 there were immense floods in low-lying districts, the waters reaching up to the third storey. The town of Mumby, near Alford, was entirely destroyed, and 1,100 sheep drowned. Near Stamford the water flowed midway of the height of a church. This is the flood referred to in Jean Ingelow's famous poem "The High Tide."

In 1766 several villages between Lincoln and Peterborough were three or four feet under water, and great quantities of cattle were carried away by the flood. Four years later, the inhabitants from Brayford to the village of Thorne, were compelled to seek refuge in the upper rooms of their dwellings, owing to a tremendous inundation, and there were great fears that the High Bridge at Lincoln would be carried away. Other floods occurred, and we have much cause for gratitude that in our day floods of such severity are unknown in the home county.

To return to the Witham. In 1655 the Commissioners of Sewers caused the river from Brayford Head, through the city, and seaward, to be cut about 2ft. deeper, magnanimously allowing the cost to be borne by the frontagers. The year 1740 was also an important one in local navigation. In that year a lease of two-thirds of the navigation of the Fossdyke was granted to Richard Ellison, of Thorne, for 999 years, at a rental of £50. Subsequently, during the same year, the remaining third was assigned him for 99 years, at £25 a year. We may note, in passing, that a remarkable frost set in during that year. A sheep was roasted on the ice, and sold on Brayford at eightpence a pound, on January 12th, while a fortnight later an ox was roasted, and afterwards sold at a shilling a pound.

The grants to Richard Ellison resulted in the waterway being made new in four years, and the first coals that came to Lincoln by it were sold at thirteen shillings a chaldron, the previous price having been a guinea.

We have treated fully of the ford, which really stopped navigation, in our article on the High Bridge, and of the subsequent development of the Witham through Lincoln. It will suffice, therefore, if we say now that towards the end of the last century vessels had their cargoes emptied in Brayford, and re-shipped on the east side of this ford, if intended for the country eastward. The deepening of the water and destruction of the ford were actually opposed by the local authorities, and it was not until Sir Joseph Banks appeared on the scene that the much-needed improvement became an accomplished fact.

About 1794, however, the river beneath the High Bridge was made navigable, two years after the passing of the Horncastle Navigation Act, which provided, amongst other things, that the Witham should be connected with the Fossdyke by deepening its narrow parts through the city. Previous to this, at certain times of the year, vehicles could often pass under the High Bridge. But in 1771 the Stamp End Lock was finished, a dance being held in it by way of signalising the auspicious event.

While mentioning dances, we may recall the fact that previous to the deepening of the bed of the river beneath the High Bridge, planks were laid down, and a ball actually held there. Picture the difference in the state of this part of the Witham at that time and in our own day, after a heavy rainfall, when hundreds of tons of water rush through the confining arch with a roar like a cascade, and when the body of an unfortunate individual falling into the torrent would be whirled away like a straw.

Two stone pillars, erected at the Bridge in 1725 with a chain between, marked municipal divisions, but both chains and divisions are now things of the past.

We have said little of the Sincil Dyke, that modest stream which chooses the rear side of the town for its meandering course, but it is certainly worthy attention. There seems to have been at one time considerable dispute as to the meaning of the word "gowt," applied to Gowts' Bridge. Of course, the city did not formerly extend so far below it as it does now, hence many people were of opinion that it meant near where a person "goes out" of the city. But the generally accepted meaning now is that it signifies a watercourse or channel. It must not be supposed that it is the only stream with the name "gowt" in the county, for, as a matter of fact, there are many such.

The present bridge was erected by the Corporation in 1813, and Alderman W. Hayward was the architect. It re-placed bridges which were spoken of as a disgrace to the city. However, we may take it now that our bridges are both substantial and goodly to look upon, though there is a building upon the High Bridge—extended a very few months back—that a great many people think mars the appearance of the noble old arch, and which the bridge gains nothing by supporting.

By the side of the Witham there have sprung into existence, extending to great proportions, a number of foundries, the products from which are known wherever machinery has been brought into use. These buildings, past which the watercourse we have inadequately described flows, have each a high name in the world of machinery, and the waters of the old river are drawn up to assist an industry which has done more than anything else to make the name of Lincoln as important in the eyes of the modern business man, as it has always been in the eyes of the historical student and antiquarian.

XIX.—THE STORY OF THE MARKETS.

How far shall we look back to find the first market held in Lincoln? We have now our produce markets, our cattle, corn, meat, and fruit markets—how long have these ben established, how long held on their present premises, and which stands first in point of antiquity?

It is rather a large order. The markets of present-day Lincoln have grown with the city itself, to a very large extent. Remains found in Bailgate—bricks, to be exact, now in the possession of Mr. Allis—point to shops having existed in Lindum Colonia, and there is evidence, not conclusive enough, perhaps, for some authorities, to the effect that a market was held there, too. If this be so, we think there is no question that this would be the first market held on the site of our own city.

We must, however, come down to the 14th century for really definite data concerning local markets. In the year 1352, the 26th of Edward III.'s reign, the staple of wool was removed from Flanders to England, and upon six towns the staple was conferred in our own land, these being Westminster, Chichester, Canterbury, Bristol, Hull, and Lincoln. It should be noted that at this time Lincoln ranked as the fourth seaport of England. Lincoln a seaport! Yet this is quite accurate—the record of Quinzeme duties paid by the ports of England shows that only London, Boston, and Southampton ranked before our own city. Of course, as we have previously written, the tide flowed up to Lincoln until a considerably later period than Edward's reign, and vessels sailed between the city and the sea.

During the time that Lincoln was a staple town for the sale of wool, there was an officer called the Mayor of the Staple, who presided over the trade. Lincoln was also made a staple for leather, lead, and various other articles, and the result of this proved of very great benefit to the town, which advanced in prosperity in a very satisfactory degree.

We must not omit to mention Act 18, Charles II., c. 4, passed in 1666, to encourage the English staple of wool, confirmed by Act 30, Charles 11., c. 3, in 1677, by which it enacted that all persons should be buried in wool under a penalty of £5—a large sum at that period. Although the custom fell, probably by degrees, into abeyance, the Act was not formally repealed until the time of George III. (54 G. III., c. 108) in 1814.

Earlier than this, and before Royal assent had been given to the various staples, there had been no little contraband traffic going on in Lincoln—not, we are pleased to add, strictly conducted by citizens themselves. A number of wealthy Florentines had taken up their abode in the city, under the Charter of the First Edward. These fellows, it appears, were inveterate smugglers, and it was not very long before they began their nefarious practices in the city of their adoption. A great number of instances of contraband shipments of wool on the Witham are recorded in the Hundred Rolls, and this despite the fact that there were Customs officers ever on the alert, and that the law enacted that were any goods exported without an account being given for the duties, the whole would be forfeited to the Crown. Wary, foxy old smugglers! Have we not a saying that a coach and four can be driven through any Act of Parliament in our own day? Who shall say how much wool was exported from Lincoln under the very noses of the vigilant Customs officers, duty free? Wary old Florentines!

As showing the prosperity of Lincoln during the reign of cruel John—and it was not every town or city that prospered under his rule—it may be mentioned that Lincoln paid the sum of £656 12s 2d annually to the Crown. The value of this money was, of course, largely in excess of its modern worth, and is shown very markedly in the statement that at the period in which it was paid the sum would have been amply sufficient to purchase 13,000 acres of land. Agricultural depression? It has not yet got so low that land can be purchased at about £50 per 1,000 acres! As we have just said, it was not given to every town to prosper during the reign of King John.

Lincoln's prosperity may be, in some measure, attributed to the fact that the town was an emporium for the merchants of Europe. Being accessible from the eastern coast, it possessed advantages that were shared by but few other towns, and distance counted for something when steam for the sea journey and iron rails for travel by land were unknown and undreamed of.

Our Cornhill is a prominent modern market-place in the city. Before the Reformation, the church and churchyard of St. John stood here. From the City Records we learn that it was sold to Mr. George Stampe, conditionally that he built on the site a good house, facing towards the street. For some reason this bargain was not carried out, for in June, 1560, there is entered an order for taking the church down. On the 6th of July of the same year is another order, this time making an end with the chanter for his claim to the chancel, and on February 16th, 1597, is one for purchasing in the lease for the use of the Common Chamber. Then, on September 2nd, 1598, we find an order for keeping the corn market there, for all manner of grain with the exception of oats and ground meal, which were ordered to be sold upon the "Old Hill," and nowhere else.

The "Old Hill," says an authority, appears to have been a little lower down. Simpson says that in his time the oat market was held against the churchyard wall of St. Mary-le-Wigford. We rather fancy our present-day corn dealers prefer the shelter of the Corn Exchange to the open street.

Just on the south side of Gowt's Bridge stood the church of the Holy Rood, or Holy Cross, part of the site being now crossed by the Boultham private road. In 1551 the Town Council gave it over to a party of cloth workers, whom they had invited over to settle in the city, so that a clothing trade might be established here. These men turned the church into a dye-house, and erected their frames in the adjoining churchyard, and for a time there seemed a possibility that the coveted trade would be established. Seven years later, however, Queen Elizabeth came to the throne, and an inquiry was set on foot as to the product of the looms, when it was found that the venture was a complete failure. As the conditions under which the cloth-makers held the premises had not been carried out, and few of the broad cloths promised had appeared, their occupation was brought to an abrupt close, and Lincoln's chance of becoming an important cloth centre was gone.

Tentercroft-street, by the way, takes its name from the field where cloths made in the looms were "tented"—stretched on long wooden frames, to which they were hung by tenterhooks, in order that they might recover the breadth lost in the operation of "fulling."

In 1516 a skilled clothmaker had been persuaded by the Mayor to come to Lincoln and instruct the citizens in the art, and considerable efforts were made to induce wool-spinners and others engaged in the manufacture to settle in Lincoln, the freedom of the city being included in the offers made, but all attempts appear to have resulted the same, and the cloth-making trade was not to be established. At one time, however, there appears to have been a cloth market on the site of the present Drapery.

And here notice how our markets have been changed from their former positions. They were held in the open thoroughfares, and, curious to state, in the steepest parts. Both the Corn Market and the Poultry Market were once held on the Steep Hill, just above the Jew's House. The Fish Market was on the site of the Bishop's Hostel, and subsequently in the High-street somewhere near the High Bridge. Unity-square was once "Jobbers' Square," where the pig-jobbers met, and the Sheep Market was held on the site where St. Swithin's Church now stands.

We have mentioned the attempt to introduce the cloth trade into Lincoln. In the crypt of the Grey Friary—near the old Sheep Market, and now called the Lincoln Middle School—was the "Jersey School," where an attempt was made to spin and knit hosiery in the style of Leicester. But, like the other attempt, it ended in ignominious failure. The Meat Market was also held in High-street, between the lower end of the present Strait and the Monson Arms Hotel. The "Peltry"—the skin market—occupied part of the site of our modern Butter Market, and near was held the Butter Market proper, having been removed from Newland, where the Butter Cross, of which we shall have something to write later, had stood to shelter the market women, but which was razed to the ground as being a "monument of superstition" during the Reformation. The present building, which we term the Butter Market, was erected in 1736, at the instance of the Mayor, Mr. John Lobsey, who actually persuaded the Corporation to suspend their civic banquet for ten years in order that a shelter for the market-women might be built. Another sacrifice on their part is recorded eighteen years earlier, when they voted £1,000 towards the erecting of the adjoining church of St. Peter-at-Arches.

Over the Butter Market Hall is the Lincoln Free Library, this part of the building having been added in 1757, and used as the City Assembly Rooms, and then, until recent years, as the Mechanics' Institution. The City Assembly Rooms were built because people living below-hill were not permitted to set foot in the County Assembly Rooms (built in 1744), which was erected, if you please, for the above-hill and county people. The City Assembly Rooms were built by public subscription. Within living memory a Dispensary Ball has been held there the night after the "Color" Ball at the County Rooms. It must be noted that some very elegant decorations were contributed by the generosity of Countess of Warwick, formerly Lady Monson.

These records have rather led us away from our subject, but are almost inseparable from it. However, we will solicit the reader's indulgence, and return. The Butchery which fronts the street bearing the same name was built by the Corporation in 1774. An old Corporation by-law enacted that no butcher should sell bull-beef unless it had been previously baited, and near the present Guild Court was the Bull-ring, where the animals were regularly baited for the public diversion. Strange as it may seem, it was not until 1827 that the cruel practice was put down. Occasionally the huge delight of the crowd was turned into terror. For instance, in 1802, a bull, torn and worried by dogs on Castle Hill, plunged madly about, and succeeded in breaking loose, and dashed away amongst the crowd, down Steep Hill, through the confined Strait, and into the High-street, scattering the terrified market folk hither and thither, ending literally in a china shop near the Stonebow. Many fled with their screeching poultry into St. Peter-at-Arches Church, where service was being performed. The bull was eventually caught, and baited in Magpie-square, where, after some hours of torture, it at last fell dead.

By a Charter dated December 17th, 1685, a Tuesday market was granted to Lincoln for the sale of fish, dairy produce, and poultry, rabbits, and herbs. Another annual fair was also granted. The Charter was received at St. Catherine's Green, and openly carried through the city to the Guildhall, accompanied by the ringing of bells, the beating of drums, and the blare of trumpets, while bonfires gleamed on every hand at night.

Journeyings to market nearly a century later could not have been altogether pleasant. Besides the uncomfortable conveyances, there were risks to run. It is recorded that in 1744 the Northern Mail was stopped by a daring highwayman—not a number as was generally the case, and the passengers robbed, besides which the unwelcome intruder, who was evidently a man of business, carried off the Lincoln, Stamford, Horncastle, Boston, Louth, Spalding, and Bourne letter bags! Seven years later Dunston Pillar was erected, with a lantern at top to guide wayfarers over the Heath, though the Earl of Buckingham removed the lantern in November, 1810.

There is a record of a post-boy being told to keep the pillar on his right hand on his way home, and who drove round and round the pillar all night.

An interesting story in connection with Lincoln markets is recorded in an old issue of the local "Date-book." It appears that in 1753 a tradesman carrying on a business as a baker in Eastgate, took a boy named Holmes from the Workhouse (then near the sheep market) as an apprentice. One morning the boy was missing, and unfavourable reports being raised against the master, even going so far as to hint that he had burnt the boy alive in the oven, he gradually lost the whole of his business, and became a ruined man. Some time afterwards the missing apprentice was found in Billingsgate, and apprehended on the warrant of a Lincolnshire magistrate. He was sent down to Lincoln, and it is recorded that for three consecutive market-days the apprentice and his master appeared in the corn market, elevated on a cart, the latter crying "Here is Tom; I am innocent!"

On January 6th, 1786, it is recorded that so terrible a storm prevailed that it was found impossible to hold a market at all, and Lincoln, accordingly, has missed at least one day whereon the tradesmen might expect to be busy.

In 1847 the New Markets were opened, and three years later the Corporation built a Fish Market upon the site of a newly-made street called Witham-street. This market—or rather series of shops—is now disused, with two exceptions, and the place has a "forgotten" look indeed. It seems remarkable that property within hail of the Stonebow should be neglected and practically falling to pieces, yet such is the case.

Lincoln markets of to-day are widely different from those of the old town. It is no longer necessary for the old market people to sit in the open street, exposed to the elements; a house has been found for each, sheltered, convenient, and worthy the city.

XX.—ROYAL VISITS TO LINCOLN.

Everybody, surely, is convinced that the present Ruler of our Realms, the great Queen-Mother, has the best as well as the longest reign to her credit amongst all the Kings and Queens who, for better or worse ,have occupied the throne of our land. The story of the visits to Lincoln of Royalties, on errands of peace or war, is lengthy and interesting.

In the year 494 A.D., Ambrosius re-took Lincoln from the Saxons. Ambrosius, if not of the blood-royal, had might, and, some will say, right on his side, and his visit would be welcomed by many of the citizens of that day.

Seven years later King Arthur found Cerdic (afterwards the founder of Wessex) layin siege to Lincoln, and, after a stubborn resistance, obliged him to flee with the loss of 6,000 men slain in battle or drowned in the wild retreat. Indeed, Arthur seems to have guarded Lincoln pretty well, for in 514 we find him within our gates again, this time driving out the Saxons, who were making a strong effort to regain the place.

In 1013, Swayne, King of Denmark, invaded Lindsey, sailing up the Trent with a strong fleet, and the people of Gainsborough and Lincoln were obliged to do him homage to escape a very unpleasant visit, and by this humiliation escaped plundering—for a time. There were visits of contending Royalties to Lincoln in 1121 and 1140, but these were of a particularly warlike character, and will be dealt with in our next article.

We have previously quoted the saying :

" The first crowned head that enters Lincoln's walls,
His reign proves stormy, and his kingdom falls,"

which is forcibly recalled to mind when we contemplate the repeated visits of King Stephen and his ultimate downfall. Not only in his case, however, but in others, was the couplet verified, and little wonder that the superstitious men and women of mediæval times believed in it implicitly. Even we, in our nineteenth century and enlightenment, are not altogether free from it, and in their day, in the "dark ages," a saying handed down from generation to generation, and bearing about it even slight rudiments of truth, found general, almost universal, acceptance. However, it does not seem to have impressed Stephen very greatly, for after he had been restored to his throne we find him spending Christmas, 1144, within the walls of Linciln. Aye, and doubtless when the boar's head was brought in, and the merry jest went round, his laugh was as hearty as the rest, and the old couplet's ominous meaning was banished from his memory. In defiance of it he wore his crown in State at Lincoln three Christmasses later.

When Henry II. came to the throne he was crowned in London, and afterwards in 1155 or 1158—the date is uncertain—went through the ceremony in Lincoln, not, be it noted, within the city proper, but in Wickenford, now St. Mary-le-Wigford's parish, but at that time a suburb. In the latter year Henry spent Christmas at Lincoln, and went through the coronation ceremony with Eleanor, his Queen, in Wickenford. Lincoln seems to have been a favourite resort for a Royal Christmas, and is evidence that the citizens treated their monarchs well. Can we doubt that if our Queen graciously visited it during this auspicious year she would receive such a welcome as no city, be its pretensions what they may, could excel, at least in point of loyalty? King Henry again came to Lincoln in 1170, but possibly only on a brief private visit, as the accounts of it are very meagre.

Thirty years later on, on Bore Hill or Bower Hill, just outside the city, somewhere near the Union Workhouse, William the Lion, King of Scotland, did homage to King John for the lands of Lothair and his earldom of Huntingdon. William took the oath of allegiance on the crosier of Archbishop Hubert, and the scene was one of great impressiveness and magnificence. Both Kings visited Lincoln two years afterwards, in 1202. There is an old record which gives the same act of homage from William to John, on Hubert's crosier, in 1203, but possibly the two dates refer to the same event. At any rate, in the last-named year King David of Scotland did homage to John at Lincoln, in probably the same manner.

Edward I. visited Lincoln in 1290, and his visit was a sad one. It was on the occasion of his Queen's death, after only a short illness, her body being subsequently embalmed at St. Catherine's Priory. Afterwards it was taken on the dreary journey to its resting-place in Westminster Abbey, the bereaved King himself following in the funeral train. The series of Crosses, previously described in these articles, mark the various stages of probably the saddest journey in all our English history. Sad, because he was a King and she was a Queen of considerable promise, and because that other King, he with the raven cloak and fleshless head, visited the indisposed Queen so suddenly, and when he was so little expected. The exquisite beauty of the crosses is admired by every historian who mentions them, and must be taken as some token of Edward's deep sorrow at the loss of his life-partner.

The second Edward visited Lincoln in 1309, and of Edward III.'s favourable regard for the city we have already written in connection with the staple of wool.

In 1386, Richard II. came to the city, and granted to the then Mayor, John Sutton, and his successors, the right of having a sword carried before them in their civic processions. The right—and, we believe, the original sword also—is still preserved.

We take a great leap now, and come down to 1485, in which year Henry VII. proceeded to Lincoln after the famous battle on Bosworth Field, and it is recorded that he spent three days in thanksgiving and in making processions, which were marked by much ceremonial and splendour. He again visited the city a year later, for what purpose is not recorded, and in 1532 the Merry Monarch came. His purpose, however, was not for thanksgiving, or, for the matter of that, for giving at all. In fact, he came to take away, and seems to have done so fairly thoroughly, as he seized a considerable amount of church property. Besides this, he visited the Cathedral on two separate occasions—in 1514 and 1540—and robbed it extensively. Whenever the citizens heard that their licentious King was in diffi-culties, we can well imagine that they trembled for the safety of their goods, and not improbably hid them until Henry was "solvent" once more! In 1541, Henry passed through Lincoln on his way from South Carlton to Nocton, during a tour of part of his dominions, and de-putations from various towns had to make humble submission to him. That this submission took the form most acceptable to his Majesty may best be gathered from the statement that the Lincoln deputa-tion presented him with £40, and Boston with £50. His Majesty graciously accepted their offerings. In this same year, Henry and his newly-wedded Queen, Katherine Howard, stayed at the Episcopal Palace, and here, as well as at Gainsborough, it was that the mis-conduct with the young courtier Culpepper took place, which, with other charges, resulted in her being put to death in the year following. But the reign of this monarch is not one of the most pleasant to dwell upon, and we may well take leave of him who spoke of Lincolnshire as "one of the most brute and beastly shires in the whole realm"— this upon an occasion when indignation at the kingly licentiousness had caused his will to be disregarded—and pass on to lighter scenes.

James the First—more buffoon, some go so far as to declare, than King—came to Lincoln on March 27th, 1617. "His Majesty hunted along the Heath, and came not by the highway, and so the Sheriffs (William Solomon and Roger Beck) removed   .   .   .   near the Cross of the Cliff, where his Majesty could not miss them, the Sheriffs being hindmost." The civic authorities were in "long cloth clothes of purple in grain," the Sheriffs carried white staves of office, and the others javelins fringed with red and white. He stayed in St. Katherine's, at the house of the Granthams—we have now a street called after this family, at a place where was their earlier residence, known as the "Cardinal's Cap." On Sunday the King went to the Bishop's Palace, and on Tuesday the Rev. Eland, Rector of Kettle-thorpe and Chancellor of Lincoln, preached before his Majesty, in his Chamber of Presence, after which the King "did touch 53 for the evil." On Wednesday James came to the George Inn, near the Stonebow, to see a cock-fight. His Majesty commanded four cocks to be put into the pit at once, and the resulting uproar gave him huge delight. From here he went to the Spread Eagle "to see a prize player by a fensor of the city and a servant of some attendant at the Court." The Lincolner got the best of it. Next day there was a horse race on the Heath, on Friday a great hunting and "a race be-tween three Irishmen and an Englishman, and the Englishman wonne the race." Next day his Majesty left for Newark, with much cere-mony. Truly James was a monarch who loved his pleasures, and we can imagine the Mayor and his Sheriffs had a full day's rest after their monarch's departure.

In 1640 his son, Charles I., whose reign has inspired song and story more, perhaps, than that of any other English monarch, came to our city on Saints Simon and Jude's day, and presented to the Corporation the Mace, which, we believe, is the one yet used in civic processions. Charles came again a year later, and yet again in 1642, on the latter occasion to summon the gentry and freeholders to his assitance. Ther were disturbances in that year, and the Mayor, John Becke, had to appear before his King at York to answer a charge of favouring the rebels, but "returned safely.'

In 1657—though this does not come exactly under a head of Royalty—Cromwell was proclaimed Lord Protector at Lincoln, and dying in the following year, his son was proclaimed here in his succession.

In 1695 William the Third visited Lincoln, and, arriving between six and seven o'clock in the evening of October 29th, was met by the Mayor and other officials on horseback. The town was so full with visitors that there was no lodging to be had anywhere, and the illuminations in honour of his Majesty must have been on a particularly gorgeous scale. "The town was glorious," we read, "with candles in everybody's window, so that a pin might have been seen and picked up." At the Cathedral next day his Majesty put in an appearance, and granted an annual September fair. He brought his own provisions, says one writer, but ate nothing. The fact was that at Belton the night previous the King had got "exceedingly merry, and drank freely, which was the occasion when he came to Lincoln he could take but a porringer of milk." He left Lincoln in his coach for Welbeck.

Coming down to 1766, we find that in September of that year the then Duke of York came through the city, and bespoke the opera "Midas' from players then in Lincoln. Afterwards he went to the County Assembly Rooms, and footed it in the merry dance, opening the ball with a minuet with Lady Scarbrough.

We take another long leap now, and come to 1849, in which year Prince Albert passed through Lincoln to lay the foundation stone of Grimsby Docks. This brief glimpse, however, was not all that Lincoln saw of the Prince Consort, for he came through again two years later (August 27th, 1851, is the exact date), and this time he was accompanied bv her Majesty the Queen, with the Prince of Wales and other Royal children. An address was presented by the Corporation, and the day was a red-letter one indeed in Lincoln's history.

But though we cannot say that the Queen has ridden through our streets, it is, perhaps, not too late to hope that, despite her age, infirmity, and shrinking from public appearances, we may yet have the felicity of welcoming in the city the august lady upon whose empire the sun never sets. It is doubtful, of course—extremely doubtful—but, as we have said earlier in the present article, if she came she would have a reception worthy the exalted position she holds. But, at any rate, we can join heartily in this, the 61st year of her unprecedentedly glorious reign, in wishing her a long continuance of health and the love of her many peoples the world over.

The Prince of Wales has visited Lincoln on several occasions, though not for some years now, chiefly at the Spring Race Meetings, as the guest of Mr. Chaplin. His visits, we believe without exception, have been of a private character.

XXI.—LINCOLN IN TIME OF WAR.

These are the piping times of peace. We come forth to the day's toil in the morning, greet our friends, and go about our business, tranquil and serene, in the calm assurance that there is no enemy at our gates—how the old term lasts, for "gates" are no longer used as a means of defence—and retire to our rest at night without our slumbers being rudely disturbed by the clangour of armed retainers engaged in hand-to-hand conflict in our streets, or the fear of the same at any moment.

No, the enemy is not only kept from the heart of the land, but the British Lion's paws stretch beyond our shores, and the enemy, however he may boast and express contempt for him, takes particular care to keep beyond the reach of the talons within their velvet sheath, the power of which he knows and respects. But when—if the term is permissible—the British Lion was only a cub, when armaments were infantile compared with our modern accoutrements and appliances, there were, as everyone knows, times when England was looked upon, to a very large extent, as the prey of any country of sufficient military force to overcome the rude battalions opposed to it. And when the invaders swarmed over England, it could but follow that Lincoln had her share in the light and shade of the various epochs. And, later, when the country was stirred to its depths by civil strife, which, after all, can be more dangerous than the fiercest attack of a foreign force, Lincoln was still one of the principal scenes wherein the battle of king and commoner, baron and burgher, was fought to the bitter, bitter end.

We have already dealt to a large extent with the strife of the Roman period, when Cæsar's forces landed on Albion's shores, and gradually forced a way into the heart and vitals of the land. We have seen, too, (second article) how home affairs demanded a withdrawal of their armies here, and that the country became a prey to the quickly succeeding Saxons and Normans. Among these early fighters there stands out one name beyond the rest, as that of a man who struggled hard against the invaders in defence of his country, and who eventually died in 475, and was buried in Lincoln. Vortimer, son of Vortigern, was the type of man of whom the bards loved to write and sing, extolling his deeds when the historian had not yet brought his screed to commemorate the events of the times. Indeed, the historian is indebted to these old-time minstrels (and markedly to the Welsh bards) for a great proportion of what light can be thrown upon the otherwise dark ages.

There can be little doubt that the city was looked upon as one of great value and importance, and that its possession gave, in a measure, the command, or at least the influence, over a wide radius. In 584 we read of Mercia being one of the Saxon kingdoms of the Heptarchy, founded by Crida, who incorporated Lindsey with it. It is stated by some that Lincoln was the capital; and though there is no absolute testimony of this, it is quite within the bounds of possibility that such was the case. Indeed, in the absence of convincing proof to the contrary, and in the light of preceding and succeeding events, we should be quite ready to accept Lincoln as having been virtually the capital, and, most probably, nominally also. A year later comes this record: "Lincoln, as capital of Mercia, compelled to receive a Saxon Sovereign."

In the year 754 we again find the city attacked, this time by Bernwulf, who ravaged Lincoln, according to some historians, completely. But the great invasion of the Danes in Lincolnshire appears to have been from 865 to 867, when the famous chiefs Hingvar and Hubba and their forces poured into Northumbria to avenge the death of Regner Lodbrog, whom Ella, King of Northumbria, had captured and tortured. They advanced upon York, and captured that city, then continued their devastating course to the Humber. They crossed the water and came as near Lincoln as Bardney, where they demolished the Abbey, and, some say, Stow church. Then Osgot, Sheriff of Lin-coln, appears to have thought it time to take action, and accordingly, in concert with Earl Algar, Wibert, Leofric, and Morcar (Lord of Bourne), sallied forth with 500 men. A fight ensued, and a tough one, too, but the Danes were routed, and three of their kings slain Not to be denied, however, the Danes rallied and "came again." This time (869) victory smiled upon them, and it is recorded that Lincoln was sacked by them. From this time they gradually spread over the land. We have earlier remarked that the village of Threekingham takts its name from the three Danish kings or chiefs slain. It is worthy of note, also, that Algar, Wibert, and Leofric, the valiant Saxon leaders, are commemorated in Algarkirk, Wyberton, and Leverington.

The Danish supremacy in the north and east of England became practically established in 873, and Lincolnshire became a part of the Danelaga, which also included York, Stamford, Leicester, Derby, and Nottingham.

Lincoln avoided war in 1013 by submitting to Swayne, the Danish King, but in 1121 came the great conflict between the forces of the Empress Maud and the party of King Stephen, the latter being routed and captured. In 1140 we find the Empress Matilda seizing Lincoln, which she strongly fortified and stored abundantly with provisions. But Matilda was by no means popular with her compulsory subjects, and they invited Stephen to come to their assistance. The Castle, let us hasten to add, was already in the possession of the Earls of Chester and Lincoln, so that the citizens were in the predicament of the gentlemen in the renowned song, who was "blest if 'e could call 'sself 'is own." Stephen came. As the Castle could not be taken, the King calmly fortified the Minster, with the greatest disregard for the sanctity of the place, and stationed his smart bowmen along the parapets, while he erected his engines of war on the summit of Remigius' walls, thus commanding a fine prospect of the enemy's stronghold

But despite all efforts, the forces in the Castle sturdily held their own, and the Earl of Chester let himself down over the walls to carry the news of the siege to Robert, Earl of Gloucester, whose auxiliary forces were anxiously watched for and expected. The army, together with a large body of savage Welshmen, swam the Trent, and arrived on Candlemas Eve, February 1st, 1141. Next morning, ere going to battle, Stephen apparently recollected the sacred character of the building he had garrisoned, and heard Mass, Bishop Alexander officiating. Many shook their heads at Stephen's profanity, and made much of the ill omens which attended the service, for when Stephen, in accordance with the custom of the Festival, offered the huge waxen taper "worthy of a king," it broke asunder as the Bishop received it. Nor was this all. The chain by which the pyx holding the consecrated wafer was suspended over the altar suddenly snapped in twain, and the sacred Body crashed on to the Holy Table. The predictions of those who witnessed this were verified when, a few hours later, Stephen was dragged roughly back, a prisoner, and conveyed across to Bristol to be confined in the Castle.

Yet the defeated king seems to have fought well. It is recorded that after the two wings of his party had been put to flight, Stephen fought on, though surrounded by the enemy, and performed great feats of strength and valour before being finally borne down by his two weapons breaking and by sheer weight of numbers. Matthew Westminster writes graphically of him, and as we read, we can seem to see the kingly dignity and intrepid endurance of the man, fighting hopelessly against overwhelming odds, grandly brought before us. "King Stephen," says Matthew, "being deserted by his army, and left almost alone in the field of battle, yet no man dared approach him, while grinding his teeth and foaming like a mad boar, he drove back with his battle-axe whole troops who came to assail him, and killed the bravest of them, to the eternal renown of his courage; and if a hundred such men had been there with him, a whole army could not have surprised his person; but his battle-axe and sword breaking, he was stricken down with a stone, and seized by William de Kahæms."

This memorable battle was fought outside Newport gate on "Lincoln Plain," and great wreck and ruin befel our city on that same day. "The citizens," Wiliam of Malmesbury assures us, "were slaughtered on all sides by the just indignation of the victims, and without gaining any pity from the conquered, as they had been themselves the origin and fomentors of this calamity." The loss of life was not great in the battle, but the historian Orderic, writing of the suffering of the citizens afterwards, says the men left their houses and their wives and ran for boats to escape, but, by hastening in too fast, overset them, and almost all, nearly five hundred, were drowned.

It is a matter of history how the Earl of Chester ultimately fell into Stephen's power, and was kept in prison until he restored to the king Lincoln Castle and other fortresses. Chester, however, neglecting his oath to Stephen, treacherously attempted to re-take the place but was beaten back, and lost a general and many men at North (Newport?) Gate.

A dramatic scene, which, if not one of war, is one of strife, is recorded on the occasion of the murder of the Sub-Dean Bramfield, who was slain by one of the Vicars while kneeling in prayer in the Minster. "Their master's death was immediately avenged by the Sub-Dean's servants," the late Precentor Venables tells us, "the wretched murdere was so roughly handled that little life was left in the lacerated body, which, tied to the tail of a horse, was dragged through the streets of the city to the public gallows on the brow of Canwick Hill."

We come now to the year 1217, and the panic-stricken rush of the French to the Bargates. The Dauphin's troops, under Count de Percne, had been defeated and driven down the hill by the Royal troops under the Regent, William Marshall, Earl of Pembroke. The doors of the Bargates closed inwardly with a spring, penning the Frenchmen in like frightened sheep, nearly the whole being taken prisoners. Then in 1265 occurred the fearful massacre of Lincoln Jews, nearly all the hated race in the city perishing.

Another scene of bloodshed comes next, connected with our beloved Minster. On St. John's Day, December 27th, 1392, while Vespers were being sung, Robert Pakynton, a servant of the Dean, violently assaulted the Treasurer's man, Thomas, and five days later (New Year's Day) also during Vespers, Simon, the bellringer, was attacked by a party of the Dean's men, and the poor fellow fled to the church for shelter, but the door was closed against him, and he received some dangerous wounds. The result was that the guilty parties were excommunicated, and the church prounced polluted and suspended from Divine service for a time.

XXII.—FOR CROMWELL OR THE CROWN?

On Sunday, March 27th, 1625, closed the life of King James the First. His disease was called tertian ague, but modern science would have called it a particularly bad form of gout. His death may be said to have been the chief incident in the prologue to the great drama between Royalist and Roundhead, Prince and Puritan. After lying in state for a long time in Westminster Abbey, James was buried, and Charles the First "reigned in his stead.".There is a curious little anecdote recorded in connection with Charles' proclamation, which shows up strangely in regard to his after-life. The knight marshal proclaimed Prince Charles, "the right and dubitable heir," to be King of England, Scotland, France, and Ireland. Mr. Secretary Conway hastily put him right, and he then said "indubitable heir." Next day Charles went with the Duke of Buckingham to Whitehall, and was proclaimed at Whitehall-gate and in Cheapside "amid a sad shower of rain." It also rained heavily when he brought his French bride to London. Ominous beginnings to a reign destined to be one of the stormiest in the history of our land !

Then a plague broke out in Whitechapel, and, as if this were not enough, there were indications that the nation was on the eve of a great social and political change. How came this change about? What was the cause of this mighty upheaval of the whole country, north, south, east, and west, in which Lincoln played an important part? We cannot give a record of the local doings without first indicating the general aspect of the civil rising. So we must briefly sketch the developments of the Great Rebellion as a whole.

Charles was hardly an ideal King. Amiable and excellent as a man, he had not the innate strength of purpose and self-reliance of a true king. His advisers quickly discovered this, and, little by little, he came under their influence, and what was nominally their advice became in practice the commands of the king. And this because Charles was unable to think for himself, or afraid to trust his own opinions on State affairs. The commands which he was advised to give set him before his people as a very stern monarch, whereas he was really vacillating and uncertain in himself, and the majority, at any rate, of the mandates issued from the Royal House came, in the first instance, from his advisers. Particularly was the Royal support given to the Archbishop of Canterbury in his claim to put down all forms of religious worship except that of which he was the head, and a great deal of persecution resulted. It became quite a frequent thing to see prisoners, bound together by the wrists, driven through the streets of London to Lambeth Palace, where, very often, they were imprisoned for their religious opinions. Another circumstance giving offence to the people was that Charles's Queen, Henrietta Maria, who was a Frenchwoman, had a certain number of priests to wait upon her, celebrated mass in her private apartments, and exercised her own religion.

The beginning of the dissension between the King and Parliament was Charles's requirement of money.   He had told them that his father's debts amounted to £700,000 ; but Parliament only granted him two supplies amounting to about £140,000.   Then strife arose at Rochelle, in France, and by his conduct in this matter, the Duke of Buckingham earned the cordial hate of the English people, and a quarrel arose between the king and his people, for the monarch supported his favourite.   The name of John Hampden, a Buckinghamshire gentleman, will always be remembered as a strong bulwark on the side of the people.   The murder of Dr. Lamb by a mob would have operated as a warning to some rulers, but Charles, incensed against the city of London, imposed a fine of £6,000 upon the citizens.   A few days later a placard was posted up in Coleman-street, bearing these words :

Who rules the kingdom?   The King.
Who rules the King?   The Duke.
Who rules the Duke?   The Devil—

which may be taken as expressing the general hatred of the Duke at the time.

Buckingham became more and more unpopular, but the King still clung to him, infatuated.   At length the Duke was slain by one John Felton—out of revenge, some have it.   For eleven years Charles governed without a Parliament, but financial affairs at length compelled him to summon one, and this, which assembled on Nov. 3rd, 1640, was called the Long Parliament, for it lasted long after Charles's head was severed from his body.   Parliament and King soon disagreed, and the outcome of it was that Charles left London for York, where he raised money and soldiers, while Parliament trained its militia.   Charles came to Lincoln in 1642 to summon to his assistance "the well-affected gentry and freeholders of his county," and to consult upon the best means of suppressing the rebellious outbreaks of the Puritans.   The Royalists, under the King and Prince Rupert, first met the Parliamentarians, under the Earl of Essex, at Edgehill, in Warwickshire, and in this battle 4,000 men were killed.   Oliver Cromwell, the Member of Parliament for Cambridge—popularly known as the "Lord of the Fens," by reason of his having successfully defended a part of the fens against certain avaricious landholders—was a prominent man in these early struggles. Raising a troop of horse himself, he speedily acquired such a reputation by his command of it that in 1643 he was raised to the rank of Colonel of the Parliamentary Army.

In this year Cromwell and Sir Thomas Fairfax found it necessary to call in the assistance of the Earl of Manchester to oppose the Royal forces in Lincolnshire.   This was because the prospects of Charles had become very promising in these parts.   Lincoln was in the Royal possession, Sir William (afterwards Lord) Widdrington, of Blankney, being the Governor.   The castles of Bolingbroke and Newark were also held for the King.   Several troops of horse and a large body of foot, under Sir John Henderson, compelled the Parliamentarians to retreat towards Louth. The rebels, however, under Cromwell, had defeated "the gallant Cavendish" in July of that year, at Lea, near Gainsborough. Boston appears to have been a Parliamentary stronghold.

Obeying Cromwell's call, the Earl of Manchester, with his whole force, advanced from Lynn, and came by way of Boston to Bolingbroke. On Monday, October 9th apparently (though it has also been given as the 6th), the Earl of Manchester brought out all his forces from Boston, placing ten companies of foot at Bolingbroke, a regiment of infantry at Stickford, and his own men at Stickney—the horse being disposed of in the surrounding villages. Royalists forces from Lincoln, Newark, and Gainsborough came out to meet the enemy. Sir Thomas Fairfax was next sent forward to Horncastle, with his advance guard about two miles nearer Lincoln, at Edlington. Intelligence was brought to Sir Thomas of the advance of the Royal troops, and communicated by him to the Earl of Manchester, but as the news was as yet uncertain, the Earl decided to call all his forces together, and make Horncastle his headquarters.

While on his way, however, fresh news was brought him. The Royalists had fallen upon Fairfax's advanced posts, and were now making for Horncastle. He advanced near enough to see his own outposts driven in, and then decided to make Kirkby and Bolingbroke the place of union. This caused some confusion, as some of the troops did not receive notice of the alteration. These—three troops of horse—had to break through a strong section of the Royal forces at Thimbleby, and then, on advancing to Horncastle, were astounded to find the place in possession of—not the Earl of Manchester, but the enemy!

Eventually the opposing forces met at Winceby, a terrific battle, after the fortune of war had temporarily wavered between them, resulting in favour of Cromwell, who himself fought like a very demon. It was in the flying retreat from the field that the Royalists became penned in a corner, seeking to open a gate, at the boundary between Winceby and Scrafield, and where the victorious Parliamentarians cut numbers of them to pieces. This lane thus obtained the name of "Slash-lane," which it retains to this day. The Castle of Bolingbroke immediately surrendered, and practically all Lincolnshire became lost to the Royal cause.

On the 24th of October, 1643—a fortnight after the battle of Winceby—the Earl of Manchester advanced upon Lincoln. That, at least, is the date given by the old writer, John Vicars, who was on the side of the Parliamentarians, as quoted in a paper read by Mr. F. C. Massingberd to the annual meeting of the Archæological Institute of Great Britain and Ireland at Lincoln in July, 1848. Precentor Venables gives the date as "Monday, May 6th, 1644—a few days after Winceby fight." In Horncastle Church there was preserved a monumental hatchment to the memory of Sir Ingram Hopton, and the date of Winceby fight (in which the Knight fell) was given there as October 6th, 1643.

The Parliamentary troops were posted on the top of Canwick Hill. All had been ready for attack on the Sunday, but the Puritans had, of course, a profound regard for the Sabbath. So at three o'clock on Monday morning they came down the hill, made a rush at the Bargate, forced an entry, and from thence dashed up the High-street and had secured the Castle in a wonderfully short time. After this they captured the Cathedral, wherein they stabled their horses, and ransacked it thoroughly. The old church of St. Martin suffered very greatly from the effects of their cannon; it lay unroofed and in ruins until the early part of last century, when it was restored, chiefly by the efforts of a gardener who had been appointed churchwarden St. Peter's-in-Eastgate Church also suffered very much, being dismantled and sacked by the Parliamentarians. Indeed, they seem to have walked roughshod everywhere through the city, the Cathedral, as may be supposed, coming in for principal attention. Here they melted down a number of valuable vessels, shattered many of the statues (largely accounting for the lamentably numerous empty niches of to-day), stripped the place—and other churches, too—of much lead, and but for the courageous interposition of Mr. Original Peart, "Sheriff and Mayor of the city, and Parliament man" for Lincoln, would have done boundless and irreparable injury to the noble pile. Mr. Peart, however, sought an interview with Cromwell, and this had the desired result. Before this satisfactory concession, the soldiers had torn up all the monumental brasses and defaced many tombs—that of Bishop Grostete for one—practically destroyed the Chapter House on the west side of the Castle, and had threatened the Cathedral's entire demolition.

The Earl of Manchester, says Vicars, "found and forced to be left in the City Close and Minster of Lincoln arms for at least 2,500 men, 28 or 30 colours, three pieces of ordnance, and great store of ammunition; the cormorants or cavalier officers having leave to depart on horseback with their swords, the common soldiers having only sticks." They retired first to Gainsborough, but soon abandoned the town, and retreated to Newark. In 1657 Oliver Cromwell was proclaimed Lord Protector at Lincoln.

We do not propose to follow the great Civil War further. Lincoln was hardly concerned with the remainder of it. In 1644 the Scottish army crossed the border to assist the Parliamentarians, and everyone has heard of the fights at Marston Moor and Naseby. Charles was defeated, and fled to Scotland, after hiding for a time near Newark. But he was given up to his enemies, and in 1649 was "tried" before Parliament. This was on January 19th, and on the 30th of the same month he was beheaded, an Act being also issued on the same date prohibiting the proclamation of the Prince of Wales. Thus England became, for the time being, a Republic. Stirring times, indeed, were these. Whatever opinions one may hold on the rights and wrongs of the Great Rebellion, who can but see the striking contrast between the characters of the vacillating Charles and the ambitious Cromwell? Nor will admiration be withheld from the Lord Protector by his determination and struggles to achieve the fulfilment of his paramount desire—that bubble which burst almost as he clutched it, for during the short time he was Lord Protector, it is stated, so unpopular did he become that he always went about clad in armour (under his ordinary clothes), and even slept in a shirt of chain mail. What is more fickle than the public favour? The struggling, ambitious peasant has railed against it; kings have waxed great in their zenith, and fallen mightily. And the Lord Protector was no exception. Truly is Power a fiery weapon, and most dangerous to its possessor!

XXIII.—ST. MARY'S GUILD AND JOHN OF GAUNT'S PALACE.

The old building which stands next to the County Police station in High-street has a particularly interesting history. It is popularly known as John of Gaunt's stables, but as a matter of fact it was built for a widely different purpose, this being as the Hall of St. Mary's Guild. Erected in the twelfth century, the building is one of the oldest in the city, which is saying a good deal. The exact date of its erection is uncertain; various chroniclers, in fact, have given it as Norman and Transition-Norman period. Says one authority, "We do not know when it (the Guild) was founded, but it must have been at a very early time, for the edifice belongs to the Transition-Norman style, and cannot be later than 1150 or 1160." Says another, "It is one of the most ancient of the city buildings, the semi-circular arch and shallow pilaster buttress marking the Norman period. The lower storey only remains, and the "Pictorial History of England" quotes it as an instance of the peculiar arrangement of Norman buildings, the only light admitted being through a narrow slit—fair evidence that the ground floor was not inhabited, but a mere storeroom for fuel, etc.

It need hardly be said, perhaps, that the building, as we see it to-day, is but a fragment of its former dimensions. Stukeley, writing about the year 1730, states that the bow-window through which Lord Hussey was brought out for execution had just been taken down. The unfortunate nobleman, it appears, was suspected of conniving at or being privy to the notable Lincolnshire rising against the suppression of Monasteries in the reign of Henry the Eighth.

The court or quadrangle at the rear of the building is of Norman architecture, and (we are still adhering to Stukeley) the same style might have been traced in more or less degree in the whole range of buildings as far as the adjoining churchyard of St. Peter-at-Gowt's. A rare old compilation of the late Mr. W. Brooke, printer, alludes to the Hall being "better known as the Sweep's House, from being so occupied for many years." We may be permitted to doubt whether this was really so. That it has been called John of Gaunt's stables we know, and it is equally possible that it may have been popularly styled the Sweep's House at some period. There certainly was, up to the houses adjoining being removed rather more than a year back, a sweep living in one of the dwellings, but this, let us point out, was not in one of the houses really part of the Hall. At the same time, the sweep whom Mr. Brooke affirms to have given his name to the building may have been another person living quite out of memory, and whose name and deeds are not handed down to us. But, all things considered, we fail to see how the place could have been widely known as the Sweep's House at any period whatever.

Recent improvements in the neighbourhood have swept away much of the old place, but there is still a portion standing, and this includes a gateway which, if not noble, is of interesting appearance. May we pause to consider what contrasting classes of men have passed through that gateway? A stretch of the imagination, and we may hark back to the twelfth century, and see the men entering the portal for whose use the building was originally designed. St. Mary's Guild, we may here state, was the principal, but not the only trading guild in the city for the protection of the citizens individually, and jointly against the tyranny af the barons and nobility. It was, in fact, the forerunner, or, if we may so term it, the chrysalis of the trades union of the present day. But this our local trades unionist, perhaps, needs hardly to be told. He will have traced the defensive union back to its earliest date, and will have watched its workings, doubtless, from remotest ages down to modern times. If so, he will have regarded the faults and failings of these old guilds, and will have had an eye upon the reformations made to adapt them to changing eras and contending minds of men. It is not too much to hope that if he has observed all this, he may have profited by it. If he has not, however, his observance has been mere waste of time. It may not be out of place here to point out that St. Mary's Guild was semi-religious and semi-mercantile. Can it be that the religious element has not sufficiently entered into the modern trades union—using the word religion as meaning brotherly forbearance and friendship—as a means of approaching the settlement of a dispute rather than putting forward the contentious side of the matter, and giving prominence to peremptory demands and threats of cessation of labour? There is much food for thought here—thought of which we may thus suggest the source and outline, but may not stay to further consider. Yet the subject is certainly tempting. In these days of strikes and continual strife between employer and employed it may be that the modern trades union is not all that it might be, and that it is then that the "semi-religious" side of its working would be best advanced, and avert many a bitter struggle of starving breadwinner and wan-cheeked wife and piteously appealing children against mighty, impregnable Capital !

To our subject. We were considering the differing classes of men who have passed beneath the gateway of the Hall of St. Mary's Guild. We have said that a stretch of imagination would depict the men of the twelfth century entering in ; solemn-visaged, earnest, calculating traders they would be, too, for fortunes were not too easily made when Henry the Eighth and his successors ruled the realm. We cannot imagine that Cromwell's Ironsides would pass the gateway ; they would certainly take a look inside, and very bare the place must have been if they did not find something worth bringing away, while subsequent generations would also find a use for the old building. Let us take a big leap down to our time, when in fast-fading recent years (all too soon to be engulfed in that "forgotten Lincoln" we are endeavouring to write down in permanent form) the field beyond the arch has been used for athletic purposes. Through the archway, to the stirring music of their band, and the imposing rat-a-tat-tat of the drums, have marched the A, B, and C (Lincoln) Companies of the 1st Lincolnshire Rifle Volunteers for drill, and through here, also, have streamed hundreds of workmen intent on seeing the Lincoln City football team play in League and other matches.

But the eye of the builder caught that field. To-day a broad road-way runs down, and John of Gaunt's field has become Sibthorp-street, while smaller streets are to branch from it. Our citizen soldiers have had to seek literally a fresh field, and the leather-hunters have found a new home on Sincil Bank, but alas, appear to have left the cream of their old success behind them. Many a stirring scene has been witnessed in the football arena on John of Gaunt's field, many a keen fight, many a brilliant triumph for the old red-and-whites. Citizens now of ripe years, whose days of donning the jersey are over, will remember the gallant battles fought and won here when the "Lincoln City" team was composed of Lincolners—not outsiders. We have a dozen names of respected citizens in our mind as we write these lines, men who have been as successful in the battle of life as in the mimic fight of the football field. So do athletics fit the man in the struggle for existence in these days of hurry and competition.

Speaking of John of Gaunt's field naturally brings us to the man himself and to his palace, which stood opposite the Hall of St. Mary's Guild. Of John of Gaunt himself the discreet historian, as a rule, says little. Shakespeare's "Time-honoured Lancaster" had a history rather dark than otherwise, and not always creditable The fourth son of Edward III., brother to the ever-famous Black Prince (yet were ever brothers so different?) and father of our "Lincolnshire born king," Henry III., who was born at Bolingbroke, John of Gaunt is yet a direct ancestor of our own Queen. The present Royal family, as a matter of fact, is derived through the daughters of James the First and Henry the Seventh from the Earl of Somerset, who was the eldest son of John of Gaunt, by Catherine Swynford, daughter of Sir Payn de Rouet and widow of Sir Hugh Swynton, of Kettlethorpe. John and Catherine were made one in Lincoln Cathedral, January 13th, 1396. Two years previous their son Henry became Bishop of Lincoln, and three years after this, his third marriage, John died, while Catherine survived him until 1403, her defaced tomb and that of her daughter, the Countess of Westmorland, yet remaining on the south side of the Choir of the Cathedral.

Of John of Gaunt's Palace nearly all traces were removed in the last century. However, many historians speak of a magnificent oriel window which stood at the south end, and was afterwards re-moved to the Castle, being bought in 1849 by the Lord-Lieutenant of the County, Earl Brownlow, who took this means of preserving the interesting and valuable relic for the county. Another fine win-dow is spoken of as being in the kitchen, which is stated to have borne some magnificent tracery. These windows, however, belong to a later period than John of Gaunt. Some attribute the erection of the building to the want of a more sheltered site than the Castle for the winter season. An old print by the brothers Buck, taken in 1727, shows an extended front, with battlements, pinnacles, mullioned window, etc., and the arms of John of Gaunt, Duke of Lancaster, carved in stone, affixed on what appears in the print to be a receding wing towards the north. These arms are declared to have been standing until 1737, when the wing was probably taken down in the extensive alterations then made. There were further demolitions in 1783.

In 1386, Richard II. visited his uncle here (that uncle by whose son he was to be dethroned and imprisoned, if not murdered!) and upon the occasion of this visit granted the Mayor, one John Sutton, the right of having a sword borne before him, the right of which still exists, and is invariably observed in civic processions and ceremonials.

XXIV.—THE MINSTER CLOSE.

When Lincoln was yet in its youth, and when the Castle became a stronghold, it was divided into three distinct parts. These were the Bail, the Close, and the City. The Bail consisted of the upper portion of the town; the Close was a walled enclosure, the habitation of the priests when certain colleges, schools, and chantries existed there; and the City consisted of the portion of the town below Bailgate and beyond Newport.

Of the gate-houses of the Close we have already made mention, and also alluded to the fact that it was in consequence of a petition addressed to Edward I. that the wall was built, though not really completed until Edward II. had ascended the throne, as a protection against audacious robbers. The principal entrance seems to have been Exchequer-gate. Our reason for returning to the subject is to make mention of certain old houses which stood in the Close until so recently as March, 1892(?) and we are largely indebted for the information to a paper of the late Precentor Venables (that matchless local antiquary and historian) on the matter.

The houses in question were eight dwellings situated between the Deanery and Chapter House. Two at least of these houses were of considerable interest. The first two to be demolished were No. 1, Minster-yard, immediately adjacent to the Chapter House on the north, and No. 6, Priory-gate. In the 17th century these two dwellings formed one tenement, and this was known as "College House." The term "College," of course, has not the modern educational meaning pure and simple, but was applied to the whole Cathedral body, with its College (or Society) of Canons and Senior and Junior Vicars. The dwelling had first a dining-hall to the north, the main tenement being added after the dining-hall had ceased to be used for its original purpose. The Parliamentary Survey of 1649-51 makes mention of it thus: "All that mansion or dwelling-house"—it opens quite like an auctioneer's advertisement!—"near the North Gate of the Minster Close commonly called the Colledge House. The same consisteth of a hall 6 yards long" (this appears to be an error, as it is stated elsewhere the length was 12 yards) "and 6 yards broad by estimation, with a parlour and other convenient rooms. Also with two cellars and buttery, a coal house, a wood house, with a cross building of stables. In the second storey of the said Mansion a dining-room wainscoated, with 4 lodging chambers, and 2 chambers in the garrets. All the said house is of stone building and covered with tyle. There's also a gatehouse of stone building with one chamber over the same."

The gatehouse here referred to was removed many years previous to the demolition of the building proper. The house was divided into two, with a very modern brick front to No. 1, Minster-yard, and a large bow-windowed parlour was added on the south side. It appears that the hall was erected some time in the 13th century by the Dean and Chapter for use as a refectory for the subordinate members of their body. Sympson writes that it was here that the Residentiaries "formerly entertained and fed their Vicars and officers in lieu of which feedings they have now a stated allowance in money paid them annually by the Dean and Chapter." It is to be hoped that the change was satisfactory to both parties; doubtless it was.

Another well-known- antiquary, Mr. Willson, tells us that later on the College House served for a considerable number of years as the Judges' Lodgings. Later still, Arthur Place (No. 32, Eastgate), was used as the Judges' Lodgings, and the College House seems to have been transformed into the Minster School-room. While it was the temporary residence of the judicial representatives of Her Majesty, the apartments, says Willson, "were only furnished in a homely fashion, the floor of the dining-room being scoured and sifted over with sand, without any carpet." It is a pity that at least something of this hall has not been preserved ,for it appears to have been an early English building of considerable size and beauty.

The length of it was 37ft. 10in., and its breadth was 21ft. 6in., while the walls rose to a height of 20ft. to the tablecourse. The building ran from north to south, the chief elevation being to the east, and the rear to the west. The chief entrance, which was at the northern extremity of the east wall, was 4ft. wide in the clear and 11ft. high, and is spoken of as a very good example of a plainish early English archway (of which, by the way, we have none too many in Lincoln), and had chamfered orders and nook shafts, of which, however, only the foliage capitals remained at the period of demolition. There were on this side, too, a couple of rather large windows, with some fine foliage capitals.

The west side, as intimated, was plainer, but there were traces of some notable architectural features.

Another of these old houses was the Dolphins Inn, to which considerable interest attaches, but which must be left to our special articles on "Inns that have gone out" for full notice.

Up to within a few years of 1856, according to an old guide book, there were gateways at either end of the Exchequer Church. The intermediate portion was until 1816 occupied by a row of "the finest specimens of old houses the city contained." Very picturesque they must have appeared, standing, as the houses did, on wooden pillars, forming a sort of rude piazza. Somewhat similar houses may be found in different parts of the country at the present day. There are two at Gainsborough, with an archway between, but these dwellings, or rather the upper portion of them—are upon pillars of stone —and being now of a yellow colour have not the handsomest appearance.

A stirring scene was witnessed at the entrance to the Close on September 20th, 1727. The citizens had aparently an even greater regard for the Cathedral than we modern citizens, and when the news spread that the Dean and Chapter had commenced taking down the tall spires of timber covered with lead, which then crowned the two western towers, their indignation was instantly roused. Shouts of anger against the Cathedral authorities were raised, and the greatest disapproval of the work was expressed. Ultimately, a mob of between 400 and 500 people collected together, and when the dusk came these marched up the hill, ascended what now termed the "Greestone" Stairs, and thundered at the little postern gate which formed the entry into the Close at this part. A great uproar also prevailed, and the mob evinced the strongest intentions of preventing, by force, if necessary, the mutilation of the towers of their beloved Minster. The authorities, however, had been forewarned of their approach, and as forewarned is proverbially forearmed, set out in defence of the Close and the Minster. The gates were hurriedly closed and secured, and men placed at each to guard them against the expected attack.

Strangely enough, the little postern gate at the head of the stairs was left unguarded, either because it was overlooked in the haste of the defensive preparations, or because it was expected that this would be the least likely to be the scene of assault, and the none too large body of defenders congregated elsewhere. With comparative ease, therefore, the assailants battered down the gate, and surged through into the Close, creating a deafening din, which re-echoed strangely from the walls of the Minster, looming vast and high above them in the half-darkness. Some of the mob rushed into Vicar's-court, where they attacked the house of one of the "Old Vicars," Mr. Cunnington, who was Receiver-General of the Chapter, and acted as a kind of secretary, treasurer, etc., all rolled into one. Mr. Cunnington was at home, and the mob entered his house, and seized him, dragging him thence to the Minster Green, where they are stated to have formed a ring round him, and goaded him into dancing for their diversion. The Minster Green, it is affirmed, rang with their cry:

> "High Church, Low Church,
> Jump again, Cunnington!"

At any rate this demonstration had the desired effect, for an assurance was given, and published abroad by the Town Crier the next day, to the effect that the Dean and Chapter would respect the wishes of the citizens, and that the spires should remain unmolested. The Chancellor, who probably knew the class of people forming the mob very well, opened his beer cellars, and the rioters refreshed themselves after their exertions. The gates were then thrown open, and the mob dispersed with more or less quietness. Whether any recompense was accorded the unfortunate Receiver-General is not stated, but he certainly deserved considerable compensation, both for the injuries bestowed on him and for the loss of dignity in the disgraceful scene on the Minster Green.

It is curious to note the difference between the conduct of the townspeople on this occasion and less than a century later (in 1807), when the Dean and Chapter decided upon the same act of vandalism as their predecessors, and, what is more, carried it out, to the great regret of many who admired the lofty, graceful spires. The storm of protest raised recently against the alterations at Peterborough Cathedral forms an excellent example of popular feeling at the present day, when one of our old Cathedrals is threatened by the hand of the destroyer or mutilator, for the latter is often worse than the first, in that he shows really less mercy.

XXV.—THE PARLIAMENTS OF LINCOLN.

It is always interesting to trace the development of any great system back to its source; to note, first, the greatness and smoothness of its present working, and then look back through long years, and observe how one generation and another has contributed to make the original idea perfected and extended, the full fruits of which we ourselves are permitted to enjoy.

We are fully aware that our present Parliamentary system is not perfection. There is a party whose continual cry is for a redistribution of seats, and another who call for the principle of one vote for one man. But though in these points the English Parliament does not give complete satisfaction to all whom it professes to represent, it is unquestionably the outcome of much thought, and labour, and battle, extending now well over six centuries.

What was the earliest form of the system?

Prior to the reign of Henry III., the voice of the city was made known through a purely local assembly, which met on emergencies —such as in financial crises, or when war threatened the country, internally or externally—and was really a kind of mediæval City Council. But in 1265 we read that the first writs of a general summons to Parliament were issued by the Crown, and it is decidedly worthy of note here that Lincoln and York were the only cities actually named as being required to send two burgesses. Of course, at this early period, and even for a great part of the following reign, the mode of election was crude, uncertain, and unsatisfactory. It could hardly be otherwise. But about 1295 we find Edward the First with the glimmer of an idea of improving his Parliament, and from this time forward the system underwent gradual changes and advancement. The number of representatives too, was extended, and in Edward's time the Parliament was composed of the three estates of the realm, the lords spiritual and temporal, knights, and burgesses, acting under his Majesty.

This time, however, was one of trouble. Edward was constantly at war with Scotland, and, a misunderstanding arising between himself and the King of France, Philip seized the kingdom of Guienne, and formed an offensive alliance with the Scots. Battles followed between the rival nations at Berwick, Dunbar, Stirling, Falkirk, and elsewhere, and in its great peril Scotland appealed to Pope Boniface the Eighth for intervention. The Pope did intervene, and boldly put forward a claim to the kingdom of Scotland, sending a Bull to Edward, in which he reminded the English monarch that the kingdom of Scotland had always belonged to the Church of Rome.

The pompous missive was conveyed by the Archbishop of Canterbury, who seems to have done his best to induce Edward to submit without reserve, but Edward's reply had all the dignity and defiance of a wrathful and determined English King. After mature consideration, he issued writs of summons for a great "general" Parlia-

ment to be held at Lincoln in the octaves of St. Hilary, 1301, when
the pretensions of the See of Rome to the kingdom of Scotland were
to receive full consideration. Special writs were sent to several
deans, abbots, and priors, enjoining them to diligently search in all
the chronicles, archives, and secret muniments of their houses for
information concerning the claimed kingdom. Further special writs
were directed to those who had attended the former Parliament at
Westminster, but if any happened to be dead or infirm, authority
was given to the sheriffs to cause another person to be elected in
their stead, and all were to have reasonable expenses paid in going
to and from the great Parliament.

From all this it will be seen that the Parliament convened to be
held at Lincoln was, most probably, the most important of Edward's
reign. There were summoned to attend it the two archbishops,
eighteen bishops, eighty abbots, the masters of Sempringham, the
Temple and the prior of St. John of Jerusalem, eighty-nine knights
and barons, forty-six representatives from counties where there were
forests, and twenty-six where there were none, sixteen masters
"learned in the law," twenty-two of the council, the Chancellors of
Oxford and Cambridge, with a few from both Universities "who
were skilled in the written law," making in all rather more than
three hundred persons. The forest laws had been quite a thorn
in the side of several kings, and were at this period, and we find
that persons having complaints to make in this respect were desired
to attend this Parliameont at Lincoln.

Of course the great business was the consideration of the claims
of Pope Boniface to Scotland. The Bull was ready, and an angry
discussion ensued as to the kind of a reply the king should return,
or whether, indeed, he would condescend to return any. Finally,
an epistle was drawn up, informing the Pope that the King of
England had immemorially enjoyed the right of sovereignty over
Scotland, as its leige lord, and that, by no kind of title, had its
temporalities even pertained to the See of Rome. The unanimous
judgment of Parliament would never permit these rights to be
called into question hereafter, or that ambassadors should go to
Rome. They furthermore strenuously asserted their resolution to
defend them, and requested the Pope to allow them the full exercise
of their ancient privileges. Two copies of this document yet exist,
we believe, in the Chapter House at Westminster, and are about 18
by 12 inches in size.

It appears doubtful, however, whether a copy was ever sent to
Rome. Some have thought that the two were drawn up for the purpose of keeping one and sending the other, while others have been
of opinion that the manifesto was intended as much for an appeal
to the public mind at home as against the apostolic authority. King
Edward was in the North of England when he summoned this Parliament. He journeyed down to the Royal Palace at Nettleham, arriving there on the 25th of January, and stayed there until the 12th
of February, when he took up his quarters in Lincoln, leaving the
city on the 4th of March, when he left by way of Grantham for
Northampton. It may be mentioned in passing that Edward granted
amongst other things at the Lincoln Parliament, a grant of six years
pavage for the city.

Peter Langtoft, a rhyming chronicler of the period, writes thus of the Parliament:

At the Pask afterward, his Parlement set he, The gode King Edward, at Lyncoln his cite. At Sant Katerine hous the Erle Marschalle lay, In the broad gate lay the Brus, Erle was he that day; The Kyng lay at Netilham, it is the Bisshopes toun, And other Lordes there cam in the cuntre up and down.

In the reign of Edward the Second, Parliaments were convened at Lincoln in January and July, 1316. The former sat twenty-five days, and its chief feature of local interest was the payment of a fine of £300 for a confirmation of the city charters and extension of privileges. Another Parliament was held at Lincoln in the second year of the reign of Edward III.

But it is the Parliament of Edward First, held in 1301, that is the most important. It not only established the claim of King Edward and his successors on the throne to the fullest extent over the country of Scotland, but embodied, in unanimous and spirited protest against the Pope's usurpation, a resolute determination to resist his claims. On this memorable epistle—memorable for its ardent patriotism and unswerving strength of intention—attempts have been made at various times to establish evidence to make good certain claims to peerages by reason of tenures. Assertions have also been advanced that all the persons whose names appear in the instruments were as earls and barons of the places in connection with their names, summoned as such to the Parliament of Lincoln—and this though the names of no less than thirty-four do not occur on the roll of writs of summons to that assembly, and though no evidence is in existence, so far as the assiduous researches of a committee on the dignity of the peerage have been able to discover, that several of the persons so named were ever called to any Parliament either before or after the one to which they laid claim.

An induction that has been drawn from the transactions of this Parliament consists in its being called a "General Parliament," and that they whose names were inserted in, and whose seals were affixed to the letter, appear to have assumed a power of addressing the Pope for themselves and the whole community, without the open show of any delegated authority to do so from the knights, citizens, and burgesses then met together. But this, the Rev. C. H. Hartshorne. M.A., and other authorities have pointed out, might have happened in consequence of the signatures of the most influential portion of representatives being deemed sufficiently weighty and authoritative in themselves as to make others unnecessary, or because the commonalty were engaged more particularly in drawing up and discussing the bill of provisions.

A Parliamentary assembly of over 300 persons takes some victualling, and some figures and other information concerning this great Parliament at Lincoln will not be out of place. Nearly £17 was expended on the carriage of the corn, oats, and malt, carcases of oxen, sheep, and pigs consumed. They came from Kesteven, Holland, and other districts. The following is an example of the bills submitted for the conveyance of the edibles, etc: "Walter de Auclound seeks payment for the four carcases of oxen, and ten carcases of mutton, carried by land from Bourne to Lincoln, for thirty miles, 2s 8d." Another bill shows that the Sheriff delivered to Walter Waldeshef, the King's baker, 356 quarters and two bushels of corn, for making bread ; 83 quarters and six bushels at an advanced price, and 90 quarters and two bushels of malt. To the clerk of the kitchen was delivered oxen, sheep, and pigs, value £77 5s 10d ; and the clerk of the market, for oats for the horses during the first three months of the year received £139 3s 5½d.

Flesh, fish, corn, firewood, and hay totals up to £226 0s 7d, the scullery required £57 16s 3d for coal, brushwood, and that ominous item "sundries." It is also interesting to learn that 3,121 gallons of ale, at a penny a gallon, were drunk between Sunday, the 19th of February, and the 1st of March, inclusive, which reckons out at the undoubtedly liberal allowance of about a gallon a day for each representative during the eleven days on which he sat. A Lincoln merchant's bill, that of Stephen Stanham, who had been elected one of its representatives, was for £96 14s 5d for sugar, figs, etc. ; another was for £54 10s for fish, and £6 16s for herrings and stock fish, this latter having been supplied during the month of February for the entertainment of the King's son, an apparently voracious youngster then not quite seventeen years old. Fifty-one horses and fifty horses cost £21 3s 4d—not hired, be it noticed, but purchased, and this is certainly moderate.

At the period of the Parliament wheat stood at 4s a quarter ; malt at 3s 2d ; sheep at 1s 6d each ; oxen at two marcs ; pigs from 2s to 4s ; a cart and four horses were purchased for 5 marcs ; and a horse was bought by Roger, a doorkeeper, for 10s.

But whatever the items of cost, the great Parliament of 1301 was undoubtedly worth it. We have not, it will be noticed, stated where in the city it was held, but general opinion seems to point to the Chapter House. Wherever it was, however, it was one of which not only Lincoln, but the nation may be proud, and to which, moreover, the country should be distinctly grateful. It was, indeed, an epoch-making Parliament, for it not only hurled the glove in the face of Pope Boniface, but strengthened and confirmed the existing liberties in our land.

We boast now of our Parliament, and of the great Bills passed by the Party whose creed and policy we admire, and of the zeal and work of the men who lead and who follow. But it is good sometimes to look back to these early times when the Parliament was but a germ, and note that though the conduct of the system was unpolished and altogether infantile compared with the manners of St. Stephen's, yet there was the same resolute ring, the same outspoken earnestness of purpose for the welfare of godliness, of monarch, and of the country which our Parliament professes to-day. Edward and his Parliament sleep, and have slept for six centuries, yet, though that fateful assembly at Lincoln may be forgotten by the people, they have its benefits, the freedom it established, and the boons that it conferred. May that strong and stern old manhood ever arm our Parliament.

" Nought shall make us rue,
If England to itself do rest but true."

XXVI.—MAYORS OF LINCOLN.

The Governorship or Mayoralty of a town or city is the highest civic honour that can be bestowed, and therefore it is the occasion for not a little righteous pride when a citizen is elected by the unanimous vote of his fellows to the civic chair for the ensuing year. The Mayoralty of Lincoln is of very ancient institution, and one which has ever been filled by men who have had the highest sense of the honour of their position, and have filled the chair to the best of their ability. Never once during nearly six hundred years has the office been degraded by any flagrant misdemeanour of the Mayor for the time being, and it has often happened that during his year of office his Worship has done some goodly act for the benefit of his fellow-citizens. Occasionally, too, he has found himself the mark for an unpleasant demonstration, and it is even on record that a Mayor has been deposed from his office, and imprisoned until the term for which he was elected has expired.

The Roman colony of Lindum had, of course, its Governor, and then came the Port-reeve, an officer appointed by the Saxons, whose duty it was to guard the gates of the city or town where he resided. In the year 1314, however, a Mayor was appointed, from which date we are able to trace their Worships right down to the present year of grace. The first Mayor of Lincoln was named Henry Best, and there have certainly been none better since—in name. We read of no great achievement by his worship to signalise so great an event; indeed, the history of the city for that year is nearly a blank. Perhaps we are indebted to Mr. Mayor for this, however, and some people would take it for an excellent sign as to the prosperity of the city at the period. If the old proverb that "no news is good news" has any truth in it, this may be so.

The first item of importance in connection with the Mayoralty is in 1386, in which year King Richard II. visited Lincoln, and granted to the Mayor (Mr. John Sutton) the right to have carried before him and his successors in that office, a sword in civic processions. The sword presented to his Worship on that occasion by the King is still preserved.

Then in 1409 we read of the Mayor (Mr. Richard Carlton) and the citizens memorialising the newly-crowned Henry IV. to ratify and confirm a charter and grants previousy made to them, and the King was graciously pleased to listen to their petition. Another petition was presented to the King (Henry VI. thi stime) in 1447 for assistance under the impoverished conditions beneath which the city had fallen, and the King granted certain appreciable easements. Further grants to the Mayor and citizens were made by Richard the Third in 1484, including the holding of an additional fair—always the occasion of considerable profit—and another grant is dated July, 1499.

The Mayoralty of Mr. John Emerson in 1553 is notable by the fact that in this year the parishes of the city were consolidated from 52 to 15, a very necessary proceeding. The parishes previous to this had, of course, been small, and it would hardly be possible to keep a keen and clear oversight upon them all .

In the Mayoralty of Mr. John Welcombe (1569), at a Common Council on September 1st, an ordinance was made on behalf of orphans and for the especial protection of Lincoln-born children, or children belonging to parents formerly citizens. All administrators and executors of the property of orphan children of above £10 were to produce a copy of the will, which they were to submit for the Mayor's inspection, and being sureties for its carrying out.

Charles I. sent for the Mayor of Lincoln in 1642 (Mr. John Becke), on an accusation of his favouring the Protector. Doubtless his Worship made good his case and proved his loyalty, for the significant record is that he "returned safe."

In the following year Mr. Edward Blow, the Mayor, was "in prison most of the year by Parliament, or absent with the King's party." Verily, in those days it were best for a Mayor to be as far above suspicion as Cæsar's wife !

The year 1650 is notable as being that of the Mayoralty of Mr. Original Peart, a sturdy yeoman whose name stands out boldly in the history of the city at this period. He had previously been Sheriff (Lincoln had two Sheriffs then), and was subsequently Member of Parliament for the city. It was the Mayor who fearlessly bearded Cromwell, and complained of the conduct of the soldiers in their wanton destruction in the churches and houses of the city, and it is pleasing to record that his Worship's intervention was not without effect.

In 1710 the first Town Clerk of Lincoln was appointed—Mr. Francis Harvey, who held it from 1710 to 1725, when his son John succeeded him. The latter held office until 1758, and was followed by Mr. Joshua Peart, the office being contested by Mr. Newesman.

We all know the "Mayor's Chair." Mr. William White was the Mayor, and in 1732 the year in which it was erected "to prevent accidents, and as a place for porters to rest their loads on." In 1737, during the Mayoralty of Mr. Robert Obbinson, an Act of Common Council was passed to exclude those born out of the city of their freedom. Mr. Richard Ruxton, as Mayor of Lincoln in 1762, laid the first stone of the conduit on the High Bridge. In 1795, it is gratifying to find the Corporation heading a subscription list for the poor with £100 ; three years later they voted 500 guineas to Government towards the expenses of the great war. The Corporation also gave £100 and £200 to the poor on subsequent occasions. At a Council meeting of May 31, 1810, under the Mayoralty of Mr. George Steel, it was resolved, by 22 votes to 14, to take down the Stonebow, but the resolution was rescinded at a meeting on July 22 of the year following. So near has the old arch been to demolition !

Of the reception of Royalty in various epochs by our Mayors we have already spoken, and there is at least one past Mayor yet living who has experienced the necessity for the reading of the Riot Act when the recklessness of the mob has got beyond the control of the police.

One name will long remain green in the memory of present-day inhabitants, as one who was ever kindness itself to the poor, whose purse was always open whenever a charitable demand was made upon it, and who was probably the greatest popular favourite as Mayor that Lincoln has ever had. We mean Francis Jonathan Clarke, Mayor in 1879, 1884, and 1885. Alderman Brogden was a Mayor of another class, and one who stood up sturdily for the rights of the public. Many yet living recollect his summary treatment of the fences and barriers erected to stop certain footpaths over which there had previously been a public way. The Mayor, in company with others, took hatchets and bars, and removed the offending obstacles by force! Mr. Bernard Cannon was another popular Mayor—indeed, in recent years, Lincoln's civic chair has been filled by gentlemen of whom the old city has every right to be proud.

The following is a complete list of the Mayors of Lincoln from the institution of the office down to the present time. The years given are the dates of election :—

1314 Henry Best	Simon de Eglinton 1315
1316 Gilbert de Weatherby	John Vincent 1317
1318 Robert de Bardney	Hugh de Russels 1319
1320 Richard de Blackenben.	John de Nova Castro 1321
1322 Hugh de Eglinton	John de Tame 1323
1324 William de Snarford	Robert de Omer 1325
1326 Hugh Taylor	William Blyton 1327
1328 Thomas de Keel	Robert Benson 1329
1330 Richard de Keel	Hugh de Eglinton 1331
1332 John Blyton	John Lavender 1333
1334 Richard Long	Robert Quirrell 1335
1336 William Humberstone	William de Rastle 1337
1338 Thomas Russell	Henry Fillingham 1339
1340 Robert Dalderby	Robert Hudlestone 1341
1342 John Wilger	John de Ashby 1343
1344 Robert Chesterfield	Roger Windeck 1345
1346 Richard Tooke	John Fenton 1347
1348 John de Outhorpe	Walter de Keelby 1349
1350 Thomas de Exton	William de Harpswell 1351
1352 William de Snellsband	Peter de Thornton 1353
1354 John de Burgess	Walter d'Orsby 1355
1356 Robert de Volme	Roger de Thorold 1357
1358 Huge de Bardney	Peter Canoiss 1359
1360 John Cole	John de Harpswell 1361
1362 William Thormisth	John de Rhaodes 1363
1364 John de Welton	Thomas Elshand 1365
1366 Richard Thorpe	John Sutton 1367
1368 Roger Torrington	Joseph Collingham 1369
1370 William Juggill	William Belly 1371
1372 John Thock	Hugh Cornwall 1373
1374 John Huddlestone	Thomas Horncastle 1375
1376 John Hopperstone	Thomas Bannam 1377

1378 John Blyton	Robert Sutton	1379
1380 Gilbert Boothby	Simon Massingham	1381
1382 William Sevelstone	Robert Salterby	1383
1384 William Dalby	John Norman	1385
1386 John Sutton	Robert Read	1387
1388 Robert de Massingham	Simon de Laxfield	1389
1390 Thomas de Thornby	John Winfield	1391
1392 Henry Harwood	Robert Harwood	1393
1394 John Belasis	Henry de Reepham	1395
1396 John Shipham	John Thurlby	1397
1398 John de Searby	John Balderton	1399
1400 Robert Brough	William Blyton	1401
1402 Robert Appleby	John Houghton	1403
1404 Peter Saltby	N. Huddlestone	1405
1406 William Bunkworth	Wiliam de Fordinworth	1407
1408 Robert Rathby	Richard Carlton	1409
1410 John Ryles	William Caden	1411
1412 Thomas Foster	Ralph Curtois	1413
1414 Dennis Salasby	Richard Cooke	1415
1416 Thomas Archer	William Markby	1417
1418 H. Tamworth	John Hogleton	1419
1420 Thomas Seringo	John Sparrow	1421
1422 Roger Garmstone	William Blyton	1423
1424 John Huddlestone	John Locking	1425
1426 John Rouse	Roger Knight	1427
1428 Robert Hawarby	Simon Grantham	1429
1430 William Saxilby	Walter Linwood	1431
1432 J. Griffington	John Clifton	1433
1434 J. Tettlethorpe	John Durkett	1435
1436 William Bane	Thomas Reeve	1437
1438 William Hawarby	John Rouse	1439
1440 William Markvoy	Edward Copjoy	1441
1442 John Hoyden	John Witter	1443
1444 John Ossin	Edward Burton	1445
1446 John Raithby	Thos. Boston	1447
1448 John Carburton	Richard Popplewick	1449
1450 Simon Grantham	Richard Barnard	1451
1452 Robert Bright	Robert Buckley	1453
1454 John Allen	William Haltham	1455
1456 J. Huddlestone	William Hoone	1457
1458 Robert Bright	John Williamson	1459
1460 Robert Beadle	William Simpson	1461
1462 James Wilton	Thomas Hornsey	1463
1464 Richard Bolton	Thomas Grantham	1465
1466 Thomas Belsby	John Sleaford	1467
1468 Richard Coates	Robert Crabden	1469
1470 William Toft	John Elston	1471
1472 William Browne	Oliver Frank	1473
1474 Ralph Huddlestone	William Killingworth	1475
1476 Thomas Knight	Wiliam Winess	1477
1478 John Otligee	W. Chambers	1479
1480 R. Huddlestone	Thomas Baitland	1481

1482	John Stanley	Edward Browne	1483
1484	Robert Bate	John Bilby	1485
1486	John Poll	William Long	1487
1488	John Dixon	Henry Hogden	1489
1490	Robert C...	William Bell	1491
1492	Edward Grantham	Robert Hutchinson	1493
1494	Robert Dighton	John Watson	1495
1496	Richard Paley	Robert Clarke	1497
1498	William Hutchinhead	William Lee	1499
1500	Richard Codd	Rowland Huddlestone	1501
1502	Robert Allenson	Edward Brown	1503
1504	John Stanley	Edward Grantham	1505
1506	Robert Dighton	Roger Alded	1507
1508	Thomas Norton	John Pickard	1509
1510	Robert Veighton	Robert Allenson	1511
1512	Thomas Vessey	Thomas Barton	1513
1514	William Inchment	Watland Love	1515
1516	Wiliam Pearson	John Poplewick	1517
1518	William Fox	John Talboys	1519
1520	Peter Elford	Robert Smith	1521
1522	John Holland	George Browne	1523
1524	Robert Allenson	Edward Smith	1525
1526	Thomas Burton	Vincent Grantham	1527
1528	Thomas	George Grissingham	1529
1530	Robert Urry	Peter Elford	1531
1532	John Popplewick	George Sapscotts	1533
1534	W. Palfreeman	Ralph Goodnap	1535
1536	Robert Allenson	Edward Smith	1537
1538	John Faulkner	Wiliam Gate	1539
1540	Peter Elford	Vincent Grantham	1541
1542	William Allenson	William Smith	1543
1544	Henry Sapcotts	Thomas Wright	1545
1546	Edward Smith	Christopher Branston	1547
1548	George Stamp	William Yates	1549
1550	Edward Atkinson	John Falkner	1551
1552	William Hutchinson	John Emerson	1553
1554	William Rotherum	George Porter	1555
1556	John Hutchinson	Thomas Grantham	1557
1558	Nicholas Falkner	William Goodnap	559
1560	Martin Hollingworth	Richard Miller	1561
1562	William Kent	William Carter	1563
1564	J. Hutchinson	Thomas Fulbeck	1565
1566	Leonard Ellis	Edward Hallyley	1567
1568	John Welcombe	Martin Mason	1569
1570	John Wilson	Thomas Dawson	1571
1572	William Kent	Edward Knight	1573
1574	Thomas Hanson	George Porter	1575
1576	William Schoolfield	Richard Carter	1577
1578	Thomas Winterbottom	R. Hawke	1579
1580	Martin Mason	William Kent	1581
1582	John Emerson	Robert Rushforth	1583
1584	William Yates	Henry Blow	1585

1586	William Chelfin	Edward Dennis	1587
1588	Thomas Hanson	William Wharton	1589
1590	Robert Mason	Roger Tonge	1591
1592	William Goss	John Beck	1593
1594	Leonard Hollingworth	John Redfern	1595
1596	George Dickinson	Wiliam Yates	1597
1598	Abraham Metcalf	Robert Rushworth	1599
1600	William Wharton	Edward Dennis	1601
1602	John Beck	Robert Mason	1603
1604	Leonard Hollingworth	Thomas Swift	1605
1606	Robert Hartley	Robert Moorecroft	1607
1608	Jeffrey Wilson	E. Shuttleworth	1609
1610	Richard Knightsmith	George Dickenson	1611
1612	Rowland Lilly	William Wharton	1613
1614	Thomas Swift	William Mitchell	1615
1616	Robert Mason	Robert Moorecroft	1617
1618	Edward Hawley	Edward Oakley	1619
1620	William Solomon	Edward Blow	1621
1622	Anthony Hare	Edward Brough	1623
1624	William Mitchell	Robert Becke	1625
1626	Richard Knightsmith	Thomas Swift	1627
1628	Ambrose Rycroft	Richard Somerby	1629
1630	Wiliam Kent	Richard White	1631
1632	Robert Marshall	William Urry	1633
1634	William Watson	R. Bartholomew	1635
1636	Stephen Dawson	Anthony Kent	1637
1638	William Brown	William Bishop	1639
1640	Robert Becke	John Becke	1641
1642	William Marshall	Edward Blow	1643
1644	Robert Marshall	George Bracebridge	1645
1646	William Goodnap	Edward Emiss	1647
1648	Richard Ward	John Ollerton	1649
1650	Original Peart	Thomas Dawson	1651
1652	Alexander Newcombe	William Dawson	1653
1654	John Oliver	William Hall	1655
1656	John Becke	Stephen Fowles	1657
1658	John Leach	William Suttaby	1659
1660	S. Luddington	Richard Wetherall	1661
1662	Robert Ross	Richard Kite	1663
1664	John Kent	G. Bracebridge	1665
1666	T. Hadney	Edward Cheals	1667
1668	William Hooton	Thomas Bishop	1669
1670	Rowland Curtis	Thomas Townrow	1671
1672	G. Bracebridge	Richard Winn	1673
1674	William Kelsey	Joseph Luddington	1675
1676	J. Carr	Edward Green	1677
1678	Ralph Burnett	Enoch Malton	1679
1680	John Bate	Robert Vergette	1681
1682	Charles Allison	S. Luddington	1683
1684	Thomas Kent	John Coxhall	1685
1686	Samuel Gibbeson	Thomas Mawmell	1687
1688	T. Nicholson	Richard Dawson	1689

1690 Thomas Mawmell	William Hooton 1691
1692 William Cockle	T. Townrow 1693
1694 Robert Mason	John Martin 1695
1696 G. Bracebridge	George Skelton 1697
1698 John Bates	William Faulks 1699
1700 John Garnon	John Rutledge 1701
1702 William Watson	John Harness 1703
1704 Charles Johnson	B. Harrison 1705
1706 Thomas Hooton	G. Newcomen 1707
1708 G. Bracebridge	John Garnon 1709
1710 George Kent	Henry Wilson 1711
1712 Hezekiah Brown	Robert Hobman 1713
1714 John Cooke	Nathaniel Knight 1715
1716 Thomas Nicholson	John Martin 1717
1718 John Lobsey	John Durance 1719
1720 Robert Obbinson	Timothy Ward 1721
1722 Benjamin Harrison	Thomas Hooton 1723
1724 G. Bracebridge	George Kent 1725
1726 Hezekiah Brown	John Becke 1727
1728 John Wetherall	Thomas Wilson 1729
1730 George Brown	William Raynor 1731
1732 William White	John Cooke 1733
1734 John Kent	John Hooton 1735
1736 John Lobsey	Robert Obbinson 1737
1738 Timothy Ward	Gervase Raynes 1739
1740 John Durance	Thomas Wells 1741
1742 John Wetherall	Edward Drake 1743
1744 Robert Thickston	George Brown 1745
1746 William Johnston	John Davis 1747
1748 William Rayner	Gervase Gibson 1749
1750 Edward Fowler	John Wilson 1751
1752 Henry Goateman	Edward Leatherland 1753
1754 Robert Drewry	John Cockle 1755
1756 John Brown	Broxholme Brown 1757
1758 Robert Obbinson	John Becke 1759
1760 John Hooton	Robert Drewry 1761
1762 Richard Ruxton	Robert Thickston 1763
1764 John Bennett	John Davis 1765
1766 John Kent	Gervase Gibson 1767
1768 Joseph Dell	Phillip Bullen 1769
1770 John Wilson	E. Leatherland 1771
1772 John Brown	Broxholme Brown 1773
1774 Robert Obbinson	Richard Ruxton 1775
1776 John Bennett	John Kent 1777
1778 Joseph Dell	Henry Swan 1779
1780 George Dent	Henry Bullen 1781
1782 Thomas Foster	Richard Gibbeson 1783
1784 John Cockle	Henry Swan 1785
1786 Joshua Morris	George Kent 1787
1788 Thomas Porter	John Parsons 1789
1790 Thomas Jepson	Tyrwhitt Smith 1791
1792 Thomas Preston	Thomas Foster 1793

1794 Richard Gibbeson	Butter Hunnings 1795
1796 John Straw	Henry Swan 1797
1798 Thomas Porter	Philip Bullen 1799
1800 John Parsons	Joseph Jepson 1801
1802 Tyrwhitt Smith	Thomas Preston 1803
1804 Robert Fowler	John Straw 1805
1806 John Hett	John Hayward 1807
1808 Thomas Colton	Robert Featherby 1809
1810 George Steel	William Featherby 1811
1812 Robert Fowler	John Hett 1813
1814 Matthew Sewell	William Hall 1815
1816 John Hayward	William Hayward 1817
1818 Robert Featherby	Henry Swan 1819
1820 George Steel	William Featherby 1821
1822 Wiliam Hall	Henry Swan 1823
1824 William Wrigglesworth	James Snow 1825
1826 Page Cartledge	Thomas Norton 1827
1828 Charles Hayward	Wm. Huddleston 1829
1830 Thomas Winn	William Wrigglesworth 1831
1832 James Snow	Page Cartledge 1833
1834 Thomas Norton	Robert Fowler 1835
1836 John Rudgard	Charles Beaty 1837
1838 William Wrigglesworth	Wm. Rudgard 1839
1840 Charles Seely	George W. Hebb 1841
1842 Thomas Wetherell	Richard S. Harvey 1843
1844 John Stevenson	James Bruce 1845
1846 Richard Carline	William Marshall 1847
1848 Richard Whitton	James Snow 1849
1850 Charles Ward	Edward J. Wilson 1851
1852 Robert G. Hill	John Thomas Tweed 1853
1854 T. J. N. Brogden	Wm. Cooke Norton 1855
1856 Nathaniel Clayton	Richard Carline 1857
1858 Joseph Shuttleworth	Charles Ward 1859
1860 Richard Sutton Harvey	John Cooper Torry 1861
1862 Charles Doughty	William Foster 1863
1864 Richard Sutton Harvey	Richard Hall 1865
1866 Wiliam Ashley	John Richard Battle 1867
1868 George Glasier	Joseph Ruston 1869
1870 Charles Pratt	William Harrison 1871
1872 Charles Leadbitter Hughes	Joseph Maltby 1873
1874 William Battle Maltby	William Beard 1875
1876 Peter Platts Dickinson	William Cottingham 1877
1878 Francis Jonathan Clarke	T. J. N. Brogden 1879
1880 Bernard Cannon	Wm. John Warrener 1881
1882 William Tomlinson Page, jun.,	Francis J. Clarke 1883
1884 Francis J. Clarke	Hugh Wyatt 1885
1886 Hugh Wyatt	Thomas Martin 1887
1888 William Watkins	Edwin Pratt 1889
1890 Edwin Pratt	William Wright Richardson 1891
1892 Thomas Wallis	Albert Wingfield Hall 1893
1894 Albert Wingfield Hall	Edward Harrison 1895
1896 Thomas Wallis	Hugh Wyatt 1897

XXVII.—SHERIFFS OF THE CITY.

Next in civic importance to the Mayoralty comes the honourable office of Sheriff. It is an ancient office, too, for Sheriffs were first appointed to the city of Lincoln in the ninth year of the reign of Henry the Fourth. From 1408 right down to 1835, two years before the accession of our beloved Queen Victoria, Lincoln had two Sheriffs, elected annually—one by the Mayor, Aldermen, and Common Council, and the other nominated by the Mayor alone. Thus, as will be seen, the list of Sheriffs is an extremely lengthy one, over 900 names appearing therein, but we believe we are correct in saying that it now appears complete for the first time in any modern publication, so that for purposes of reference it has a distinct value.

Naturally, the Sheriff has played a conspicuous part in the affairs of the city in his year of office. Upon numerous occasions, referred to in other portions of the present work, he has gone out in pomp and state to meet the King or Queen coming to Lincoln on a visit of a more or less welcome character, while in sterner times he has nobly borne his part in defending the city and citizens from the intended ravages of the foe. In or about 866, for instance, Osgot, who was then Sheriff of Lincoln—though of the office and its holders at this period little can be told—went forth in company with others, and defeated the Danes completely. But this, of course, was long before the re-established office came into being. One name stands out clearly among those of mediæval times, and it is that of Original Peart, who during his eventful lifetime successively held the offices of "Mayor, Sheriff, and Parliament Man," and who will always be entitled to our gratitude as the man who boldly faced Cromwell, and asked for a cessation of the destruction being wrought in the city by the victorious Ironsides, and, moreover, gained what he sought. Peart's must have been a striking personality, and though the information given us concerning him is fitful and fragmentary, we can piece them together very readily, and almost exactly define the grand and vigorous character of Lincoln's champion at the time when she so sorely needed him.

The mode of electing the two Sheriffs was not perfection, and in 1659 another Peart—Robert of that ilk—died, and one Robert Helsey, was appointed. It happened that Peart had been the Mayor's nominee. Upon his nominating Helsey, the new Sheriff claimed precedence over the other, elected by the full Council. But the latter was unwilling to concede anything to Helsey, alleging that priority of election should give precedence. Thereupon the Mayor ordered a re-election, in order, as the historian puts it (with a startling absence of impartiality) "to favour his officer." But the Council-elected Sheriff would not agree to this, and declined to be re-elected upon any consideration. What is more, he insisted on retaining the office and holding the priority till the termination of his office, and actually carried out this determination. So equal appeared the claims of the two Sheriffs, we are told, that the Judges to whom the dispute was referred at the following Assizes, could not agree to whom to award the precedence. It is rather amusing to find one of the disputants severing the Gordian knot so decisively, to say the least.

A couple of years later, when Charles II. came to the throne, John Middlebrooke and John Goodknap were Sheriffs of Lincoln. They had favoured Parliament, it appeared, and therefore the King turned them out of office, and re-placed them with John Townson and Henry Mozley. A glance through the list in later years shows local names now held in high respect cropping up here and there, particularly after the Mayor's nominee was dispensed with, and one Sheriff only chosen. In our own time the office has been offered to gentlemen of the greatest ability, and for many years the succeeding Sheriffs have won for themselves the highest possible popularity by the discharge of the duties falling to their lot. The following is a complete list of the Sheriffs, from Henry IV. granting the office in a special charter. The dates given are the years of election : —

1408 John Hycon and Richard Covell.
1409 T. Collington and J. Sparrow.
1410 Richard Barnby and W. Saxelby.
1411 John Huddlestone and Wm. Hawarby.
1412 John Ryles and Wm. Kerby.
1413 S. Winflow and T. Broomhead.
1414 Thomas Canterbury and T. Rose.
1415 Robert Alaster and Roger Dawquell.
1416 W. Seaton and W. Cawdwarill.
1417 Stephen Skelton and Gilbert Read.
1418 Thomas Terrige and Robert Nainby.
1419 Robert Toynton and H. Harvy.
1420 R. Hawarby and W. Linwood.
1421 John Newcome and Robert How.
1422 W. Bracebridge and E. Colton.
1423 Thomas Kermond and Joseph Rately.
1424 William Beefe and Joseph Russel.
1425 Simon Grantham and John Thethethorpe.
1426 John Clifton and Richard Sturton.
1427 John Swan and John Rausby.
1428 Robert Effinwell and Joseph Syson.
1429 Joseph Furforth and Ed. Copjoy.
1430 Rh. Smallwood and T. Darby.
1431 Wm. Bayne and Joseph Headon.
1432 Robert Constable and Joseph Smith.
1433 R. Ranesby and W. Woltham.
1434 Ralph Saenby and Thomas Seer.
1435 R. Rarnard and W. Maskham.
1436 John Winter and Joseph Walden.
1437 Robert Cato and John Frank.

1438 Rd. Garner and John Gibbon.
1439 Ed. Tonnard and Joseph Burton.
1440 Ed. Burton and Joseph Tonnard.
1441 John Ossin and Thos. Bastin.
1442 R. Popplewick and J. Barge.
1443 Cuthbert Skelton and J. Raithby.
1444 John Allen and Robert Bright.
1445 J. Braieworth and Robert Octoby.
1446 J. Scarborough and R. Bonnington.
1447 W. Maynard and J. Housholder.
1448 Robert Buckley and Robert Scapholm.
1449 Wm. Verris and John Title.
1450 J. Williamson and Robert Beadle.
1451 R. Wright and J. Margretton.
1452 Wm. Hoine and Thos. Browell.
1453 Wm. Chapman and R. Wake.
1454 Thos Hornsey and John Gray.
1455 John Parke and William Smith.
1456 Richard Ranph and John Sleeford.
1457 Robert Grabden and J. Taylor.
1458 W. Primpton and Edward Though.
1459 T. Martin and W. Bootenhall.
1460 Jacob Witton and Robert Green.
1461 W. Killingworth and J. Elstane.
1462 Robert Bright and Wm. Walter.
1463 Joseph Colbeck and Thomas Besby.
1464 Wm. Toft and R. Huddlestone.
1465 Richard Othwood and Thomas Beech.
1466 Wm. Browne and Oliver Frank.
1467 John Poll and John Othenn.
1468 John Toft and P. Dickinson.
1469 Robert Peart and W. Achambers
1470 W. Harley and W. Richardson.
1471 John Oldway and Thomas Birde.
1472 Wm. Hall and Wm. Read.
1473 Edward Browne and Joseph Sparrow.
1474 R. Huddlestone and T. Britland.
1475 T. Dalewent and J. Robinson.
1476 J. Clavelder and R. Raughton.
1477 John Ripler and John Tainton.
1478 R. Stainfield and Coos. Colsey.
1479 Wm. Neele and Richard Fox.
1480 Wm. Long and Henry Hogden.
1481 R. Hutchinson and Thomas Hird.
1482 Wm. Jinley and Richard Paley.
1483 John Watson and H. Brinkley.
1484 Robert Clarke and Robert Dighton.
1485 W. Hullyman and Robert Othose.
1486 W. Miller and T. Evenwood.
1487 T. Welbourne and T. Barrow.

1488 John Burnet and Joseph Brownell.
1489 W. Hutchinhead and R. Codd.
1490 Wm. English and W. Orrans.
1491 Richard Ratcliff and Thomas Norton.
1492 Wm. Ley and R. Whymark.
1493 Joseph Drybar and W. Grantham.
1494 T. Langton and R. Allenson.
1495 H. Willoughby and T. Sayle.
1496 Richard Pecher and Robert Fowler.
1497 John Talboys and Wm. Sams.
1498 John Percer and John Hinto.
1499 Richard Disney and Joseph Halvester.
1500 A. Dawson and W. Humphry.
1501 John Bryant and John Barton.
1502 F. Mooreing and R. Dallington.
1503 Thomas Bearbox and T .Elstone.
1504 John Fox and John Huffey.
1505 Henry Catley and Hugh Fox.
1506 R. Johnson and J. Popplewick.
1507 Rd. Mason and Wm .Pearson.
1508 Thomas Vessey and Thomas Rainton.
-509 W. Westcome and G. Browne.
1510 Wm. Fox and Robert Wheman.
1511 Robert Miller and C. Barton.
1512 R. Calgarth and W. Hutchinson.
1513 John Haltham and Robert Lever.
1514 W .Barker and Edward Freefoot.
1515 Robert Smith and Thomas Suffenan.
1516 C. Branston and W. Robson.
1517 Robert Verey and P. Watkinson.
1518 Robert Staines and Robert Oulett.
1519 J. Grissington and E. Dawson.
1520 Edward Smith and Thomas Power.
1521 Joseph Johnson and Joseph Hutchinson.
1522 R. Goodknap and J. Clarke.
1523 Richard Taylor and W. Palfreeman.
1524 Robert Wright and Richard Horne.
1525 John Burd and Richard Baynard.
1526 Wm. Latch and Robert Semer.
1527 H. Sapscotts and John Aile.
1528 John Gatt and Robert Miller.
1529 W. Bailey and J. Rotterdam.
1530 John Falkner and Wm. Smith.
1531 C. Haltby and John Emerson.
1532 Thomas Burton and Robert Skinner.
1533 J. Collinghig and W. Dighton.
1534 C. Smith and A. Huddleston.
1535 George Sample and Edward Glover.
1536 John Smith and Wm. Miller.
1537 Thos. Hanson and John Beck.

1538 W. Wheeler and N. Falkner.
1539 George Smith and Thos. Wright.
1540 Wm. Alleson and J. Plumtree.
1541 W. Simkinson and George Porter.
1542 J. Goodknap and W. Hudson.
1543 H. Hallyley and Richard Drewry.
1544 J. Skinner and Edward Crosfield.
1545 W. Rotherham and W. Hill.
1546 C. Winley and Wm. Cliffe.
1547 R. Miller and J. Hutchinson.
1548 T. Beverley and W. Madenwell.
1549 Richard Carter and Wm. Clarke.
1550 Martin Hollingsworth and Wm. Newcome.
1551 Wm. Goodknap and R. Dove
1552 Ralph Stubs and Wm. Crowne.
1553 Rd. Orrell and C. Johnson.
1554 Rd. Kent and Leonard Ellis.
1555 W. Vergette and W. Schoolfield.
1556 John Westcome and G. Brough.
1557 John Green and Rd. Crossfield.
1558 Richard Smith and Anthony Hare.
1559 E. Hallyley and T. Winterborne.
1560 John Wilson and Rd. Hawkes.
1561 M. Mason and Edward Knight.
1562 T. Dawson and John Harwood.
1563 Joseph Cockle and Christopher Hutchinson.
1564 John Cockle and Christopher Hutchinson.
1565 Thomas Hodgson and W. Scoffin.
1566 Thomas Knight and Wm. Yates.
1567 Thomas Hanson and W. Langton.
1568 J. Emerson and W. Hutchinson.
1569 Thos. Barker and John Pearson.
1570 Silvester Wilford and T. Knight.
1571 C. Rotherham and N. Horner.
1572 L. Lawcock and Geo. Kent.
1573 Robert Hemswell and C. Wilson.
1574 Robert Rushfurth and H. Blow.
1575 T. Wingreen and W. Miller.
1576 John Scrimore and R. Mason.
1577 John Smith and T. Goodknap.
1578 C. Lathcopp and M. Hammond.
1579 Edward Dennis and Chris. Dobson.
1580 R. Tongue and Thomas Emerson.
1581 Wm. Wharton and R. Redfern.
1582 John Beck and Robert Osgerby.
1583 John Clarke and Wm. Goss.
1584 Rd. Smith and A. Gabbatiss.
1585 A. Metcalf and Orman Hill.
1586 Geo. Dickenson and Edward Fowler.
1587 Rd. Subdean and Stephen Cooke.

1588 Thos Swift and Jeffrey Wilson.
1589 A. Osgerby and Chris. Paley.
1590 S. Shawcock and W. Solomon.
1591 E. Dawson and L. Hollingworth.
1592 Rd. Lilly and Rd. Beresford.
1593 Rd. Auckland and P. Wilson.
1594 E. Hollingworth and J. White.
1595 John Howe and R. Wingreen.
1596 John Hanson and Robert Perkins.
1597 Robert Tongue and Robert Lauton.
1598 Joseph Fieldhouse and J. Barton.
1599 Joseph Fieldhouse and J. Barton.
1600 Roger Morecroft and G. Baines.
1601 T. Newcome and Richard Parry.
1602 W. Mitchell and John Dawson.
1603 R. Knightsmith and E. Brough.
1604 E. Shuttleworth and W. Yates.
1605 Edward Blow and George Knight.
1606 John Fern and Thomas Sawer.
1607 Stephen Mason and Rowd. Lilly.
1608 Edward Hawley and Robert Marshall.
1609 Richard Somerby and S. Houghton.
1610 Ed. Oakley and Robert Beck.
1611 Edward Griffin and A. Rycroft.
1612 Bennat Auton and H. Kendall.
1613 James Newhouse and Thos. Chamberlain.
1614 Thos. Bishop and T. Dawson.
1615 Robert Smith and Rd. Whitby.
1616 Wm. Solomon and Roger Beck.
1617 Edward Booth and A. Hare.
1618 Mark Lemsley and Thomas Rose.
1619 R. Marshall and R. Bartlemew.
1620 Robert Kelke and Wm. Wray.
1621 Jeffrey Wilson and S. Dawson.
1622 Richard White and George Beck.
1623 George Clarke and Wm. Watson.
1624 Wm. Kent and Edward Beck.
1625 Edward Trawley and Chris Sawer.
1626 Geo. Wray and Edward Hill.
1627 Jeffrey Wing and Anthony Kent.
1628 Alexander Jolly and Thomas Field.
1629 R. Hird and J. Laws.
1630 Wm. Hooker and Mark Fenn.
1631 Wm. Bishop and E. Dawson.
1632 W. Marshall and Edward Blow.
1633 John Beck and John Tooley.
1634 G. Bracebridge and M. Laws.
1635 H. Phillips and A. Newcome.
1636 J. Willerton and A. Browne.
1637 James Laws and H. Scupholme.

1638 Richard Ward and Enoch Malton.
1639 W. Goodknap and R. Leach.
1640 R. Wetherall and Original Peart.
1641 Edward Emiss and Thomas Ross.
1642 Thomas Gray and Thomas Snell.
1643 Wm. Pell and Thomas Blithe.
1644 Wm. Dawson and Robert Middlebrooke.
1645 Nicholas Nixon and T. Dawson.
1646 Wm. Hall and John Oliver.
1647 S. Luddington and T. White.
1648 Stephen Fowler and John Rass.
1649 Joseph Watson and Edward Hooton.
1650 Ralph Burnett and W. White.
1651 Wm. Lamb and Wm. Suttaby.
1652 Joseph Johnson and George Bennet.
1653 Edward Cheales and Edward Tuffin.
1654 Robert Craven and Thos. Hadney.
1655 T. Ward and Roger Preston.
1656 John Leach and John Legat.
1657 Rowland Curtois and Joseph Urry.
1658 Robert Peart and George Skelton.
1659 J. Luddington and W. Hooton.
1660 Robert Beck and Richd. Kite.
1661 John Middlebrooke and John Goodknap.
1662 Ed. Fauks and Thos. Walker.
1663 Thos Townrow and W. Tooley.
1664 Nevil Lilley and Edward Green.
1665 John Saul and Robert Vergette.
1666 Robert Hall and John Carr.
1667 H. Lamb and G. Bracebridge.
1668 Ralph Burnet and J. Johnson.
1669 E. Malton and John Newcome.
1670 Joseph Bate and Stephen Harrison.
1671 John Hare and Richard Dawson.
1672 Samuel Booth and John Jackson.
1673 O. Laurence and Thomas Hare.
1674 Thos. Green and Wm. Derrick.
1675 Joseph Martin and Sam. Rydatt.
1676 T. Langley and James Garnon.
1677 W. Bishop and W. Holmes.
1678 C. Allinson and Stephen Malton.
1679 W. Browne and T. Newcome.
1680 Joseph Coxall and Thos. Maumell.
1681 Thos. Kent and Stephen Luddington.
1682 Samuel Gibson and John Hall.
1683 Robert Mason and Thomas Kidd.
1684 T. Nicholson and T. Barrat.
1685 Robert Peart and Robert Obbinson.
1686 Wm. Cockle and W. Ruxton.
1687 F. Allen and Ben. Harrison.

1688 Bryan Lamb and M. Dry.
1689 W. Watson and Joseph Rutledge.
1690 John Beck and Nathaniel Knight.
1691 George Skelton and Saml. Dodson.
1692 Daniel Blithe and Wm. Harby.
1693 George Kent and John Norton.
1694 John Sibray and Wm. Fauks.
1695 Henry Green and Thomas Colson.
1696 Wm. Brookes and Joseph Norton.
1697 C. Johnson and Joseph Harness.
1698 Stephen Dawson and Thos. Ferris.
1699 John Garnon and John Mason.
1700 Henry Wilson and John Cooke.
1701 Thomas Hooton and John Urry.
1702 Michael Dawson and Robert Hobman.
1703 Chas. Newcomen and J. Fauks.
1704 George Bracebridge and John Thompson.
1705 Robert Bradshaw and H. Saul.
1706 John Lobsey and Robert Colson.
1707 John Martin and Joseph Maumell.
1708 H. Brown and Robert Obbinson.
1709 Joseph Hobman and Joseph Holmes.
1710 Thomas Kent and Enoch Malton.
1711 John Parson and Joseph Durance.
1712 John Colson and Thos. Ward.
1713 G. Wilson and T. Walmsley.
1714 Henry Kidd and Henry Lamb.
1715 John Dymoke and J. Garnon.
1716 — Wray and George Brown.
1717 W. Sharpe and John Johnson.
1718 Joseph Wetherall and T. Wilson.
1719 John Hye and Timothy Ward.
1720 George Grey and Wm. Dawson.
1721 J. Wickham and Enoch Malton.
1722 Nathaniel Knight and John Becke.
1723 Wm. Rayner and Wm. White.
1724 James Garnon and J. Cockle.
1725 Wm. Colson and Joseph Durance.
1726 Gerald Raines and Wm. Taylor.
1727 Thos Wells and Thos. Knight.
1728 John Trawley and John Kent.
1729 Y. Sudbury and Robert Seeley.
1730 Thos. Parsons and Samuel Trotter.
1731 John Hooton and W. Westby.
1732 T. Obbinson and J. Barnes.
1733 W. Johnston and J. Garthwaite.
1734 Robert Drewry and John Parsons.
1735 E. Leatherland and W. Parson.
1736 John Wilson and H. Goakman.
1737 Jno. Bailey and Wm. Seeley.

1738 Wm. Proctor and Edward Fowler. ,
1739 Robert Thickston and Edward Drake.
1740 Chas. Foster and G. Durance.
1741 Chas. Concy and Ed. Holland.
1742 John Cockle and John Davies.
1743 Geo. Smith and Gervase Gibson.
1744 Mark Mowbray and Joseph Wells.
1745 Robert Waterman and W. Wood.
1746 Jonathan Durance and Ernest Audley.
1747 Wm. Johnsone and W. Hare.
1748 E. Stephenson and R. Ruxton.
1749 Philip Pym and Robert Smeeton.
1750 Robert Obbinson and John Brown.
1751 James Cockle and John Swan.
1752 John Becke and Broxholme Brown.
1753 R. Drewry, jun., and J. Bennet.
1754 Daniel Caparn and Francis Kirk.
1755 Joseph Durance and Richard Smith.
1756 Geo. Westby and J. Thickston.
1757 Samuel Trotter and John Martin.
1758 B. Hunnings and F. Toyne.
1759 John Parson and John Kent.
1760 George Kent and Philip Bullen.
1761 W. Wetherall and T. Foster.
1762 Joseph Proctor and H. Millington.
1763 George Brown and J. Waterman.
1764 Henry Swan and Joseph Dell.
1765 J. Tombleson and R. Vergette.
1766 H. Bullen and Richard Gibbeson.
1767 Richard Picksley and Zachariah Tesh.
1768 Richard Town and Wm. Pear.
1769 Thomas Dawson and Wm. Seely.
1770 Joseph Cockle and Ward Mason.
1771 B. Wetherall and W. Molson.
1772 Joshua Morris and John Cappe.
1773 H. Swan and Wm. Eastland.
1774 Thos. Porter and John Lamb.
1775 Robert Low and John Straw.
1776 Richard Hare and Thomas Hill.
1777 J. Wrigglesworth and R. Holmes.
1778 Wm. Wood and Gentle Brown.
1779 Geo. Bennet and H. Stanley.
1780 John Hattersley and Patrick Drummond.
1781 Wm. Cappe and Joseph Hayward.
1782 Thos. Jepson and John Proctor.
1783 James Cuttill and Thos. Preston.
1784 Richard Gibbeson and John Straw.
1785 John Hall and Broxholm Fox.
1786 Richard Bullen and Chas. Foster.
1787 Tyrwhitt Smith and John Steel.

1788 Edward Mossom and Daniel Caparn.
1789 Wm. Walker and P. Bullen.
1790 W. Porter and C. Foster sen.
1791 Henry Hett and Robert Fowler.
1792 John Drury and Thomas Colton.
1793 Joseph Lee and Robert Featherby.
1794 Samuel Trotter and John Hett.
1795 John Bullen and John Spyve.
1796 W. Hayward and T. Brown.
1797 Henry Blyth and John Allison.
1798 J. Glenn and Matthew Sewell.
1799 J. Caparn and W. Featherby.
1800 Robert Bunyan, jun., and Wm. Woodall.
1801 B. Wetherall and W. Patrick.
1802 Geo. Steel and John Spicer.
1803 Thos. Foster and Matthew Wrigglesworth.
1804 Thomas Norton and George Brown.
1805 Charles Hayward and Robert Read.
1806 Silvanus Cartledge, jun., and W. Wood.
1807 Wm. Hall and John Winn.
1808 Thos. Winn and Wm. Norton.
1809 James Snow and Samuel Trotter.
1810 Henry Swan and John Straw.
1811 Wm. Stainby and Thos. Preston.
1812 Page Cartledge and Daniel Hill Davis.
1813 Job Cartledge and John Keyworth.
1814 Chas. Foster and Jonothan Glenn.
1815 James Bruce and John Brow.
1816 Robert Bristowe and Wm. Trotter.
1817 Thos. Jepson and James Sympson.
1818 Richard Gibbeson and Wm. Huddleston.
1819 Robert Swann and James Beck Horner.
1820 Luke Trotter and John Asher.
1821 Hadnah Yates and Richard Whitton.
1822 Thos. Skepper and Richard Nicholson.
1823 Wm. Seely and Geo. Sprague.
1824 Fredk. Burton and Wm. Berridge.
1825 Thos. Picksley and Wm. Wilkinson.
1826 John Hayward and Wm. Hickson.
1827 Ed. Parker Charlesworth and Wm. Cappe.
1828 Geo. Narr and Wm. Cooke Norton.
1829 Henry Blythe and Wm. Noah Jepson.
1830 Matthew Smith and Rd. Whitton.
1831 Fredk. Burton and Wm. Berridge.
1832 Ed. Edman and Joseph H. Keyworth.
1833 John Stevenson and Frederick Kent.
1834 Richard Carline and John Smith.

1835 Thos Newton	Thos. M. Keyworth 1836
1837 Wm. Gresham	John Sharpe 1838
1839 Geo. Bailey	Wm. Cappe 1840
1841 Michael Penistan, sen.,	Frederick Allen Sayles 1842
1843 Gent. Huddlestone	John Summerscales 1844
1845 Henry Moss	Wm. Hy. Johnson 1846
1847 Thos. J. N. Brogden	Chas. Allison. 1848
1849 Stephen Harrison	Matthew Turton 1850
1851 John Middleton	Benjamin Wilson 1852
1853 Theodore Trotter	Chas. Doughty 1854
1855 Wm. Kirk	Richard Hall 1856
1857 Wm. Ashley	John Smith 1858
1859 Samuel D. Roome	John Norton, jun. 1860
1861 Reuben Trotter	Wm. Huddleston 1862
1863 Geo. Wm. Fox	Thos. Heffernan 1864
1865 Thos. Pilkington	John Hall 1866
1867 C. L. Hughes	C. Akrill 1868
1869 Wm. Parry	Thos. Foster 1870
1871 John Giles	Wm. Rainforth 1872
1873 R. C. Odling	Wm. Ashton 1874
1875 Hy. Newsum	Geo. Bainbridge 1876
1877 C. Duckering	H. Pratt 1878
1879 E. Waterhouse	Gilbert J. Dashper 1880
1881 Benj. Vickers	F. R. Larken 1882
1883 W. W. Richardson	Thos. Bell 1884
1885 A. McKerchar	T. M. Wilkinson 1886
1887 H. E. Cousans	Richard Whitton 1888
1889 W. Rainforth, jun.,	Arthur C. Newsum 1890
1891 Alexander Trotter	J. W. Shepherd 1892
1893 J. W. Ruddock	T. H. White 1894
1895 Joseph Bentley	W. Mortimer 1896
1897 F. C. Brogden	

XXVIII.—" INNS " THAT HAVE GONE " OUT."

In the days when the railway and the consequent "hotel" was undreamed of, when the face of Britain was not crossed and re-crossed here, there, and everywhere by a multiplicity of steel rails whereon wondrous machines sped at a still more wondrous pace, and when our fathers used the horse and the coach for the transit of themselves and their goods, then the wayside inn played a conspicuous part in the history of our land. The evolution of the bicycle is doing much now to bring into our notice again many of the inns scattered over the country which had been some years practically buried in oblivion But the inns we propose to treat of in this chapter once stood in all their pride and prosperity within the confines of our own Lincoln, and that at not so very distant a period after all

The importance in which the inn was held in the " good old days" may be gathered by a perusal of the works of any author of the period. Take the immortal and unapproachable Dickens as an instance. Many of the most delightful of Pickwick's adventures occurred within their hospitable walls. Sam Weller is introduced to us there, so are several other characters in the book. Cap'en Cuttle doesn't manage to quite steer clear of the swinging sign, nor do the Crummles, nor Micawber, nor the Artful Dodger. Henry Cockton gets some fine fun out of Valentine Vox by placing him in the bar parlour of an inn,, and we may go right back to Shakespeare and the jovial, burly Falstaff and his boon companions and find the same thing. Leaving fiction for history, we may find not a few dramatic scenes and momentous meetings transpiring within the walls of an inn. So that the hostelry, in short, held a foremost place in the institutions of the land. Now we may come to particulars.

Everybody in Lincoln recollects the demolition of the Dolphins, after its purchase by Mr. Alfred Shuttleworth, J.P., seven years ago. There has long hovered over it a vaguely-understood tradition that its name was derived from a Dauphin of France, who lodged within its walls during the time that the French King John the Good was a prisoner at Somerton Castle—that is from August 4th, 1359, to the 21st day of the following March. The tradition is positively affirmed by a document which formerly existed in the inn, but is nevertheless a fiction. The document, however, is interesting, and runs thus :

"The sign of this Inn was the Minster Hostelry at the middle of the 14th century. The tenants of the Cathedral Church, after paying their rents in the Common Chamber between the Minster and the Chapter House hard by were here entertained. As the rents were paid in corn and wool from the scarcity of coin, the landowners had large store houses on the west side hereof leading to the Deanery. In the month of September, in the year of our Lord 1356, the 28th year of the reign of King Edward III., his son Edward Prince of Wales, commonly called the Black Prince from the colour of his armour, fought and won the battle of Poictiers in France, and took King John and his son the Dauphin prisoners. The Prince brought them to England, where they were put in charge of Saier de Rochford, the owner of Somerton Castle, near this city, who undertook to keep them for two shillings per day; a goodly sum when sheep were only 4d each. The following Easter Sir Saier de Rochford brought the King of France and the Dauphin to the Dean of this city, and after attending the Cathedral service they put up their horses and spent two days at this ancient inn, since which its sign has been the Dolphins."

History does not contradict the first part of the document, that relating to the Minster tenants, but the account of King John's captivity, published by the Duc d'Aumale makes no mention of the Royal prisoner s visit to the Inn. But even were this true, the fact remains that the Dauphin stayed in France during the whole period of his father's captivity. The lad who was taken with his Royal father on the field of Poictiers was not the Dauphin at all, but the youngest of his four sons, Philip—a boy of about 15 years—after-wards Duke of Burgundy. Again, the King and his son were placed under the care of William, Baron Deyncourt—not Sir Saier de Rochford, and the latter was not the owner of Somerton, but one of the knights entrusted with the keeping of the captives under the Baron.

The old building, which stood very low, was not a little pictur-esque, and not a few lovers of the ancient houses of Lincoln expressed keen regret when it was taken down. However, the improved ap-proach to the Cathedral and the generally brightened and broadened aspect of the site is truly a welcome change, and we doubt if any would now wish to see the old Inn back again.

The shop of Messrs. Holmes and Rosser in the Bail was no doubt once an Inn, and was originally named "The Swan;" it was probably a timber building formerly. The eastern "Chequer" gate was divided into tenements at one time, and that on the northern side was used as a public-house, and called "The Sign of Great Tom." It seems a wonder that the name is not perpetuated in some modern hostelry. Can it be that our innkeepers are wanting in local patriot-ism? The name is certainly appropriate and attractive. "The Black Horse," leased to Mr. Cracroft, woollen draper, in the Bail, in 1674, the "George," the "Antelope," and the "Blue Bell" have also dis-appeared.

Then there stood in the last century, a fine hostelry in the Bail, called the "Angel," very near to the present "White Hart." It was leased in 1580 by the Dean and Chapter to Justice Robert Monson, who had been M.P. for the city in 1563 and 1571, and Recorder in 1569. Part of the reserved rent in the lease was "one cagg of fatt, sweet, and good wholesome sturgeon, with a jowl in it, which was to be presented yearly to the provost of the Cathedral on the Monday next before Holy Rood Day." The "Angel" seems to have flourished until 1792, when the property began to decline. Both this Inn and its rival, the "White Hart," are rated at £24 in 1738, but in 1792 the latter was £25, and the "Angel" had sunk to £10. Later than this it ceased to be an Inn at all, and gradually evolved into small tenements. A fallen "Angel," indeed!

A very interesting old Inn is that which formerly bore the name of the "Ram" and afterwards (probably by amalgamation with another tenement) of the "Lyon." In 1741 the "Snake" is added to the title in a lease granted to Clement Wood, Governor of the Castle, of the "Red Lyon and Snake." The Inn was known at one time as the Earl of Scarborough's Arms," but probably only for a short period between 1757 and 1783. Afterwards an Inn on the other side of the street was given the title, and the "Lion and Snake" remains as the name of the old building.

The existing "King's Arms" preserves the name of one of the chief Inns of the city, now divided into three houses.

The "George" Inn stood at the south-west corner of Guildhall-street, and seems to have been an old timber building of great size. It was re-built by the Corporation in 1741, and christened the "Reindeer," becoming known later as the "City Arms." Sympson mentions it in a letter to Browne Willis as having been purchased and re-built by the Common Chamber in 1741 "with brick and stone in a grand manner. It is not yet finished"—the letter is written in September, 1743—"and will cost the city upwards of £2,000. There is one chamber in which the city purposes to have the public feasts, which is 63 feet long, 21 feet wide, and 16 feet high." Some historians declared the church of St. Peter at Placita to have been on this site, while others positively affirmed it to have been on the site of the Butter House, a long controversy being waged between the disputants. We believe it is now generally conceded that the church really did exist on the Butter House site.

High old times, they had, too, at the "George," or rather the "Reindeer," sometimes. As already recorded during the course of this compilation, King James the First visited it in 1617, and enjoyed a cockfight there uproariously. Of course, in those days mine host provided various entertainments for the edification of his patrons, and of these cock-fighting no doubt formed a prominent feature. At all events, during the reign of James it would do so, and not only in Lincoln, but all over the realm, for the sport affected by Royalty is always one of the delights of the people.

But cock-fighting was not the only sport by any means. Bull-baiting was another, and a disgraceful one. There was a Bull-ring near the Jew's House, and the practice was not put down until so late as 1827.

A far honester and, to modern minds, more enjoyable pastime was quarter-staff. Two men, armed with long staves would face each other, and a fine display of skill and judgment would result, though the battles were not without the elements of danger, broken heads being quite of ordinary occurrence. Not very far from the old "Reindeer" stood the Town Pillory, which also formed a subject for the attention of the customers of the worthy host. Here notorious perjurers, fraudulent bankrupts, and others were fastened, and exposed to the rough badinage of the mob. "Election" eggs, cabbage-stalks, and missiles of a harder description were often hurled at the miserable wretch figuring for the time being in the pillory, who was, of course, totally unable to resist or avert the flying objects.

The Old Saracen's Head and the King's Head were principally known as coaching inns. At the former, probably, was enacted the tragedy wherein two unfortunate priests were seized during the cruel persecutions of "Good" Queen Bess's reign, and subsequently executed. One of them, Thomas Hurt, was a Norfolk man, we are told, and had but lately escaped from Wisbech Castle. These were dragged before the Mayor, and from thence to the Court of Assize, where Judge Glandvil convicted them as "Seminary Priests, and consequently traitors." These men, like, not merely odd ones, but many hundreds of others suffered a martyrdom for their religion, and were executed at Lincoln in 1600.

Innkeeping was not always the class of business it is now. Nowadays a publican may exercise some discrimination as to whether he shall or shall not serve a customer who has evidently already peered deeply into the tankard. But fifty or a hundred years ago it was different. A roystering blade whose demands for liquor were not instantly supplied would as likely as not enforce the application by the exhibition of weapons, and, possibly, of his prowess with them into the bargain. Moreover, when his tankard was empty, his lofty contempt for the necessarily obsequious innkeeper would not always permit him to pay for what he had consumed, so that he was at best a somewhat unprofitable customer. In time of war, too, a landlord might find a dozen brawny, hungry, and thirsty soldiers march into his parlour with loud demands for refreshments for themselves and horses, and accommodation for the night. To do this good paying customers might have to be turned away from the beds they had engaged, and the landlord knew well that he would be lucky indeed if he saw any of his abruptly quartered customers' gold. Yet it was wiser and safer to keep on the right side of the heroes of the battle-field and the beerhouse. If a fight occurred and his furniture was damaged, or even his house set on fire, the best thing to do was to bear it with all the equanimity possible. There was power indeed in the command to set forth his best for the military "In the King's Name!"

XXIX.—VANISHED CHURCHES.

" Vanished Churches !" What a world of mystery such a title
suggests ! Not only have the devout bands of worshippers of past
ages gone for ever, but the very buildings in which the services were
held are gone also, in many cases, to the foundation stones. When it
is considered that prior to the Reformation there were no less than
fifty-two churches in the city of Lincoln, some idea may be gained
of the sweeping destruction which has befallen many of them. A
number have perished utterly. Others still exist in name, though
the actual buildings have disappeared, others, perhaps, being erected
on or near the site of the original church.

For it has not always necessarily followed that when one church
has been pulled down, a new one has been built upon its ashes, so to
speak. St. Swithin's is a case in point. The quaint old church or
churches wherein the forefathers of the present-day parishioners
worshipped stood to the westward of the present handsome edifice,
which is built on the site of an old sheep market, as many yet living
will remember.

The first "vanished" church of importance, it will be generally
conceded, is that which first stood on the site of the present church
of St. Paul's, in the Bail ; for here was erected the first Christian
Church in the county, by the great Paulinus, Bishop of York, chaplain of Queen Ethelburga, who was assisted by his first Lincoln
convert, Blecca, the reeve or governor of the city. In the walls of
this same church in 627 Paulinus consecrated Honorius, the fifth
Archbishop of Canterbury. The church was called "Paulinus's,"
which has since become contracted to St. Paul's. Writes Precentor
Venables : "From the time that Blecca . . . built the first
church of St. Paul, of all the fifty-two churches once standing here
no single church in our city ever owed its origin to the State. If
founded and endowed by Kings, it was in their individual capacity,
not as sovereigns, out of their own personal estate, 'rerum suarum,'
not in any way out of national property. The endowments have
been repeatedly protected by the enactments of the State, just as all
other property has been protected, but there are no enactments creating those endowments. They are always spoken of and treated just
as any other property which has come down to its owner by a rightful
title, which the State might recognise and affirm, but which it had
no claim to have created and no power to annul." The gifted Precentor was always enthusiastic and convincing in the defence of the
status of his church.

What St. Paul's is to the upper town, St. Martin's is to the lower.
Only the tower now remains of the edifice, which was re-built by
public subscription in 1740, and for this we have to thank Ald. P. P.
Dickinson, who was Mayor at the time the church was demolished,
but whose efforts preserved the tower as a striking memorial of what
old St. Martin's had been. It was a custom generally followed in

England at one period to dedicate the first church built in any town to St. Martin of Tours, "as a token of dutiful affection of a daughter church to its mother." This custom was followed at Oxford, Canterbury, Leicester, and elsewhere. St. Martin's suffered severely in the attack of Cromwell's Ironsides on the city in 1644, and being unroofed, like so many Lincoln churches at this time, by the combined attack of cannon and predatory soldiers, it lay in ruins till the early part of the last century. Then a local gardener was appointed churchwarden, and set zealously to work to restore the edifice, with such good results that it was soon put into a condition fit to receive worshippers. The alabaster figures of Sir Thomas and Lady Grantham (after whom Grantham-street is named, and in which thoroughfare they had a fine mansion) were placed in the basement of the tower. They had been badly damaged by the fall of the canopy which had been constructed above them.

When Remigius set to work to build his Cathedral he swept away the church of St. Mary Magdalen. Whether this was the church of which Bede writes, or whether it stood where St. Paul's now does, is doubtful. History is by no means clear on the point.

We have said that fifty-two churches existed previous to the Reformation. There seems a general conviction that some of these must have contained much rich Norman work, in addition to somewhat elaborate details of a latter period, judging by the numerous fragments which have been discovered in excavating from time to time. Many of them, however, were in a decaying state subsequent to the Wars of the Roses, when the prosperity of the city had suffered a decline. They were reduced to twelve in the reign of Edward V.

St. Botolph's Church, both the present and past buildings, are interesting. The ancient church is recorded to have been a fine building, the finest in the city after the Cathedral, built, in fact, cathedralwise, with the tower in the centre, the body and side aisles being vaulted with stone. In 1644, the destructive Parliamentary forces noticed the lead roof, and stripped it off completely, to convert it into bullets. This seems to have weakened the structure, for the roof, which was replaced with tiles, thatch, etc., fell down two years later—on Sunday, August 6th, 1646. The walls gradually fell into disrepair, and the whole building became a practical ruin. Mr. Thomas Andrews, the parish clerk, preserved the dimensions, which are given as follows: Length from east to west, 123 feet; breadth of middle aisle, 20 feet; side aisles, 14 feet; length of transept, 73 feet; breadth, 34 feet; square of tower, 22 feet.

In the early part of the last century, however, the parishioners bestirred themselves—it was a period when many churches rose Phœnix-like from their ruins—and with the aid of the neighbouring gentry set about constructing a new church with the stones of the old one. This became an accomplished fact in 1721. The Corporation refused their assistance on account of the great expenditure caused by the building of St. Peter at Arches, towards which they had given £1,000. However, in 1723, when Mr. Thomas Hooton was Mayor, the city agreed to give £200 towards the minister's salary in order to obtain the Queen's bounty towards the same. The new St. Botolph's was but a small church at first, but during the incumbency of the Rev. W. J. Hathway a chancel was added, and other improvements made. In 1878 a new aisle was added, and by degrees the church attained its present comely appearance. The south aisle has a special interest, inasmuch as it was the last gift of the late Bishop Wordsworth to his See. The church owes much to the late Vicar, the Rev. A. C. Ramsay, who was, perhaps, the most popular incumbent the parish has ever known—though the present Vicar, the Rev. Dr. Ellis, is extremely well liked, and his powerful sermons draw hearers from a long distance.

It is not, perhaps, widely known that a church dedicated to St. Botolph was usually the nearest to the entrance of a town, this saint being regarded as the special protector of travellers. When persons came in from a journey, it was their first duty to give thanks to the saint who had guarded and guided them through all the perils and mazes of the way.

Just below Gowt's Bridge stood the church of the Holy Rood (or Holy Cross), the site being crossed by the present private road to Boultham. The church was turned in 1551 to a use it was certainly never intended for when built, viz., given over to a party of cloth-workers, who had been invited by the Corporation to settle in the city. We have already treated of the unsuccessful attempts to establish a cloth-manufacturing trade in Lincoln.

The old church of St. Swithin's is spoken of as one of the finest in the city, and its destruction came about in a somewhat unique manner. During the great Civil War—on May 30th, 1644, to give the exact date—some troopers were drying a quantity of gunpowder on the Cornhill, when by some means the mass exploded. Embers were scattered far and wide, and some falling on the roof of St. Swithin's Church, it took fire. Any effort made to save the building proved futile, and the edifice was quickly reduced to a heap of ruins, the walls remaining standing in part. It stood in this fashion until 1718, when the south aisle was restored to some extent, and served as a place of worship until 1801, when a small church was built, and this lasted until the present fine bilding was erected. The chancel was constructed mainly through the liberality of Messrs. Clayton and Shuttleworth, and the glorious tower and spire—without a doubt the finest in the city—is due to the generosity of Mr. Alfred Shuttleworth, J.P., who had it built to the designs of Mr. Fowler, Louth, as a memorial to his late father, Mr. Joseph Shuttleworth. St. Swithin's parish, as indeed the Church in Lincoln, owes a deep debt of gratitude towards this gentleman. He has recognised the vast extension of the parish in the east, and has promised £1,150 towards the erection of a church and mission hall there, with a further £500 for the building of a mission hall until the church is ready.

Quite close to St. Swithin's stood the church of St. Denis, in Thorngate, commemorating Dionysius the Areopagite, patron saint of France. The name yet survives in a prebendal stall in the Cathedral, though the church was demolished and even its site forgotten by James the First's time. St. Rumbold's Church was also in the vicinity.

The Church of Saint Peter-at-Pleas (ad Placita) was in very early times known as St. Peter-atte-Stancheked, Stanthaked, or

Staynshed, a name no doubt received from its proximity to the Stoneshade or mural protection, which the Romans constructed when they extended their colony down to the water. Afterwards it became known as St. Peter-ad-Placita, from the time of City Pleadings or Placita being removed from elsewhere to be carried on at the Guildhall close by. It is further distinguished as St. Peter-the Little, or Upper Saint Peter, and as St. Peter ad Forum Pellium, from the Skin Market held near it. The church had been given to the Abbot and Convent of Sey in Normandy at a very early period, and like many other churches belonging to those foreign establishments, it became a rectory, the whole profits being oppropriated to the use of the incumbent. But in 1384 Richard II took all the English property belonging to the French Monasteries, among them the Priory of Wingate,, the Superior of which, being subordinate of the Convent of Sey, had the appointment of the rectory of this church. From this year the King himself presented, and after the suppression of alien monasteries in 1414 the patronage of this church was made over to the Nuns of Sion (Middlesex), the Nns of Heynings having a pension at a later date of two shillings yearly. There was attached to St. Peter-at-Pleas a Chapel known as Hodyleston's Chauntrie, originally founded by Robert de Huddlestone a woolstapler of Lincoln, in 1375. The name Huddlestone occurs in the Mayoralty several times about this period; Robert would probably be a member of the same family. The endowment was augmented by certain benefactions made to the Dean and Chapter, who appointed the Chantry-priest, but in 1484, when the rectory became impoverished by lack of tithes and offerings, the Chantry was united to it, and the rector officiated.

The church stood close by that known as St. Peter at Arches, in the same churchyard, and part of the Butter House was erected on it in 1724. Robert Anesley, the last Rector, was appointed in 1475, and an order was made on June 10th, 1542, for pulling down the church, and directing that the lead, bells, carved benches, etc., be sold for the use of the Common Chamber. For information concerning this church we are greatly indebted to the courteous assistance of the Rector of St. Peter-at-Arches, Canon T. S. Nelson, M.A.

The church of St. Mary Crackpool (or Creekpool) stood slightly north of Guildhall-street, then known as Baxter Gate or Baker-street, in which the chief bakeries of Lincoln were situated, and was so called because it was built on the bank of a creek or inlet of deep water, which had served the Romans as a landing-stage.

St. Thomas of Canterbury, on the High Bridge, has already received notice. The "brothers" and "sisters" of the Cordwainers' confraternity, in company with the "graceman," went in procession from this chapel to the Cathedral annually, and there made an offer of one farthing.

The church of St. John, according to some authorities, stood behind the shop of Mr. Hugh Wyatt, High-street, while others affirm that it stood on the Cornhill. Certainly the cemetery attached to the church stood on the latter square, but we must admit a certain amount of doubt as to whether the edifice itself really stood there. St. John's, which was constructed in the Gothic style, was secularised in the 16th century, the cemetery being purchased by the Corporation, and devoted to the purposes of a corn market.

A drawing by Grimm is still existent, we believe, of the old church of St. Mark standing in ruins in 1788. It was a picturesque building in the decorated style. St. Andrew's (Wickford) was at the south end of John o'Gaunt's property, in which was also St. Anne's chapel and guild. The church of St. Peter-ad-Vincula was probably near the old Fish Market above hill, though some are inclined to think St. Peter's-in-Hungate was the same, while others give it as St. Peter's-ad-Placita. St. Lawrence's stood on the site of the Theatre Royal. It withstood both the Reformation and the Civil Wars, and was formerly used as a house to receive the plague-stricken. The steeple was standing as late as 1718, and formed part of a stable.

Other churches of which not a trace remains, were All Saints, near the Deanery; All Saints, beyond the Bar Gates; the Holy Innocents, on the Green close by, in the Melandery Closes; St. Andrew in (or under) the Palace near Ventnor-terrace; St. Andrew beyond the Bar; St. Augustine; St. Bartholomew, to the west of the Castle; St. Clement, beyond the Bar; St. Clement in Westgate; St. Cuthbert; St. Edward, just below the Midland Station, in the High-street; St. Edward the King; St. Faith; St. Giles in East-gate; St. Gregory, not far from it, in Closegate; St. James, in the northern part of Newland; St. John, in the Fish Market; St. Leonard, in Eastgate; St. Margaret, south of the Minster; St. Michael, in Wigford, High-street; St. Pamond, in Broadgate; St. Peter, in Broadgate; St. Peter, by the Pump, eastward of Broadgate; St. Peter, beyond the Bar; St. Stephen, in Newland; St. Trinity, at the foot of the "Grecian" Stairs; and St. Trinity, in Closegate.

So mighty is Old Time; so do the stones of our buildings, sacred or secular, crumble away beneath the touch of his bony hand!

By the kindness of the Lord Bishop of the Diocese we are enabled to give the following information from an old manuscript, called "A true account of the accustomed service in all the Churches and Chappels in the Diocese of Lincoln. Supposed to be made out from the returns to the Queries sent out on the primary visitation of Dr. John Thomas, Lord Bishop of Lincoln, 1743."

Divine Service, we learn from this ancient record, was held in St. Benedict's Church at this period once in every month, twice on the greater Festivals, "and as often about Michaelmas." St. Mark's had services only on the three greater Festivals, and four times in the year besides. St. Martin's had services four or five times a year, St. Mary-le-Wigford once every Sunday, St. Paul's in the Bail every Sunday afternoon, and on Thursdays and Saturdays, and St. Peter-le-Goats once a month, while St. Peter-in-y-Arches had prayers early on Sunday morning, and twice every day in the year, also a sermon every Sunday afternoon. Communion and Catechism were of occasional occurrence. There were no services at St. Margaret's, and no churches for the parishes of St. Swithin, St. Botolph (?), St. John, St. Michael, St. Nicholas, and St. Peter-in-Eastgate.

XXX.—THE "GREESTONE" STAIRS.

What's in a name? Shakespeare asked the question hundreds of years ago, and it will perhaps be hardly an answer if we say that it can be very misleading. Yet that this is a truth we can find ample evidence by the consideration of our present subject. A name is given to a person, place, or article primarily as a mark of identification; when this fails to do its duty, the name is a name in spirit no longer, but a misnomer—not useful, not merely useless, but misleading and even dangerous.

We have heard people gravely assert that the derivation of the name "Greestone Stairs" was to be found in the fact (sic) that the stone used in the construction came from Greetwell, some two miles away—Greetwell Stone, Greestone. Another section have gone further afield, and solemnly declared that the proper name is the "Grecian Stairs," for the steps supply the place of the original stairs erected by the ancient Greeks! However, it will be interesting to get at the root of the actual truth.

There is a scholarly article by the late Chancellor Massingberd on the subject, which we believe may be accepted as authoritative. There is little doubt that the proper word is the "Greesen," which is the early English plural of a "gree" or step, to which "stairs" has been added without dropping the original name when this was becoming obsolete and thus the name would be "the Greesen Stairs." Stukeley's map of Lincoln has another name, "the Greestan" Stairs. If this may be taken to mean merely "greystone," the Chancellor emphatically dissents therefrom. If, however, it means the greestone (or step-stone), it makes no material difference whether it is understood to be the stepstone stairs or simply the plural of the same word explained by a repetition, the Greesen Stairs.

The word is spelt by some "gree" and by others "grize;" the former, which is more ancient, is spelt by Wiclif and Chaucer, and the latter by Shakespeare, Ben Jonson, and other writers. For instance, where in Acts xxi., 35, we now read "When Paul came upon the stairs, so it was that he was borne of the soldiers for the violence of the people," Wiclif had it, "When Poul cam to the grees it bifel that he was borun of knytys for strength of the peple." Tyndall's translation is, "When he cam unto a greece." In the last verse, where the present reading is "Paul stood on the stairs," Wiclif writes, "Poul stood on the greezen." Here is a quotation from Chauser's "Romaunt of the Rose," with the expression occurring:

"In thank thy service wol I take,
And high of gree I will thee make."

Ben Jonson has it, "The daughters of the Genius . . . in a spreading ascent, upon several grices, help to beautify both sides." Better known, perhaps, is Olivia's confession of love in Shakespeare's "Twelfth Night." In reply to her speech, "That's a degree to love," Violet says, "No, not in grize, for 'tis a vulgar proof that very oft we pity enemies." In "Timon of Athens," too, occurs the expression, "Every grize of fortune Is smoothed by that below."

In modern Danish "graa-sten" is a technical term for hard stone, and represents the "gra-steinn" of Old Norse. The word "greystein" was most certainly introduced by the ancient Norsemen into Normandy, for there is ample evidence of the existence of an Abbey of Greystern or Grestein near the mouth of the Seine, founded in the year 1040. In Craven, millstones for grinding the coarser kinds of grain are called "graystones," and in the same district stairs are yet called "grees." Further proof of this may be seen by a reference to the "Craven Dialect."

A similar instance of evolution in nomenclature is to be found in the sign of the Black Goats' Inn. It was previously the Three Goats, which was, no doubt, derived from the three gowts or drains by which the water from Swanpool was conducted into the Witham.

When we come to a consideration of the date of the stairs we are confronted by a difficulty. So far as we are aware, there is no record extant giving the actual time of their construction. Many people are agreed that they would be built at the time—or shortly after the time—that the Close was walled in. The little postern gate at the summit formed an entrance to the Close, and there is good reason for supposing that the steps were built as the readiest way of gaining access thereto from the lower part of the city, and save the journey further up the hill to Pottergate Arch.

At the foot of the stairs, as has been previously hinted, stood the Church of Holy Trinity, and the "grees" are mentioned in connection therewith as early as 1398. The legitimacy of the Lady Katherine Hebden had been called into question. A Royal brief, dated July 11th, 1398, certifies that William de Wyhom and Beatrix de Rye were married at this church after the banns had been duly published. William and Beatrix were the parents of Katherine, afterwards the wife of Sir Nicholas Hebden.

The Girls' High School has sprung up beside the stairs of recent years, and the appearance of the neighbourhood has been altered slightly, but the old steps retain a picturesque appearance, which the narrow archway at their head decidedly enhances. Of the furious rush up these stairs, the battering at the postern, and the rowdy scenes on the Minster Green when certain changes were about to be made in the towers of the ancient pile, we have already spoken. We have heard of people who entertain the belief that the Witham, when the tide flowed unchecked from Boston to Lincoln, used to rise as high as these stairs, but this belief is, of course, absolutely unfounded.

Nevertheless, they are certainly worthy the antiquarian's notice, and if the ascent is fraught with trouble to those with asthmatical tendencies, the sight of the glorious southern front of the Minster, when they reach the top, the charming peep into the grounds of the Episcopal Palace, and the calm of Vicars' Court should be ample reward.

XXXI.--THE FALL OF THE KNIGHTS TEMPLAR.

The Temple and Temple Bar are as well known to residents in London as is the Chapter House to the citizens of Lincoln; both are landmarks of history, and each is indissolubly connected with the story we have to tell—the story of the mighty order of the Red Cross Knights, and the Knights of St. John.

While the name of the Order lives, that of Odo de St. Armand, Grand Master, will also live. The brave defenders of the Holy Sepulchre had been engaged in a long and bloody war in Palestine, victory inclining sometimes to the Knights, and sometimes to the Infidels, principally the latter, especially after the renowned Saladin appeared on the scene. This resulted in fearful ravages in the ranks of the crusaders, almost totally extinguishing the faithful band, matters culminating in a particularly heavy battle on the banks of the river Jordan in 1179.

It speaks much for the valour and indomitable prowess of the Crusaders that, despite the heavy slaughter, the Saracens took but few prisoners. The Knights preferred death to captivity, and, though fearfully overmatched, proudly refused to throw down their weapons while they had the slightest strength to wield them. The few who were captured had fought until they could fight no more, and the gaps in the ranks of the victors were the clearest proof of the pluck with which they had fought to the very last a battle which from the first had been all against them.

Amongst the captured few was the Grand Master of the Order, Odo de St. Armand. He was taken before Saladin, whose nephew was in the hands of the Christians. The wily Saracen Prince commenced his interview with his prisoner by complimenting him on the vigour and valour he had exhibited on the field of battle. From this he went on to offer the Grand Master his liberty, provided his nephew was set free in return. But this, and a change of demeanour to threats of death or life-long imprisonment were equally unsuccessful. Finally Saladin sent his prisoner to the dungeons of Damascus. Here St. Armand languished for some time, ultimately dying there.

The victorious Prince had meantime entered into a truce of five years' duration. In place of the captive St. Armand, the Knights appointed Heraclius, the patriarch, as their Grand Master. Heraclius was determined to make the best use of the five years' truce, and proceeded, with the Grand Master of the Knights of St. John, to Europe, with the intention of raising all the help possible, their main hope being Henry the Second, of England, who had promised, on receiving absolution from the Pope for his share in the murder of Thomas a Becket in Canterbury Cathedral, that he would personally lead a large army to Palestine, and, furthermore, maintain two hundred Templars at his own expense.

Heraclius and the Master of the Knights of St. John arrived

safely in England in 1185, and met Henry at Reading. The King promised to bring the matter before his Parliament on the first Sunday in Lent. The Templars had, in the meantime, found that their hospital in Holborn, London, was too small for their work to be adequately conducted, and thereupon began to erect the church and other buildings which yet bear the names of their Order. When Heraclius arrived in England, they had completed the round portion of their splendid new church, and this they requested the patriarch to consecrate for them. That he acceded a tablet which existed in the church until the year 1695 records. He also consecrated the church of the rural establisment of the Knights of St. John at Clerkenwell.

Parliament assembled, and Henry,true to his promise, brought the matter of the proposed crusade before it. Henry desired to go, but the barons insisted that by his coronation oath he was bound to remain at home, and offered instead to raise the sum of fifty thousand marks to defray the expense of forming a body of troops. The King's answer is, therefore, recorded as "that he might not leave his land without keeping, or to the prey and robbery of Frenchmen, but he would give willingly of his own to such as would take upon them the voyage."

The patriarch's reply to this ,as given by the historian Fabyan, was, "We need a man, not money,. Nearly every Christian land sends money, but no land sends a prince. Therefore we ask a prince that needs money, not money that needs a prince." Ultimately he left the Royal presence, and returned to the East.

The Templars at this time began to flourish, and seem to have been fully established in England. The penetential cell of the Church, in which disobedient brethren were placed, was a most uncomfortable place, and the punishment to the body by a lenthy stay there must have been very severe. This may be gathered from the fact that it measured but four feet and a half by two feet and a half. Thus the unhappy prisoner could only lie down by placing his limbs in a very cramped position. In order that he might have religious consolation, an aperture was left through which he could see into the body of the church, and even take part in the services. Walter le Bacheler, preceptor of the Order in Ireland, was one of those confined in this fearful cell, and here he was left until he died through the strain of the punishment. He was buried in the court between the church and the hall.

The following is a copy of the tablet recording the consecration of the Church by Heraclius, alluded to above :—

ANNO : A P : INCARNA
TIONE DOMINI. MCLXXV.
DEDICATA : HEC ECCLESIA IN HONO
RE BEATE : MARIE. A. DNO : ERACTIO : DEI : GRA
SCE : RESURECTONIS : ECCLESIE PATRI
ARCHA. IIII IDVS FEBRVARI. Q. EA. ANNATIM
PETETIB DES. PENITETIA LX. DIES INDIVISIT.

It will be noticed that the date of dedication is given on the tablet as 1175, while history records the arrival of Heraclius in England as ten years later, but the latter date is probably an error.

We might write some columns on the subject of the Temple Church, but we must hurry on. Nevertheless, we cannot leave it without reference to some of the mighty men who lie beneath its stones. A peculiar circumstance is recorded in connection with a Bishop of Carlisle—a warlike prelate, killed by a fall from his horse in 1255—who was buried here. In 1810 his tomb was opened, and at the feet of the skeleton was found the perfect skeleton of a very young infant. The mystery of this has never been explained.

The Earl of Pembroke, the famous protector, is buried here; so are William Plantagenet, fifth son of Henry III; Lord de Ros, to whom the nation owes an unredeemable debt, for he was one of the bold barons who forced King John to sign Magna Charta; William Marshall, who married King John's daughter; Selden, Plowden, and many others.

Shakespeare makes the Temple Gardens the scene of the adoption of the red and white roses by the rival houses of Lancaster and York. Oliver Goldsmith dwelt in the Temple, Charles Lamb was born there, and Dr. Johnson and his biographer Boswell haunted its courts.

Being greatly popular, it naturally followed that the Templars made many enemies, who envied them the height to which they had attained. Many conspiracies were hatched in order to bring about their downfall, but the work and personalities of the Knights of the Red Cross and of St. John had made them hard to depose. Ultimately, however, their enemies gained the ear of the Pope, and once this was won, they spared no effort until he was brought to their views. The result was, that on a given day, the Templars, both in England and France, were seized and thrown into prison. The last Grand Master, James de Molay, with a number of his brethren, was seized and burnt alive, not on a huge pile, but by the torturing means of small fires of charcoal.

Up and down the realm the Templars were hunted. To such an extent was this carried on that many people who were not members of the Order were obliged to shave off their beards in order to save their lives, for a distinguishing mark of a Templar was his long, flowing beard.

In this connection it is related that the King, by whose order the Knights were destroyed, was obliged to grant a certifice to his own valet, one Peter Anger, in order to free him from suspicion of being one of the hunted brotherhood! Peter, it seems, had taken a vow that he would not cut his beard till he had made a certain journey abroad. This latter is vouched for in Dugdale's history of Warwickshire.

A number of the brethren were captured, and imprisoned at Temple Bruer and other houses of the Order in this and neighbouring counties. From these places they were brought to Lincoln, and incarcerated in the gate-house at Claxlede-gate, which stood near the Bull's Head Inn. They were taken before Bishop John of Dalderby in the Chapter House (1310), on the charges of apostacy, idolatry, and gross immorality. Idolatry! This was one of the charges brought against a body of men whose lives were avowedly devoted to the defence of the sacred traditions of the Cross, a symbol of which they wore upon their garments, and following which, too, were designed the hilts of the swords they wielded! A charge of idolatry against the remnant of a band who had fought the infidel on his own ground, given their money, and shed their blood for the truth of Holy Writ!

Truth to tell, the doom of the Knights Templar was pronounced long before the charges against them were formulated. As one sits in the quiet, grand old Chapter House of Lincoln to-day, it does not need, after all, so very great a stretch of the imagination to see the solemn scene re-enacted before one's eyes. The Bishop, with the other dignitaries of the adjoining Cathedral, sitting there in State, with the haggard faces and broken figures, yet retaining something of their old martial spirit, arrayed before him. The troop of renegades and apostates, only too ready to give their lying evidence against the prisoners. Those other men—even worse than the perjurers—who had extracted "confessions," wrung from some of the weaker brethern by most horrible tortures. Yes, all were there, and the "proofs" of the idolatry and immorality of the true men who stood there captive were given with glib tongues and plausible manner.

And what of the Bishop? Was his conscience clear? Did he know the lie from the truth, and yet, in spite of it all condemn the prisoners? Or was he deceived—as he may well have been,—by the volume of evidence brought against the Templars, the prisoners being unsupported by even their own denial, for had they not "confessed" their guilt?

Unhappy Templars—martyr Templars!

Well we know their sentence—life-long imprisonment in various monastic houses. Their church, buildings, gardens, etc., passed into the hands of the Knights Hospittalers of St. John of Jerusalem. The latter had little use for two houses, so they demised the whole of the splendid establishment, "and all the appurtenances that belonged to the Templars in London to certain students of common law.'" This took place in 1346, and the Temple became one of the Inns of Court. The idea that lawyers should reside in the same locality appears to have originated with the Court of Common Pleas, and this led to the gradual collecting in London of the whole body of lawyers, and their settlement in places best suited to their studies and practice. With the stirring scenes enacted here later we have nothing to do.

The Knights of Templar, then, vanished into life-long immurement. But to their fate they seem to have been followed by universal respect, and the popular opinion was emphatically a belief in their innocence. But what was popular opinion against Kingly decree? The story of their work is one of glorious achievement. The pity of it is that the close of the story is one of dishonour, or rather undeserved condemnation.

Yet the philosopher may well find their history a subject for moralising, even as others may find it one from which shines a grand example.

XXXII.—THE BISHOP'S PALACE.

It will be surprising to those who know the truth to learn that there are many people, even within the city itself, who imagine that Bishop King dwells in the ancient Palace of the See. The postal address—"The Old Palace, Lincoln,"—is possibly accountable for this to some extent, but whatever the cause, it is an undoubted fact that there is an impression abroad amongst a number of people to the effect that the palace now used as an episcopal residence is the original building. However, as the majority of people are aware, the Old Palace proper is a ruin—a fine, picturesque pile, but none the less a ruin.

Its picturesqueness when seen from the heights of the Canwick Hill, or even from the nearer point of Broadgate, will be unquestioned. Particularly in the summer, when the foliage on the numerous trees around and below it is most abundant, the old building is indeed a thing of beauty, and affords much charm to the viewer, which is not lessened when the eye travels upward to the massive Rood Tower of the Cathedral, standing majestically behind and above it.

It is by no means certain who built the Old Palace. Of course, its history must in some measure run along the same lines as the history of the Cathedral, of which it is, so to speak, a servant, but this does not necessarily imply that when Remigius began to build his Cathedral he also began to build himself a palace. As a matter of fact, there is not the slightest evidence to prove that he was responsible for a single stone of it. We have seen it suggested that as he set himself to build a Cathedral, he would not forget the necessity of a Bishop's house. But it may be said that his zeal for the great task which he had set himself would quite overshadow any idea of building any house for his own personal use. We may also suppose that all his efforts and all the money which he could concentrate for building purposes would be used for the erection of his great ambition—the mighty Cathedral, which to-day is a glorious fact, but which he himself was not permitted to see finished.

The successor to the founder of the Cathedral, Robert Bloet, is not recorded to have built anything at Lincoln, though Henry I. granted him a license to make a gate in the wall that ran round the Bail. Next came Alexander of Blois, surnamed "the magnificent," from the luxury of his equipage and the free manner in which he spent his money. The diocese, it must be recollected, then extended from the Humber to the Thames, and he built fortresses at Banbury (which has entirely disappeared), Sleaford (one wall of which only remains), and Newark. There is again no direct evidence that this Bishop erected the Palace, but in 1147 Bishop Robert of Chesney obtained from Henry the Second a Charter giving the boundaries of the land on which it is built. The cemetery of St. Michael's Church was the western boundary, the city wall the eastern limit, the cemetery of the vanished St. Andrew's Church the southern, and the wall running parallel to the south side of the Cathedral the northern extremity. He is given permis sion in the Charter to "perforate the wall, for his entrance and exit, towards the church," by which is understood the Cathedral. There is still existing in the wall which separates the grounds of the Palace from the Cathedral a blocked-up gateway, and it is not impossible that this may have been the identical exit which the license had authorised.

But when we come to St. Hugh of Avalon, who became Bishop in 1186, we find something more tangible, this being nothing less than a record of the commencement of building the hall. Hugh, like Remigius, died without completing his work. It is not unlikely that as the Choir of the Cathedral was at the same time in course of construction, Hugh paid more attention to that than to his Palace, more especially as he was already possessed of a house at Stow Park.

Another Hugh—he of Wells, Somerset—appears to have completed the building, but at all events it is certain that he spent a considerable sum on the buildings. In 1185 occurred the earthquake, which "rent the Cathedral from top to bottom," but we have seen no record which gives any account of damage befalling the Palace, which is somewhat strange, when it is considered a number of other buildings were thrown down, and that the Palace is virtually within the shadow of the great Church. An inspection of the hall, or rather the ruins of it, shows it to have been somewhat following the style of a church. The Parliamentary Commissioners describe it, in 1647, as having "one large middle allye, and two out iles on eyther syde with 8 gray marble pillars bearinge up the arches of freestone," while there were "large and faire freestone windows very full of stones in paynted glass of the kings of this land." There is a record that Bishop Alnwick filled the windows w'th stained glass. The size of the hall was 90ft. by 60ft .The roof was of timber, covered with lead, and the fire was used in the middle of the floor.

But the roof has gone; the gray marble pillars have gone; the glass windows have gone. Probably the first and last may be laid at the doors of the Puritans. We have remarked that the churches of the city were laid under contribution for their leaden roofs, to be used in the form of bullets and fired against the citizens, if necessary, and there seems no doubt that the leaden roof of the Episcopal Palace also went into the melting pot.

We read of little about the Palace from Hugh of Wells' time until 1320, when Henry de Burghersh obtained a license to embattle and fortify it. This was at the time when the King granted the erection of the wall round the Close to keep out marauders, cut-purses, and the unscrupulous gangs who even waylaid the clergy on their way to midnight service. St. Hugh's favourite dwelling at Stow Park, the old Grange at Nettleham, and other places were also strongly fortified at the same time.

William Alnwick, perhaps, did more for the Palace than any Bishop either previously or since. He had been a generous donor to Norwich Cathedral, and he did not withhold his munificence when he came to our own city. He added a considerable amount to the Palace, including a fine chapel dedicated to the Virgin. But all the buildings which he added have been almost completely wrecked —to such an extent, in fact, that it is stated to be difficult to point out now to a visitor what the arrangements were in those days. But from a drawing by Buck it may be gathered that the ground plan of the Palace was something after the shape of the letter L.

It must not be supposed that the only Palace in the Diocese of Lincoln was that which we are now describing. There were residences at Nettleham, Stow Park, Buckden, Sleaford, Newark, Liddington, Banbury, and Wooburn.

Bishop Longland was the last prelate to occupy the Palace before the Reformation. He was Confessor to Henry VIII., and to this fact is probably due the visit of the King and his Queen, Catherine Howard, in 1541. It was in the Palace, too, that the acts of criminality with Culpepper occurred, which led to the unhappy Queen being decapitated. Longland died, and the glories of the Palace began to fade. It had been plundered by rebels even in his episcopate, and his successor, Henry Holbecke, was coerced into surrendering the greater part of the episcopal estates, the consequence being that from one of the wealthiest Lincoln became one of the poorest Sees in the realm. With reduced money at his disposal, it is not surprising that the Bishop preferred the house at Nettleham, and that succeeding prelates followed his example.

Bishop John Williams seriously set himself to restore the fast tottering fabric, but was prevented from doing so by the Civil War breaking out, and in 1643 we find the building being used as a common prison, the Sheriff having been ordered to remove the prisoners thither from the Castle, while the latter was being fortified. The Civil War, as we have already intimated, was the cause of much injury being done to the building, and in 1720 Bishop Reynolds gave permission to the Dean and Chapter to use some of the materials for the repair of the Cathedral.

Meantime, in 1660, Bishop Saunderson had found it impossible to restore the Palace to its former grandeur, and therefore repaired and used the Palace at Buckden, Huntingdonshire, which became the recognised episcopal residence for some time. Bishop Fuller, who presided over the Diocese from 1667 to 1675, rented a house in the Close when in the city, and King William was entertained at the same house when he visited Lincoln in 1695.

Dr. Edward Nelthorpe, a physician, obtained a 21 years' lease of the Palace premises in 1727, and pulled down the patchy dwellings which had done duty during the Commonwealth, and built himself a new house on the west side of the Palace. This, added to and improved from time to time, forms the Palace as it stands to-day. In the earlier part of the present century the Ecclesiastical Commissioners built the Palace at Riseholme, though for what actual reason we are at a loss to say—it was scarcely because it was needed. But in 1886 the Riseholme Palace was sold, and the proceeds devoted to the enlargement of the Palace proper. In closing we must not omit to thank the Rev. Canon Maddison, librarian of Lincoln Cathedral, to whom we are indebted for much of the above information.

XXXIII.—THE BISHOPS OF THE DIOCESE.

Driven further and further inland by the savage attacks of the pagan Danes, who mercilessly crushed Christianity wherever they found it, the Bishops of Mercia eventually found themselves on the banks of the Thames. However, being allowed here comparative peace, they planted their "Bishop's stool" at Dwr-ceaster—"the camp by the water"—known to us now by the name of Dorchester. The modest church here became the Cathedral church of Mid-England, from Humber to Thames, and including the ten counties of Lincoln, Rutland, Northampton, Leicester, Cambridge, Bedford, Buckingham, Oxford, Huntingdon, and Hertford. Remy, or as his name is in the Latin, Remigius, an almoner of the Norman Monastery of Fescamp, by contributing to the Conqueror's fleet, earned the grateful thanks of that monarch, and a promise of the first vacant bishopric. Wulfroy, Bishop of Dorchester, dying the year after the Conquest, Remigius became Bishop of the most extensive and powerful See in England. But the Norman monk desired something better as his Cathedral, and cast about for a suitable site for a new one. He chose Lincoln; the work was commenced about 1074, and the church was ready for consecration in 1092.

This, in a nutshell, is the history of the Bishopric of Lincoln. But Remigius was not to see the consecration. Three days before the appointed time he died. "Nature," said William of Malmesbury, alluding to Remigius, "seemed to have formed him to show that the richest intellect might dwell in the most wretched body." For Remigius was dwarfish in stature, and undignified in personal appearance. In addition to the building of part of our Cathedral, he erected the Monasteries of Stow and Bardney, a Hospital for Lepers at Lincoln, and caused William the Conqueror to build Battle Abbey in England, and Caen Abbey in Normandy. Further than this, the first Bishop of Lincoln, we are told, "for three months in the year fed daily one thousand poor persons, and clothed those who were blind or lame."

Robert Bloet succeeded him, and bestowed much rich work on the Cathedral. He presided over the See 21 years, and died as he was attending Henry I. at Woodstock. "Alexander, the Magnificent," came next, the nephew of Roger of Salisbury, at one time the most powerful man in the kingdom. We alluded in our last article to his castle-building. It becoming evident that he and his uncle and his cousin, the Bishop of Ely, were too strong to be safe subjects, King Stephen eagerly caught at a pretext of a brawl raised by their retainers at Oxford to have them seized. The two Bishops were seized, and under a threat of starvation Alexander was compelled to surrender his castles in 1139.

Two years later the Cathedral suffered disastrously from fire, which burnt off the roof, and destroyed the boarded ceiling. To prevent the possibility of a recurrence of such a disaster, Alexander replaced the ceiling with stone vaulting, and at the same time added other magnificent features to the building. In 1142 Alexander visited the Court of Rome, and made a second journey there in 1144. Two years after, going to France to meet the Pope, he fell sick, returning home with great difficulty, and dying soon afterwards.

Robert de Chesney was consecrated Bishop of Lincoln in 1148, and built St. Katherine's Priory. On his death the See was vacant six years. Then Geoffrey Plantagenet became Bishop, but was never consecrated. During his nine years' presidency over the See, he cleared off the late Bishop's mortgage, recovered several lands, and added two bells to his church. Resigning in 1182, he shortly afterwards became Archbishop of York.

Next came Walter de Constantis, and after him Huge de Grenoble. The latter is perhaps the most popular with us of any of the old line of Bishops. He not only contributed largely to the development of the Cathedral from his own pocket, but helped with the labour in another equally practical way—by shouldering the hod and carrying the mortar and cut stones for the use of the builders. It is told that one day the Bishop having laid down the hod, a cripple put down his crutches and took it up. This endeavour to follow the Bishop's example was rewarded by the disappearance of his lameness, and he walked out of the Minster "whole and sound."

After William of Blois and Hugh of Wells came Grostete, another name that will long live in the annals of the Cathedral history. He was indeed a striking character. A Suffolk peasant's son to begin with, he became the most learned scholar of his day, the champion of the liberties of the Anglican Church, and a bitter enemy of the indolence and avarice which had made the clergy of that age a by-word and a reproach. The King might be king of the realm, but Grostete was king of the Cathedral; he set that as an ideal before himself, and ruled accordingly. His fearlessness is best shown by the fact that he told the Pope to his face that the deeds which he (the Pope) commanded were not the deeds of a Christian Bishop, but rather of an Anti-Christ. The story of how he said that if he were to cease calling out against the evils the very tower would fall, and how the tower actually did fall, has already received mention.

We now pass over several Bishops, and come to Henry Burghersh, who was created Bishop of Lincoln at Boulogne (France) in 1320. He was a great opposer of Edward the Second, and "was mortally hated by the King, for which reason the Parliament chose him one of those Bishops," who afterwards assisted towards that unhappy monarch's deposition.

Richard Fleming, consecrated Bishop in 1420, was the founder of Lincoln College at Oxford. Thomas Watson, consecrated in 1557, was one of the Papist Bishops chosen to dispute on religion in Westminster Abbey. The Reformation being established, the Bishop of Lincoln was deprived of his See and kept a close prisoner. He was the last Roman Catholic Bishop who presided over this Diocese.

Thomas Barlow, consecrated in 1675, is quite a remarkable Bishop. He presided over the See 15 years, during which he never once visite any part of the diocese!

It would be easy to write of various deeds in the lives of other Bishops, men of godly life and whole-hearted devotion to the Church, but the above are a few of the more remarkable. Most of the others have been prelates of the highest character, the greatest popularity, and the most thoroughly exemplary life. The late Bishop Wordsworth, installed in 1869, and our present beloved Bishop, Edward King, consecrated in 1885, are among the best examples of these.

There have been 62 Bishops of the Diocese since the removal of the See from Dorchester to Lincoln, the following being a complete list, with the dates of installation :

1067 Remigius de Fescamp	Robert Bloet 1094
1123 Alexander de Blois	Robert de Chesney 1148
(See vacant six years) Geoffrey Plantagenet (not consecrated) 1773	
1185 Walter de Constantis	(See vacant two years)
1186 Hugh de Grenoble	See vacant four years)
1203 William of Blois	(See vacant three years)
1209 Hugh of Wells	Robert Grostete 1235
1254 Henry Lexington	Richard Gravesend 1258
1280 Oliver Sutton	John of Dalderby 1300
1320 Henry Burghersh	Thomas Beck 1342
1347 John Gynwell	John Buckinham 1363
1398 Henry Beaufort	Philip Repingdon 1405
1420 Richard Fleming	William Gray 1431
1436 Wm. Alnwick	Marmaduke Lumley 1450
1452 John Chadworth	Thomas Scott, or Rotherham 1472
1480 John Russell	William Smith 1496
1514 Thos. Wolsey (afterwards Cardinal Wolsey)	
1514 Wm. Atwater	John Longlands 1521
1547 Henry Holbeach	John Taylor, or Rands 1552
1554 John White	Thomas Watson 1557
1560 Nicholas Bullingham	Thomas Cowper 1571
1584 Wm. Wickham	Wm. Chaderton 1595
1608 William Barlow	Richard Neile 1614
1617 George Mountain	John Williams 1621
1642 Thos. Winniffe	Robt. Sanderson 1660
1663 Benj. Laney	William Fuller 1667
1675 Thos. Barlow	Thos. Tenison 1692
1695 John Gardiner	William Wake 1705
1716 Edmund Gibson	Richd. Reynolds 1723
1744 John Thomas	John Green 1761
1779 Thos. Thurlow	Geo. Pretyman Tomline 1787
1820 George Pelham	John Kaye 1827
1853 John Jackson	Christopher Wordsworth 1869
1885 Edward King.	

XXXIV.—THE CASTLE.

We have left the venerable series of buildings until late, and we feel that, somehow, we owe the Castle a kind of apology for our tardiness. However, we must make amends by giving, from the many pages of its history that we propose to dip into for the purposes of this article, as comprehensive a notice as possible.

It is a remarkable fact that of the 49 Castles enumerated in Domesday Book, not less than eight were erected by William the Conqueror, which is easily a record number. One of these was at Lincoln. When William came, saw, and conquered, he very wisely decided to strengthen his captured towns as much as he could, and for the purpose of constructing a Castle at Lincoln he calmly swept away 166 houses. But, though some authorities do not mention it at all, there appears to be little doubt that a Castle existed here earlier than this. Earthworks, we are assured, from 50 to 80 yards broad, and from 20 to 30 feet in height, enclosing about six acres, existed long before the Conquest. There is little of interest to tell with regard to the Castle during William's lifetime, but when the usurper, Stephen, ascended the throne it became the scene of considerable action.

Knowing he had no just claim to the sovereignty, he found he could only support himself in it by means of the strongholds he had either built, or allowed his barons to build. Stephen was greatly assisted by the clergy, and was elevated to the throne chiefly by their instrumentality, but soon quarrelled with them. The Bishop of Salisbury espoused the cause of Matilda, the rightful heiress to the throne. After a variety of fortune, she retired from the Castle of Wallingford, and decided upon that of Lincoln as her headquarters. Here she was sharply besieged for several days, and at last articles of capitulation were drawn up, but Matilda did not fall into the hands of her waiting enemies. While the terms of surrender were yet being drawn up, she managed to escape, and left her father, the Earl of Gloucester, in charge of the fortress.

Stephen was exultant, imagining his conquest to be secure, and accordingly left the Castle in the hands of but few followers. With dramatic smartness, the Earl of Gloucester pounced upon these and overpowered them, and, to Stephen's consternation, his Majesty himself was taken prisoner. As a sequel to this, Matilda gained her rights for a time, and ascended the throne. The unfortunate lady, however, soon found how fickle is Dame Fortune. In 1143 a Papal Legate summoned a Council to Lincoln, and in 1146 the Earl of Gloucester, in his turn, was taken prisoner, and Stephen released. The latter tried several times to regain the Castle, which was now held by the Earl of Chester. By a treacherous stroke, Stephen captured the noble Earl, and demanded the Castle as the price of his ransom, which he obtained. Roger of Wendover describes this circumstance in these words: "King Stephen took Ralph, Earl of Chester, as he was coming to him in a peaceful manner to Northampton, and kept him in prison until he restored to him the Castle of Lincoln, with other fortresses which he had in hand; and thus the

King carried his crown in State at Lincoln."

During the reign of Henry the Second, the Constableship of the Castle was held by one Richard de Hay, and on his death the office descended to his daughter Nicholaa, who married Gerald de Camville. Following her husband's death, the aged Nicholaa became sheriff of the county, and this local Amazon held the Castle for King John against all the fierce attempts of the insurgent barons to gain possession of it. In 1215 the King himself came to the city, and, says the old record, the Lady Nicholaa "delivered the keys of the Castle as to its Lord, and he besought her saying, 'My beloved Nicholaa, I will that you keep that Castle as hitherto, until I shall order otherwise;' and so she retained it as long as King John lived."

Indeed, Nicholaa retained the custody of Lincoln until very near her death, which occurred in 1231. Then we find the castle a very prominent scene in the struggle between the Cromwellians and the Royalists in 1644, when the Castle was taken, and so many of the churches plundered and even partially destroyed.

The drum-tower at the north-eastern corner of the walls known by the name of "Cobb Hall," was doubtless a place of confinement. By descending through a trap-door, a number of iron rings to which the chains were fastened may still be viewed, and there are a number of drawings on the walls evidently the work of the prisoners.

A study of these is very interesting. One clearly represents a hunted stag, the neck pierced by an arrow, while the figure of a man is depicted in front. Over the top of the drawing in old English characters, are the words "Thank God." Another drawing is apparently intended to represent a centaur, and others are equally notable. The walls almost meet at an angle, the space between being but a few inches; nevertheless, each orifice is closely barred, the whole being of great strength, and one would think escape from such a place a practical impossibility. From 1815 to 1868 when the Act abolishing public executions was passed, this tower was the place of hanging those condemned to death, the gallows being erected on the leaden flat top of the tower.

Earlier than this the place of execution was at the corner of the road opposite the north-western corner of the Castle Dykings, and this spot bore the gruesome name of "Hangman's Ditch." The last person hung there was William Ward, for breaking into a shop at Mareham, April 1, 1814. This, to our modern minds, seems a light offence for the execution of the offender, but such a fate was by no means uncommon as the penalty of even lesser crimes. On March 17, 1785, for instance, nine persons were executed together, one for highway robbery, and the remainder for horse stealing and sheep stealing, and to see the horrible spectacle a crowd of 20,000 people gathered together.

Worse scenes still took place there in 1727 and 1747, when women were burned at the stake for the murder of their husbands. They were not burned alive, however, having been strangled (though this was against the strict letter of the law) by the ropes with which they were bound to the stake.

In 1815 two men were executed in the Castle yard for burglary and robbery in a Pinchbeck shop. They had conducted themselves after their conviction, we are told, in a very hardened manner, and gave reason to believe that they entertained hopes of either escape or rescue. To guard against the first an additional watch was stationed in the yard. On the Wednesday evening preceding the execution two men were found lying on the top of the south wall, and were shot at, but got away. Eventually the execution took place without any further interrupion.

In 1817, we read that on February 5th four prisoners escaped from the Castle, which is hardly complimentary to their warders. The hanging of culprits for sheep-stealing was hardly effective, either. As an instance, William Udale was hung for the offence in 1827, and the same night a Lincoln butcher had a sheep stolen from his grounds! But more amusing still—if amusement can be extracted from so grim a subject—are the following entries in the old "Date Book"—1854: July 27th, Ralph, the burglar, escaped from Lincoln Castle, re-captured at Barton, August 1st. 1854: October 3rd, Ralph, the burglar, escaped the second time from Lincoln Castle, he was re-captured at Nottingham. We believe the enterprising Ralph subsequently succeeded in breaking prison a third time, and on this occasion avoided re-capture.

The last public execution at the Castle was that of William Pickett and Henry Carey, both young men, the former aged 20, and the latter aged 24, for the murder of William Stevenson, at Sibsey, in 1859. We have heard persons yet living in the city describe the scene. The Keep, on the opposite side of the Castle grounds (or Lucy Tower, as it may be called, it having been named after the wife of one of the Earls of Lincoln), is the burial place of a number of the criminals who suffered execution there, though the graves are not easily recognisable now. The small stones bear the initials only of the persons who lie beneath. Thus it might be easy to confuse them. Priscilla Biggadike and Peter Blanchard were both buried here, and, as will be seen, the initials are identical.

The inner gateway of the Castle, the postern which faces Asylum-road, and the whole of the lower portions of the wall are Norman. The tower is partly Norman; it was added to by the Edwards, and the small observatory which now caps the whole is of modern construction. A walk round the Castle in our own day is of the very highest interest. It should not be forgotten that immediately upon entering the heavy gateway, one views on the right the much-mutilated remains of the effigy which crowned poor Queen Eleanor s Cross. A look round the comparatively modern block of buildings where the prisoners were confined, and where the Petty Sessional Courts for the divisions of Lindsey and Kesteven are now held, is also necessary, the "Black Hole," or dark cell, and the old condemned cell calling into play the imaginative faculties of the visitor to the utmost. The Courts of Assize, of course, are not of great antiquity, but when one of Her Majesty's Judges visits Lincoln and the flourish of trumpets heralds his approach to the Court of Law, it does not need any great stretch of fancy to suppose oneself back in earlier ages and witnessing quite a different scene.

It is, of course, recognised that, next to the Cathedral, the Castle is the most important place in the city to be visited, and we fail to see how anyone can spend an hour, or a few hours, for the temptation is almost irresistible to linger, within the mighty walls without profiting by and enjoying the experience. Above all, one must recognise the grand position it holds from a military point of view, which renders it almost absolutely impregnable.

XXXV.—PARLIAMENTARY REPRESENTATIVES.

The first Members of Parliament for the City of Lincoln of whom we have the names are Ricardus de Bella and Alexander Filius Johannis, and the date of their election was 1298.

Thus we may look back almost exactly 600 years, and know that during that period Lincoln has had her voice in the Parliaments of the succeeding ages, and been represented in the Council of the Nation. A glance through the local records of these gentlemen cannot fail to be interesting. It not infrequently happened, as will be seen from the record published below, that two elections occurred during the same year.

We have to come down to the last century for anything approaching lengthy records, however, and the first of interest is dated 1716. There was, we read, one of the strongest contests for the county of Lincoln ever known, nearly the whole of the voters being polled out. The candidates were Sir Neville Hickman and Mr. Vyner. Sir Neville led easily at one time, but an unlucky circumstance changed the tide, and resulted in his defeat. "Elated and exultant with the certainty of success, surrounded with enthusiastic friends, Sir Neville indulged rather too freely, and rushing out in the yard of the old Angel Inn, now extinct, knelt upon his bare knees, and drank the health of the Pretender! With the fear of præmunire before their eyes for supporting a Jacobin, his followers fell off, a knowledge of the disloyalty of the candidate was spread like wildfire, the popular indignation was aroused, and Sir Neville was defeated."

On April 15th, 1754, the candidates for the honour of representing Lincoln were the Hon. George Monson, Mr. John Chaplin, and Mr. Robert Cracroft, and this election is described as the most corrupt at that time known in the city—some freemen received as much as twenty guineas for their votes. Monson and Chaplin were elected. After the election Cracroft published a list of over 200 persons who had promised him their votes, but voted for his adversaries. The figures were as follow : Monson, 635 ; Chaplin, 617 ; Cracroft, 436.

In 1761 the Hon. George Monson again headed the poll, Mr. Coningsby Sibthorp being also elected, and Mr. Lister Scrope defeated. "A riot took place, the mob entered the Town Hall"—wherever that may have been—"with bludgeons, broke all the windows," and did so much damage that the election had to be put off until next day! Quite a record, we should think. The books had to be shut up, owing to the riot occasioned by the gallant candidate Scrope "drawing his sword to head up his men." In 1790, it may be noted in passing, an Act of Parliament for paving, lighting, and watching the city of Lincoln received the Royal assent. Probably the lowest number of votes recorded for any one candidate in a Lincoln Parliamentary election was in 1780, when the poll resulted as follows : Sir Thomas Clarges, 626 ; Robert Vyner, 616 ; Lord Lumley, 339 ; Thos. Scrope, 6.

In 1794, Mr. Charles Anderson Pelham, M.P. for Lincolnshire, was created Baron Yarborough. The following is a copy of his letter to his constituents on the occasion : "To the gentlemen, clergy, and freeholders of the county of Lincoln. Gentlemen,—His Majesty having been graciously pleased to confer a Peerage of Great Britain upon me, I am necessarily precluded the honourable distinction I have so long experienced in being one of your representatives in Parliament. Permit me to assure you that I shall entertain a very grateful sense of my obligations to you, and that I shall be ready on all occasions to promote the landed and commercial interests of the county of Lincoln to the utmost of my power. I have the honour to be , with the most respectful gratitude, gentlemen, your ever obliged and faithful humble servant, Yarborough. Arlington-street, Aug. 13, 1794." As an example of fine "old-world" (as we call it now) courtesy, the above would be distinctly hard to beat. Mr. Robert Vyner, jun., was elected in the place of the new peer. We are sorry to state that in May, 1796, one of the Members for Lincoln, Colonel Cawthorne, had to be expelled from the House for falsifying his accounts as Colonel of the Middlesex Militia.

In 1800, Colonel Sibthorp, then Member for Lincoln, gave a feast to the inhabitants at Canwick. The event would have passed off with complete success but for the intervention of a mob, whose conduct deserves the greatest denunciation. Whole joints of meat were taken from the table (provision had been made for 2,000 people), and forcibly taken from the carvers. The kitchen, larder, etc., were broken open, and much of the furniture was destroyed.

We give below a list of M.P.'s for Lincoln, with the date of their election. It is impossible to glance through the list without being struck by the recurrence of certain names—Seely, Sibthorp, and Monson, for instance. A number of Members have done much for the advancement of Lincoln. As instances of this, we need only mention the fine Drill Hall and other buildings, the gifts of the late Mr. Joseph Ruston, and the new Constitutional Club, the gift of the father of the present Member for the city.

Elections are conducted in more honourable fashion nowadays, and there are those who think that gentlemen who could stoop to the practices some of them did for the purpose of ensuring their return hardly deserved the title of "honourable member." The following is the list of Members above referred to :—

1298 Ricardus de Bella and Alexander Filius Johannis.
1300 Stephanus Stanham and Willielmus de Cause.
1302 Johannes Filius Ricardi and Willielmus de Cause.
1307 Willielmus Cousin and Alexander Filius Martini.
1308 Johannes Edwards and Alexander Filius Martini.
1310 Thomas Gamel and Henricus Windestow.
1311 Thomas Gamel and Henricus Windestow.
1311 Thomas Gamel and Rogerus de Totil.
1312 Thomas Gamel and Henricus Scoyll.
1313 Thomas Gamel and Henricus Scoyll.
1314 Willielmus de Pontefracto and Henricus Scoyll.

1314 Hugo Scarlet and Henricus Scoyll.
1318 Willielmus de Hakethorne and Johannes de Fame.
1327 Willielmus de Hakethorne and Johannes de Fame.
1327 Willielmus de Hakethorne and Walterus de Eboraco.
1328 Willielmus Nottingham and Johannes Weston.
1328 Walterus de Eboraco and Robertus Hakethorne.
1330 Hugo de Carleton and Willielmus Hakethorne
1330 Henricus Draper and Willielmus Hakethorne.
1332 Hugo de Carleton and Willielmus Virby.
1332 Thomas Cause and Willielmus Hakethorne.
1333 Thomas Carleton and Willielmus Hakethorne.
1334 Thomas de Carleton and Willielmus Hakethorne.
1335 Willielmus Virby and Willielmus Hakethorne.
1335 Simon de Grantham and Willielmus Hakethorne.
1336 Hugo de Eginton and Willielmus Hakethorne.
1337 Thomas Bottiler and Willielmus Virby.
1337 Willielmus Hakethorne and Ricardus Fitz Martin.
1338 Henricus Sales and Johannes Judkyn.
1338 Willielmus Hakethorne and Ricardus Hakethorne.
1338 Thomas Bottiler and Willielmus eVrley.
1338 Thomas Bottiler and Willielmus Verley.
1339 Robertus de Dalderby and Willielmus Verley.
1340 Willielmus Hakethorne and Willielmus Verley.
1340 Willielmus Hakethorne and Nicholas Welton.
1341 Willielmus Hakethorne and Willielmus Verley.
1343 Walterus de Ebor and Alanus de Huddleston.
1346 Willielmus de Verley and Simon Erneburgh.
1347 Robertus Dolderby and Willielmus Humberston.
1348 Walterus Kelliby and Thomas Locton.
1350 Walterus Kelliby and Robertus Dolderby.
1352 Johannes Outhorpe, only one chosen.
1353 Robertus Dadderley and Robertus Kelby.
1355 Johannes de Bolle and Walterus de Kelby.
1357 Johannes Outhorpe and Johannes Beke.
1359 Stephanus Stanham and Johannes Blake.
1360 Johannes Outhorpe and Willielmus Wisurn.
1360 Walterus Kelby and Petrus Ballasyre.
1362 Walterus de Kelby and Johannes de Bole.
1364 Walterus Kelby and Johannes de Bole.
1365 Johannes Rodes and Johannes Welton.
1368 Johannes Golderston and Johannes Dell.
1369 Walterus Kelby and Johannes Sutton.
1372 Walterus Kelby and Johannes Sutton.
1373 Rogerus Tattershall and Johannes Sutton.
1373 Rogerus Tattershall and Johannes Sutton.
1376 Willielmus Belay and Johannes de Huddleston.
1377 Hugo Garwell and Johannes Blake.
1378 Hugo Garwell and Johannes de Outhorpe.
1378 Thomas de Horncastre and Rogerus Tiryngton.
1379 Johannes de Huddleston and Johannes Duffield.

1381 Robertus de Sutton and Robertus de Leeds.
1382 Thomas de Horncastre and Robertus de Saltby.
1383 Willielmus de Snelleston and Nicholas de Werk.
1383 Willielmus de Snelleston and Johannes Prentys.
1384 Robertus Sutton and Johannes Dorfield.
1385 Robertus Sutton and Simon Messingham.
1386 Robertus Sutton and Robertus de Saltby.
1387 Thomas Thornhagh and Johannes Bellessise.
1388 Gilbertus de Baseby and Robertus de Hareworth.
1389 Nicholas de Werk and Robertus Peke.
1391　Robertus de Sutton and Robertus de Leeds.
1392 Robertus de Thornhagh and Johannes Belleshull.
1393 Robertus de Sutton and Robertus de Messingham.
1394 Robertus de Leeds and Robertus de Harworth.
1396 Robertus de Sutton and Robertus de Appleby.
1397 Semannus de Laxfield and Johannes Thorley.
1399 Willielmus de Blyton and Robertus de Sutton.
1399 Gilbertus de Beseby and Robertus de Hareworth.
1401 Willielmus de Blyton and Johannes Balderton.
1402 Willielmus de Blyton and Johannes Balderton.
1403 Semannus de Laxfield and Willielmus Dalderby.
1404 Robertus Appleby and Nicholas Huddlestone.
1406 Ricardus Worsop and Thomas Foster.
1413 Johannes Dalderby and Thomas Foster.
1414 Thomas Terring and Johannes Riley.
1415 Hamundus Sutton and Johannes Bigg.
1417 Thomas Archer and Robertus Walsh.
1419 Ricardus Worsop and Thomas Foster.
1420 Johannes Bigg and Hamo Sutton.
1421 Willielmus Ledenham and Robertus Walsh.
1422 Hamo Sutton and Robertus Walsh.
1423 Hamo Sutton and Robertus Ferriby.
1424 Henricus Sutton and Robertus Walsh.
1427 Henricus Tamworth and Robertus Walsh.
1428 Johannes Clifton and Robertus Walsh.
1432 Willielmus Markby and Robertus Walsh.
1434 Willielmus Markby and Robertus Walsh.
1441 Willielmus Stanlow and Robertus Gegg.
1446 Johannes Vavasour and Willielmus Gressington.
1448 Johannes Richby and Robertus Sutton.
1449 Johannes Richby and Robertus Sutton.
1450 Johannes Saynton and Robertus Sutton.
1472 Johannes Saynton and Johannes Putt.
1492 Thomas Knyggte and Wm. Bele.
1513 to 1523 there was no Parliament.
　　　　(A number of records are totally lost.)
1541 Anthony Myssenden.
1542 Geo. St. Poll and Thos. Grantham.
1547 Geo. St. Poll and Thos. Grantham.
1552 Geo. St. Poll and Thos. Grantham.
1553 Geo. St. Poll and Robert Ferrars.
1554 Ald Wm. Rotheram and Robert Ferrars.
1554 Geo. St. Poll and Robert Ferrars.

1555 Geo. St. Poll and Robert Ferrars.
1557 Geo. St. Poll and Francis Kempe.
1558 Robert Mounson and Robert Ferarrs.
1563 Robert Mounson and Robert Ferrars.
1571 Robert Mounson and Thos. Wilson, LL.D.
1572 John Welcome and Thos. Wilson, LL.D.
1585 Stephen Thimgolaby and John Joyce.
1586 John Saville, Recorder, and Thos. Fairfax, jun.
1888 Geo. Anton, Recorder, and Peter Evens.
1592 Geo. Anton and Chas. Dymoke.
1597 Thos. Mounson and Wm. Pelham.
1601 John Anton and Francis Bullingham.
1603 Sir Thos. Grantham and Sir Edward Tyrwhitt.
1614 Sir Lewis Watson and Sir Edward Ayscough.
1620 Sir Lewis Watson and Sir Edward Ayscough.
1623 Sir Lewis Watson and Thos. Hatcher.
1625 Sir Thos. Grantham and John Mounson.
1625 Sir Thos. Grantham and Sir Robert Mounson.
1628 Sir Thos. Grantham and Sir Edwd. Ayscough.
1640 Sir Thos. Grantham and John Farmery, LL.D.
1640 Sir Thos. Grantham and John Broxholme, in whose place
      Thos. Lyster.
1653 Members returned only for the county.
1654 Ald. Wm. Marshall and Ald. Original Peart.
1656 Humphrey Walcot and Original Peart.
1658 Ald. Robert Marshall and Thos. Meers.
1660 John Monson and Thos. Meers.
1661 Sir Robert Bowles and Thos. Meers.
1678 John Monson and Thos. Meers.
1679 John Monson and Thos. Meers.
1681 Sir Thos. Hussey and Thos Meers.
1685 Henry Monson and Sir Thos. Meers
1688 Sir Chas. Neville and Henry Monson.
1690 Sir John Bolles and Sir Edward Hussey.
1695 Sir John Bolles and Wm. Monson.
1698 Sir John Bolles and Sir Edward Hussey.
1700 Sir John Bolles and Sir Thos. Meers.
1701 Sir John Bolles and Sir Edward Hussey.
1702 Sir Thos. Meers and Sir Edward Hussey.
1705 Sir Thos. Meers and Thos. Lyster.
1708 Sir Thos. Meers and Thos. Lyster.
1710 Richard Grantham and Thos. Lyster
1713 John Sibthorp and Thos. Lyster.
1714 Richard Grantham and Sir John Tyrwhitt.
1722 John Monson and Sir John Tyrwhitt.
1727 Sir John Monson and Chas. Hall.
      The former was made a Peer, and Sir John Tyrwhitt elected.
1733 Chas. Monson and Coningsby Sibthorp.
1740 Chas. Monson and Sir John Tyrwhitt.
1746 Chas. Monson and Coningsby Sibthorp.
1753 Hon. Geo. Monson and John Chaplin.
1760 Hon. Geo. Monson and Coningsby Sibthorp.
1768 Thos. Scrope and Hon. C. J. Phipps.

1774 Lord Lumley and Robert Vyner.
1780 Sir Thos. Clarges and Robert Vyner.
 Clarges died 1782, and John F. Cawthorne elected.
1784 Sir Richard Saville and John F. Cawthorne.
 John F. Cawthorne expelled and Geo. Rawdon elected.
1790 John F. Cawthorne and Robert Hobart.
1796 Hon. Geo. Rawdon and Richard Ellison.
 Rawdon died in 1800, and Humphrey Waldo Sibthorp was elected.
1802 Richard Ellison and Humphrey W. Sibthorp.
1806 Richard Ellison and Hon. Wm. Monson.
1808 Richard Ellison and Hon. Wm. Monson.
 Monson died in 1808, and Lord Mexborough was elected.
1812 J. N. Fazakerley and Sir H. Sullivan.
 Sullivan died in 1814, and Coningsby Waldo Sibthorp was elected.
1818 Coningsby Sibthorp and Ralph Bernall.
1820 Coningsby Sibthorp and Robert Smith
1822 Sibthorp died, and John Williams was elected.
1826 John Fazakerley and Chas de Laet Sibthorp.
1830 Col. Sibthorp and J. Fardell.
1831 Col. Sibthorp and George Heneage.
1832 George Heneage and Edward Lytton Bulwer.
1835 Col. Sibthorp and Edward Lytton Bulwer.
1837 Col. Sibthorp and Edward Lytton Bulwer.
1841 Col. Sibthorp and W. R. Collett.
1847 Charles Sibthorp and Charles Seely.
 Seely was unseated in 1848, and Thos. Hobhouse elected.
1852 Col. Sibthorp and G. F. Heneage.
1856 Col. Sibthorp died Dec. 1855, and Major G. W. T. Sibthorp elected.
1857 Major G. T. W. Sibthorp and G. F. Heneage.
1859 Major G. T. W. Sibthorp and G. F. Heneage.
1861 Charles Seely elected on the death of Major Sibthorp.
1862 J. B. Moore elected on the retirement of G. F. Heneage.
1865 Charles Seely and E. Heneage.
1868 Charles Seely and J. Hinde Palmer.
1874 Charles Seely and Lieut-Col. E. Chaplin.
 We append the figures for the remainder:
1880—Charles Seely 3,401, J. Hinde Palmer 3,128, Chaplin (not elected) 2,190. Hinde Palmer died in 1884, and Joseph Ruston was elected, the following being the figures: Ruston 3,234, Richard Hall 2,263. In the following year the Redistribution of Seats Bill was passed, and Lincoln from that date had only one member. The following are results of the elections from that date up to the present: —
1885 J. Ruston 3,726, F. H. Kerans 2,701.
1886 F. H. Kerans 3,159, W. Crosfield 2,851.
1892 W. Crosfield 3,410, F. H. Kerans 3,186.
1895 Charles Hilton Seely (present member) 3,808, Crosfield 3,530.
 We are much indebted for the compilation of this list to Mr. E. Bond, of the Public Library, and Ald. J. G. Williams, who have rendered us considerable assistance in a somewhat difficult task.

XXXVI.—"THE BLUECOAT SCHOOL."

We have had in recent years many controversies in which popular local opinion has been strongly aroused—notably, the bewilderingly-numerous schemes for Public Baths—but nothing that may be compared to the display of feeling on the part of citizens when the "Bluecoat School" Charity was diverted from its original purpose to other uses. Into the merits of the case we may well devote an article to inquire; indeed, scarcely anything comes more notably into the province of the "Forgotten" Lincoln we are reproducing in compositor's type and printer's ink. But we scarcely dare trust ou 'elves to express an opinion upon the matter. That there is much to be said upon both sides is evident, and if the vox populi has been the strongest in sound, that of the Charity Commissioners was none the less the most effective. If the present uses to which the charity is put are not the ones originally intended—we are not saying that they are not—then upon those responsible for the change rests the blame, if blame there be.

In the year 1602 a benevolent Welton doctor, by name Richard Smith, bequeathed the manor and certain lands at Potter Hanworth for the erection and endowment of a school, to be used for the maintenance and education of a dozen poor boys. In later years, how-ever, the estates increased in value considerably, and a number of other bequests having been left to the Scheme, the Governors were enabled in 1815 to increase the number of boys to 50. Still the Scheme prospered, and by degrees the number ultimately reached 124. These boys were lodged, fed, clothed, and educated until they reached the age of 14 or 15, when each lad was apprenticed to a trade, with a premium of £16.

The increase in the value of the land at Potter Hanworth is largely due to drainage and other improvements. It is stated that within almost the last fifty years the land let for £300 per annum, and that, later, the rent rose to between £1,500 and £2,000. It should be noted that Dr. Smith obtained letters patent for the establishment of the Institution "for the maintenance and education in perpetuity of twelve poor boys."

The subjects taught included music (the boys had a really fine brass band during the last years of the School's existence), drawing, reading, writing, arihmetic, Euclid, mensuration, and algebra. Six of the boys, employed as monitors, also received instruction in French. A silver medal was awarded yearly to the boy most distinguished for intellectual proficiency and moral conduct, the uum of £5 being further distributed amongst those attaining a certain standard of merit.

The following is an incomplete list of bequests to the Charity—the Hospital Chest was ransacked during the Civil War, and other lists are missing :—A person or persons unknown devised estates at Frampton, Kirton, Holton-cum-Beckering, and Newark, for two boys; Ald. John Lobsey, of Lincoln, left, in 1748, the sum of £200, for one boy; Dr. Peter Richier, of the Bail, Lincoln, left, in 1732, £200 per annum, from land at Winthorp, for two boys; Edward Holland, plumber and glazier, left an estate in 1749, which sold for £250, for one boy; Ald. John Hocton left £220, in 1767, for one boy; in 1766, Richard Barker, schoolmaster, bequeathed £100, the interest arising from which was to be given every seventh year to seven poor men who had been educated at this School and had faithfully served their apprenticeships and maintained good characters; in 1798, Elizabeth Garmston left £100, in 1804 Samuel Lyon left £500, in 1806 Joseph Dear left £50, and in 1837 Charles Hayward left £2,000.

The School had to be several times enlarged to accommodate the increasing number of scholars, and this, of course, entailed considerable expense. An enlargement in 1851, for instance, cost £1,600. The Governors were seven in number—two gentlemen of the Bail and City, the junior residentiary of the Cathedral, and four members of the Corporation, who were elected yearly on the first of January, in place of the former Mayor, Recorder, Senior Alderman, and Town Clerk, who, by virtue of their respectve offices were, before the passing of the Municipal Corporations Act, ex-officio governors of the Hospital.

The dress of the boys was at first similar to that of the scholars at Christ's Hospital School in London, but this was superseded by one more healthy and convenient. A rather smart dress it was, too, and when the boys were seen out they looked a clean, intelligent, and altogether creditable troop of youngsters.

That the groundwork of a good character—a useful education, training in discipline, and the road opened for the scholar to take up a good trade—was formed in the "Bluecoat School" is thus amply proved. Many of the "old Blues" are occupying lucrative positions in the City and elsewhere to-day, and bear the greatest credit to the training they received under the provisions of the good old Scheme.

However, sad to say, the Scheme, when in the height of its prosperity and usefulness, was abruptly stopped. The beginning of this, it is to be feared, was the abuse of the Charity by those who certainly ought to have protected it most—the officials. Left absolutely for boys of the poorer class, the School began to be used for the children of really well-to-do people, who were quite able to afford the expense of educating their offspring at a private school.

The change came by the passing of the Education Act, which compelled every parent to have his child educated, and gave administrative bodies power to raise money by rates for that purpose. This Act was improved upon by the recently made Act of Free Education, by which education is bound to be provided for every child in the land. Thus, to a great extent, the need for the "Bluecoat School" is gone. The Charity Commissioners, finding the charities were being abused, decided upon a change, and the draft schemes were published in 1881. The Lincoln Charities were merged into one common scheme, the Grammar School, Middle School, and Christ's Hospital having their funds consolidated, and used to found exhibitions and scholarships at the two former schools.

The "Bluecoat School" building was sold to the Chancellor, and the proceeds put into the common fund for the Schools. Part of this re-arranged scheme, it may be noted, was the establishment of a Middle School for Girls. The present building on the Lindum-road is the outcome of this, but it is called—not the Middle—but the "High" School for Girls.

What indignation the proposed abolition of the "Bluecoat School" aroused! Practically the whole of the citizens were point blank against the change, and a deputation even went to London to inter-view Mr. Mundella on the subject.

It is, of course, very greatly a matter for one's own private opinion as to whether the purposes to which the charity are at present devoted are as useful to the class it was intended to benefit as the original Scheme.

There are several minor points in connection with this Charity on which information is far from clear. Once a year, on St. Thomas' Day, the boys went in procession to St. Mark's Church, and after the service each received a small donation there. The aggregate sum thus annually spent is put to some use now, of course, but we cannot say what it is. Each of the 12 original boys, and the Master, had a silver mug with his name engraved on it. These are still preserved.

We remember a fete in the Arboretum during the public excite-ment in connection with the proposed alteration detailed above. It had been announced that the closing set piece of the fireworks would have reference to the all-pervading topic—the Scheme to deprive the Bluecoat boys of their education and subsequent apprenticeship. The firework was lighted, and there blazed out in grim blue letters
                  "THUS LET THE SCHEME PERISH."

It is but fair to add that, recognising the success of the new scheme, all local antagonism has apparently died away.

The first Wesleyan Chapel in Lincoln was erected on the Waterside South. The first visit of John Wesley to Lincoln was in 1780, when he preached in the Castle yard. Seventy-five years previously his father had been imprisoned for debt in the Castle. While there the Rector of Epworth read prayers twice daily and preached on Sunday afternoons.

Broadgate was originally outside the city walls. Land being so valuable in the cities proper, the mediæval broad streets were usually outside. London and Oxford supply instances.

In 1035 there was a frost on Midsummer Day. So severe was it that much corn and fruit was utterly destroyed.

Lincoln was never nearer destruction by fire than in 1110. In that year a conflagration broke out that almost consumed the entire city.

The present Dean of Lincoln is not the first of his name in that office. A William Wickham became Dean in 1577, and afterwards Bishop.

In 1661 the seven Aldermen were displaced from the Bench because they favoured Oliver Cromwell. The Sheriffs were turned out of office from the same cause, and the Town Clerk also.

In 1710 Mr. Thomas Lyster gave a second donation of £50 towards the new paving of High-street.

On September 14th, 1787, is recorded the largest show of cattle at Lincoln for a number of years. This fair is called "Fools' Fair." King William and his Queen having visited Lincoln and asked the citizens if there was anything they would like, they chose a fair in the middle of harvest, when few could attend it. The town at the same time had little trade or manufacture. Thus the name arose. It is recorded that when told the people's choice, the King smiled, and, in granting the request, said it was a very humble one indeed.

On August 4th, 1803, a meeting was held in Lincoln, when it was resolved that a volunteer corps of infantry and one of cavalry should be raised in the city. The sum of £1,300 in subscriptions was announced.

The Cathedral was robbed of the whole of the Communion plate, value over £500, in 1805. Five locks were picked to obtain it.

A romantic story is related with regard to the old city prison in 1809. Tuke, a keeper, was dismissed from his office owing to the escape of two prisoners of whom he had charge. The generally-accepted opinion was that his daughter, who had become attached to one of the prisoners, took the keys from her father's pocket whilst he slept, and enabled the men to escape. One is forcibly reminded of the incident by one in the Gilbert-Sullivan opera, "The Yeomen of the Guard."

On September 7th, 1809, it is recorded that for a wager a Sleaford waiter trundled a hoop from that town to Lincoln without once letting it fall or touch his body. The distance by road is 18 miles.

The Jubilee of King George III. was celebrated on October 25, 1809, with great pomp. The Corporation gave a public breakfast at the Reindeer (not the present inn of that name, but the one where the Lincoln and Lindsey Bank now stands), and "the city perhaps never before exhibited such a scene of decorous festivity and loyalty."

A duel was fought on Canwick Common in 1816 between Mr. Samuel Gibbeson, R.N., and Mr. Edward Fowler, a merchant, a lady being the cause. Having exchanged shots the matter was settled amicably. The encounter is lifted from the level of the French duel by the fact that one of the antagonists had his neck-cloth pierced by his opponent's ball.

In 1818 Bonaparte's military carriage, taken at Waterloo and sent by Blucher to the Prince Regent, was exhibited in Lincoln, and naturally attracted the greatest attention.

On July 19, 1821, the Coronation of George the Fourth was cele-brated in the city, but appears to have ended rather discreditably. An unruly mob broke the window of the old Reindeer Inn, and committed other outrages. The military had to be called out, the Riot Act read, and the streets cleared.

Another duel, this time between Col. Sibthorp and Dr. Charles-worth, occurred in 1824. It arose out of some uncomplimentary remarks made at a Turnpike Meeting.

On November 17th, 1824, three prisoners escaped from the Castle. One got clear away, the second was re-taken, and the third was dis-covered a few days later begging for re-admittance! He said he "had only been home to see his wife and family."

Lincoln was first lighted with gas in 1829.

A stirring scene is recorded on Lincoln racecourse in 1831. A riot took place, booths were torn to shreds and carriages set on fire. About 500 thimble-riggers and others fought against the townsfolk, the riggers and others taking out the legs of their "thimble-tables" to fight with, and would certainly have won the day but for the opportune appearance of about fifty fox-hunting gentlemen and farmers, who turned the tide.

An Irish labourer was tried at Lincoln for murder in 1837. His countrymen made a subscription for his defence, to such good pur-pose that he was acquitted. As he left the prison he nonchalantly informed the keeper that "they needn't try anybody else for it!"

It is not generally known that there are some inverted arches beneath the shop of Mr. Higgs, beside the Stonebow. The arches were being dug through by some workmen who were making certain alterations, but were stopped by Mr. W. Watkins, F.R.I.B.A. By the way, it is to Mr. Watkins that lovers of the antique owe a great deal, for he has been the means of preserving not a few relics of ancient times, that must otherwise have been carelessly mutilated or utterly destroyed.

The Vicars' College, now called the Vicars' Court, formed a quad-rangle, of which there remain only three houses, occupied by the Vicars and minor canons of the Cathedral. Gough attributes its erection to Bishop Sutton, but he was probably not the founder.

Much might be written concerning the Malandery Closes, a quadranglar enclosure of some seven acres, in the north-west corner of the South Common. It marked the precincts of the Leper Hospital of the Holy Innocent, founded by Remigius, first Bishop of Lincoln. There were also St. Leonard's Leper Hospital in the north, and St. Giles' Hospital was formerly a Lazar (or Leper) House. In the wall of All Saints' Church, Bracebridge, may yet be seen a window through which the Lepers were allowed to gaze upon the Altar, for they were not, of course, permitted to enter.

The church of All Saints, Bracebridge, by the way, is one of the most interesting in the county of Lincoln. The view of the Chancel from the body of the church through a narrow archway, the "squints" on either side of it, and the hour glass beside the pulpit by which the clergy used to preach, are of great interest. By standing in a certain part of the church, near the outer door, it is remarkable that a little of everything in it may be seen, but absolutely nothing in its entirety! This view is a most striking one. The edifice owes much to the Rev. C. C. Ellison, who has restored it very greatly, and also improved it, but has exercised the wisest care in dealing with the ancient building.

It would take a great deal of time to calculate how much Lincoln owes to Mr. Goddard, senr. He was at one time Surveyor to the Lighting and Paving Commissioners, and it was upon his advice that a number of the City pavements were widened and otherwise improved.

One ofter hears of peculiar epitaphs, but the following, from an ancient headstone in St. Mary-le-Wigford's churchyard, is hard to beat:—

> Here lies one, believe it if you can,
> Who, though an attorney, was an honest man.

The earliest Nonconformist meeting-house built in Lincoln is the Presbyterian, or Unitarian Chapel, at the High-street northern corner of Monson-street. It was built by Daniel Disney and other friends about 1725, but the congregation was formed much earlier. The Disneys, a great Puritanical family, took their name from the village of Norton Disney, though they resided at Swinderby. D'Isney Place in Eastgate was erected by a member of the family.

John Disney, Daniel Disney's father, was a staunch adherent of the Parliament during the great Rebellion. On the suppression of the Dean and Chapter, he purchased the Precentory, and at the Restoration, it took the new Precentor (Dr. Featley) two years to eject him.

The Theatre Royal (not the present building) was re-built from an older building in 1806. A Roman bath had been discovered on the site, and St. Lawrence's Church formerly stood close by. The following is a copy of a playbill from the first Theatre: "For the benefit of Mr. Robertson. Theatre, Lincoln. On Friday evening, October 4, 1805, will be presented the grand drama of The Venetian Outlaw, or the Bravo's Bride. End of the Play, The Comic Song of Giles Scroggins' Ghost, by Mr. Adamson, from the Theatre Royal, Richmond. An Address in the character of a Sailor by Master

Brown.   To which will be added the new Musical Farce of Spanish Dollars, or the Priest of the Parish.   Tickets to be had at the Printing Offices. Doors opened at six, and to begin at seven." The Theatre Royal erected in 1806 was burnt down on November 26th, 1892.

Lincoln has known many dry summers, but never one when water was so scarce as in 1826.   In that year Brayford Pool was absolutely dried up, and people actually took strolls across the bed of the same. Navigation was necessarily at a standstill.   In the city the supply of water needed by residents had to be used with extreme care.   At appointed times, twice a day, the Town Crier stood at St. Mary's Conduit, and at that on the High Bridge, and doled out the water.   This condition of things continued for nearly two months.

The growth of Lincoln during the last hundred years has been very striking.   Appended is the population since 1801, up to and including the last census, taken in 1891.   From this it will be noted how rapidly the city has increased its inhabitants, the figures growing by leaps and bounds during the last forty years, wherein the population has more than doubled.   This, it need not be stated, is directly due to the establishment of those immense manufactories which have carried the name of our city throughout the civilised globe.

Year	Population.
1801	7,197
1811	8,599
1821	9,995
1831	11,217
1841	13,896
1851	17,533
1861	20,999
1871	26,766
1881	37,312
1891	41,491

Gazette and *Echo* General Printing Works, Lincoln.

XXXVIII.—BISHOPS, MPs, SHERIFFS AND MAYORS AFTER 1898.

Compiled by G. F. MORTON

BISHOPS

(*after 1885*: *Edward King*)
1920: William Shuckburgh Swayne

1942: Henry Aylmer Skelton
1947: Maurice Henry Harland

1910: Edward Lee Hicks
1933: Frederick Cyril
Nugent Hicks
1946: Leslie Owen
1956: Kenneth Riches

MEMBERS OF PARLIAMENT

(*after 1895: Charles Hilton Seely*)
1906: C. H. Roberts
1910 (December): C. H. Roberts
1922: Alfred T. Davies
1924: R. A. Taylor
1931: Walter S. Liddall
1945: George Deer
1951: Geoffrey de Freitas
1959: Geoffrey de Freitas
1964: Dick Taverne
1970: Dick Taverne

1900: C. H. Seely
1910 (January): C. H. Roberts
1918: Alfred T. Davies
1923: Alfred T. Davies
1929: R. A. Taylor
1935: Walter S. Liddall
1950: Geoffrey de Freitas
1955: Geoffrey de Freitas
1962 (by-election): Dick Taverne
1966: Dick Taverne
1973 (by-election): Dick Taverne

SHERIFFS

(*after 1897: F. C. Brogden*)
1899: Edwin Brown
1901: Clement H. Newsum
1903: Charles J. Fox
1905: Fred S. Lambert
1907: W. R. Lilly
1909: Charles Odling
1911: William Cottam
1913: Cyril Nelson

1898: John Henry Foster
1900: F. H. Livens
1902: W. H. Close
1904: Fred Stephenson
1906: E. Mansel Sympson
1908: Herbert E. Newsum
1910: W. H. B. Brook
1912: Edwin Teesdale
1914: John Kent

1915: John Harris	1916: James Ward Usher
1917: Herbert C. Wilson (1)	1918: Herbert C. Wilson (2)
1919: A. B. Porter	1920: J. W. Ashley
1921: John Sutton Baker	1922: G. J. R. Lowe
1923: Russell T. Race	1924: George Robson
1925: G. J. Bennett	1926: R. B. Purves
1927: R. C. Minton	1928: J. H. Burgess
1929: Herbert W. C. Green	1930: George Wright
1931: A. W. Foster	1932: T. O. Clapham
1933: T. W. Jessop	1934: William Goodlet
1935: Rev. Frederick Burrows	1936: Miss Emily Gilbert
1937: Charles Gilbert	1938: W. S. Maclean
1939: W. M. Schofield	1940: Arthur Moore
1941: J. Peacock Rayner	1942: T. F. Taylor
1943: George Deer	1944: Robert Humphreys
1945: G. R. Sharpley	1946: John Cochrane
*1947: P. A. Lane	1949: J. H. Smith
1950: G. C. Wells-Cole	1951: E. F. Needham
1952: C. W. Hooton	1953: R. E. M. Coombes
1954: H. A. Smith	1955: L. R. Grantham
1956: William A. Hughes	1957: S. C. Mort
1958: T. A. Drabble	1959: Frederick Hunt
1960: Arthur Sutcliffe	1961: Bernard Clarke
1962: Duncan McNab	1963: Cyril Hill
1964: S. P. Williams	1965: John B. Wilkinson
1966: W. J. Bell	1967: P. H. Newlove
1968: H. S. Scorer	1969: F. W. A. Brogden
1970: William Valentine Semple	1971: Eric Hunt
1972: Herbert Jones	† 1973: Basil Alfred Arnold

MAYORS

(*after 1897: Hugh Wyatt*)	1898: Hugh Wyatt (4)
1899: J. G. Williams	1900: C. W. Pennell
1901: J. W. Ruddock	1902: Charles Pratt
1903: Maurice H. Footman	1904: Hugh Wyatt (5)
1905: Arthur C. Newsum	1906: J. S. Ruston
1907: John Mills (1)	1908: W. S. White

*Under the Representation of the People Act 1948 the term of office of the Sheriff elected in November 1947 was extended to the annual meeting of the Council held on May 24 1949.

†The last Sheriff of the County Borough of Lincoln: From April 1 1974 under Local Government Reorganisation Lincoln becomes a District Council.

1909: C. T. Parker (1)   1910: Clement H. Newsum
1911: John Mills (2)   1912: Thomas Wallis (3)
1913: Herbert E. Newsum   1914: Merza A. Ashley
1915: C. T. Parker (2)   1916: C. T. Parker (3)
1917: C. T. Parker (4)   1918: C. T. Parker (5)
1919: H. A. Cottingham   1920: T. C. Halkes
1921: W. H. Kilmister   1922: James Smalley
1923: John Hague   1924: R. A. Taylor
1925: Miss M. E. Nevile   1926: George Robson
1927: C. E. Snook   1928: Pearce Milner
1929: Thomas Nowell   1930: C. H. Doughty
1931: W. F. Elderkin   1932: J. W. Rayment
1933: George Deer   1934: J. K. Fox
1935: J. J. Leamy   1936: J. E. Fordham
1937: William Sindell   1938: Herbert Willcock
1939: A. L. Bower   1940: Albert Tuck
1941: J. W. Preston   1942: T. H. Davy
1943: Leslie J. Mills   1944: Harold Bennett
1945: J. W. F. Hill   1946: H. H. C. Kerry
*1947: J. W. Lawson   1949: H. W. Martin
1950: Mrs. Edyth I. Cowan   1951: T. F. Taylor
1952: J. W. Giles   1953: R. E. Seely
1954: A. H. Briggs   1955: W. J. Bell
1956: C. A. Lillicrap   1957: Mrs. G. L. Murfin
1958: Leslie H. Priestley   1959: F. W. G. Todd
1960: Eric J. Richardson   1961: W. E. Herbert
1962: Mrs. Hannah M. Kerry   1963: G. W. Colls
1964: A. S. Woolhouse   1965: G. G. Elsey
1966: F. R. Eccleshare   1967: S. A. Campbell
1968: Ralph Wadsworth   1969: John H. Spence
1970: Mrs. M. R. Sookias   1971: Fred Blackbourn
1972: Wilfred Pixsley   †1973: Peter W. Archer

*Under the Representation of the People Act 1948 the term of office of the Mayor elected in November 1947 was extended to the annual meeting of the Council held on May 24 1949.

†The last Mayor of the County Borough of Lincoln: from April 1 1974, under Local Government Reorganisation, Lincoln becomes a District Council. (Note: It is likely Lincoln will continue to have a mayor but at the time of going to press the result of the District Council's application is not known.)

DATE DUE